UNIVERSITY OF HUNGER

T0347015

MARTIN CARTER

UNIVERSITY OF HUNGER

COLLECTED POEMS & SELECTED PROSE

EDITED BY GEMMA ROBINSON

BLOODAXE BOOKS

ISBN: 978 1 85224 710 2

First published 2006 by
Bloodaxe Books Ltd,
Eastburn,
South Park,
Hexham,
Northumberland NE46 1BS.

www.bloodaxebooks.com
For further information about Bloodaxe titles
please visit our website or write to
the above address for a catalogue.

Supported by
**ARTS COUNCIL
ENGLAND**

Cover design: Neil Astley & Pamela Robertson-Pearce.

This is a digital reprint of the 2006 edition.

CONTENTS

The When Time (1977)

SELECTED PROSE

A CHRONOLOGY OF MARTIN CARTER

1927: (7 June) Martin Wylde Carter born in Georgetown, Guyana to Victor Emmanuel and Violet Eugene Carter (neé Wylde).

1938: Enrols at Queen's College, Georgetown.

1942: Meets Phyllis Howard.

1947: Refuses to go to university. Joins the Civil Service.

1948: First published poem, 'From "An Ode to Midnight"', in *Kyk-Over-Al*.

1950: Founder member of the socialist and anti-colonial People's Progressive Party (PPP). Second published poem, 'The Indian Woman', in the PPP journal, *Thunder*.

1951: Self-publishes *To a Dead Slave* in Georgetown. *A Hill of Fire Glows Red* published, Georgetown.

1952: Self-publishes *The Kind Eagle (Poems of Prison)* in Georgetown. Self-publishes *The Hidden Man (More Poems of Prison)* in Georgetown. 'Poems of Prison' published, *Kyk-Over-Al*.

1953: Marries Phyllis Howard. Leaves the Civil Service and stands for PPP in the first universal suffrage elections in British Guiana. Son, Keith, is born. (31 August – 24 September) General Strike in the sugar industry. (9 October) British government calls State of Emergency in British Guiana. (26 October) Carter and comrades detained without charge at US Airbase, Atkinson Field; the authorities claim the men were 'spreading dissension'. (23 November) Hunger strike. 'University of Hunger' published in *Kyk-Over-Al*. (27 December) Hunger strike concludes.

1954: (January) Released and placed under restriction orders. *Poems of Resistance from British Guiana* published in London by Lawrence & Wishart. (May) Publishes his first editorial in *Thunder*. (June) Imprisoned for taking part in illegal procession; sentenced to six months. (December) 'Six Poems of Resistance' published in US political journal, *Masses and Mainstream*. Released from prison. Daughter, Sonia, is born.

1955: PPP splits between Cheddi Jagan and Linden Forbes Burnham; Carter joins Jagan faction. 'Three Poems of Shape and Motion' published, *Kyk-Over-Al*.

1956: Carter leaves the PPP.

1958: Employed as Information Officer in the British Council's Georgetown office.

1959: Starts employment as Information Officer at Booker, Georgetown.

1960: Publishes *Conversations* in *Kyk-Over-Al*. Travels to London for Constitutional Conference concerning electoral reform for an independent Guyana. Son, Howard, born.

1962: Riots break out in Georgetown. Governor calls state of emergency.

1964: Governor calls another state of emergency. *Jail Me Quickly* is published in *New World Fortnightly*.

1965: Becomes editor of *Booker News*.

1966: (28 May) Independence; British Guiana renamed 'Guyana'.

1967: Resigns from Booker and becomes Minister of Information and Culture in Burnham's first People's National Congress (PNC) government in the newly independent Guyana; employed as a technocrat. Leads Guyana's delegation to the United Nations.

1968: PNC wins General Elections but is accused of electoral rigging.

1970: (February) As Minister of Information opens the Conference of Caribbean Writers and Artists in Georgetown. Daughter, Michelle, born. (November) Resigns as Minister of Information.

1971: Returns to Booker's Information department.

1972: Takes part in the first Carifesta, the pan-Caribbean festival of the arts, held in Georgetown.

1975: Writer in Residence at the University of Essex, UK.

1977: *Poems of Succession* published by New Beacon, London and Port of Spain.

1978: Leaves Booker, becoming Lecturer in Creative Writing/Artist in Residence, University of Guyana. Takes part in demonstrations against the PNC. Is beaten during demonstrations. (14 July) Fr Bernard Darke, priest and photographer for the campaigning, anti-PNC *Catholic Standard*, is stabbed to death at a protest attended by Carter. Carter writes 'Bastille Day – Georgetown'.

1980: *Poems of Affinity: 1978-1980* published by Release, Georgetown. A next collection, *Poems of Mortality*, is announced. Walter Rodney, founder member of the bipartisan Working People's Alliance, killed.

1984: *Four Poems and Demerara Nigger* published in *Kyk-Over-Al*.

1985: Death of Burnham.

1986: A director of Guyana Publications Limited, publisher of independent *Stabroek News*.

1989: *Selected Poems* published by Demerara Publishers, Georgetown. Wins Guyana Prize for Literature.

1992: Travels to UK on Guyanese Writers Tour with Wilson Harris, Grace Nichols and Fred D'Aguiar. 'Free and fair' elections are restored to Guyana. The PPP wins and Jagan becomes President.

1993: Suffers a stroke, losing the ability to walk and talk. *Kyk-Over-Al Special Issue: A Martin Carter Prose Sampler* published.

1994: Receives the Order of Roraima for outstanding contribution to literature.

1996: Awarded the Gabriela Mistral gold medal from Chilean government for contribution to literature.

1997: Second edition of *Selected Poems* published by Red Thread Women's Press, Georgetown. (13 December) Dies at family home. Survived by Phyllis Carter and their four children. Given a state funeral and buried at the Place of the Seven Ponds, Georgetown.

ABOVE: *Martin Carter, circa early 1960s.*

BELOW: *Martin Carter* (RIGHT) *with Cheddi Jagan* (CENTRE) *and Rory Westmaas* (LEFT), *being taken away in a police van, 1954.*

INTRODUCTION

'I am my poem'

A photograph is taken of three young men inside a police van (*see left, below*). All look out through the grille into the camera lens, their expressions unclear, apparently neither worried, angry, happy, nor afraid. It was British Guiana, 1954, a colony living in a State of Emergency imposed by the British government. The men in the photograph were Martin Carter, Cheddi Jagan and Rory Westmaas, key activists in the People's Progressive Party (PPP). Like political parties in so many places in the British Empire, the PPP was demanding a future separated from British interests and aligned to a socialist worldview. Carter is poised. By the end of the year he would be the author of *Poems of Resistance from British Guiana*. Imprisoned for the second time by the colonial government, his name would be secured as the poet who articulated the mood of protest and independence in Guyana and throughout the West Indies.

Another photograph shows an older Carter in the late 1960s, dressed in a suit and tie, ready for the business of government (*see page 56*). Now Minister of Information in the increasingly controversial People's National Congress (PNC) government of the newly independent Guyana, Carter saw the country's declaration as a Co-operative Socialist Republic, the nationalisation of the media, as well as allegations of electoral rigging and border disputes with Venezuela. Carter remained a Minister for three years. When Phyllis Carter was asked to comment on her husband's resignation from the government she responded: 'I have lived through many crises with my husband who is a poet. Even while he was in government, things for me were quite the same. Now it is simply a continuation of the life I have been living with him as a poet... Those who know of his virtue, of his contribution to the society as a poet need no enlightenment'.[1]

For the man who wrote at the height of the Emergency in the 1950s, 'I am my poem, I come to you in particular gladness' ('I Am No Soldier'), Phyllis Carter's words ring true. Carter's commitment to a life of poetry in times of public and private crisis determines and invigorates his work. From the 1940s to the 1990s, his poetry would challenge him and his readers to be more than witnesses or bystanders in a world that he defines in 'University of Hunger' as 'the terror and the time'. In 1951 his poem 'All Are

15

Involved' articulated this challenge in the form of a riddling chant:

> This I have learnt:
> today a speck
> tomorrow a hero
> hero or monster
> you are consumed!
>
> Like a jig
> shakes the loom.
> Like a web
> is spun the pattern
> all are involved!
> all are consumed!

Carter's work creates a poetry of involvement, a poetry that helped shape the political and cultural parameters of Guyana. In 1970 the only comment that Carter offered when he resigned from the government matched his wife's understanding of the primacy of poetry and people within his life. He said he wished to live 'simply as a poet, remaining with the people'.[2]

A Poet in Colonial Guyana

Sustained claims for Guyanese poetry came first from Norman Cameron in his 1931 anthology, *Guianese Poetry (covering the hundred years' period 1831-1931)*, and then in 1945 from A.J. Seymour as editor of the literary and cultural journal, *Kyk-Over-Al*. The dominant opinion prior to these works was that Guyanese poetry did not exist. In his introduction, Cameron quotes from the preface of *Midnight Musings in Demerara*, a collection of poems published anonymously in Guyana in 1832 by 'Colonist': 'The colony, though fertile in everything else, is barren in incidents for poetical display.' Colonist continued, arguing that the colony did not have 'the haze of antiquity to shroud, and yet beautify, the records of past generations' nor 'the novelty of a lately discovered country'.[3] Yet, living in the West Indies did not, as Kenneth Ramchand has suggested, condemn people to a life of 'cultural absenteeism'.[4] Throughout the 19th century and the 20th, Guyana developed a flourishing newspaper culture, self-publishing was familiar and newspapers, such as the *Chronicle*, also acted as publishing houses. Nevertheless, the status of Guyana as a place that could produce literature and sustain a literary culture was in constant debate.

Cameron's starting-point for his anthology is important: naming poetry as 'Guianese' in 1831 matches the date that the former Dutch colonies of Demerara, Essequibo and Berbice became united as the colony, British Guiana. Colonist, writing insistently from Demerara, might well describe the one-year-old colony as lacking 'the records of past generations', but that description denied the history and cultures of the territory and the people – Amerindians, slaves, indentured labourers, colonists and workers – who inhabited this area on the north-east coast of South America. The poetry written in Guyana in the 20th century would deal directly with ideas about nation and culture. And cultural critics and writers would turn their attention to the hybrid, or more aptly, the creolised Caribbean that had been created through multiple cultural encounters over five centuries.

The founding and development of *Kyk-Over-Al*, the journal in which Carter's work first appeared, occurred simultaneously with debates about the colonial status of Guyana and a growing interest in the poetics of the colony.[5] Named after a ruined Dutch colonial fort which lies near the confluence of the Mazaruni, Essequibo and Cuyuni rivers, *Kyk-Over-Al* means 'watch over all', and the title suggests the ambassadorial intentions of the magazine. The fort became a new site of cultural cohesion – a symbol of 17th-century conflict and colonialism creolised into a symbol of collective Guyanese identity. In his first editorial in December 1945, A.J. Seymour summarised the heuristic outlook of the review: '*Kykoveral* we hope will be an instrument to help forge a Guianese people, to make them conscious of their intellectual and spiritual possibilities'.[6] *Kyk-Over-Al* became the matrix of culture in Guyana, co-ordinating new writing and plotting the features of distinctly Guyanese and Caribbean traditions.[7] Seymour's contribution was significant: he encouraged Richard Allsopp's pioneering linguistic research on Creole; he published the early work of Derek Walcott, George Lamming and Wilson Harris, and translations of Aimé Césaire.

Beginning a 20-year relationship with *Kyk-Over-Al*, Carter made a deceptive entrance into Guyanese poetry. In 1948 a 'fragment' of his poem, 'An Ode to Midnight', was published in the journal. Beginning, 'O, Midnight hour why must thy time be sad? / Art thou not like the other hours of night?',[8] the ode's deliberate archaism does little to distinguish it from the many pastiches in *Kyk-Over-Al* that cast back to classical and romantic structures of poetic expression. Carter may have been thinking of his own work when he wrote in 'Sensibility and the Search' in 1958: 'look at the poetry we call West Indian. What has the larger part been, other than a series of poor imitation of English models? If, for instance, at a

ABOVE: *A young Martin Carter, pictured with friends from Queen's College.*
BELOW: *Martin Carter as a teenager.*

given period Tennyson is the leading English Poet, then the poems written are poor copies of Tennyson.' In later poems, Carter would evolve a distinctive use for the archaisms of his juvenilia. But as a teenager, his time was absorbed by English literature. One of his favourite poets was Keats, and his younger brother Ben remembers Carter copying the dress of the 19th-century poet and wearing his hair in the style of Oscar Wilde.[9]

Carter came from a middle-class family of mixed African and European ancestry, who sent their six sons to the colony's most prestigious school, Queen's College (*see picture opposite*). He joined the school in 1938, and his contemporaries remember the quiet studiousness of the six Carter brothers.[10] With friends he founded a club called the Symposium, a forum in which they could discuss literature, culture and politics.[11] Wilson Harris in an autobiographical essay writes of Queen's College as 'a vessel of learning linking old worlds and new'; he emphasises the varied ethnic backgrounds from which both staff and pupils came and he clearly wants to reposition the colonial education he received as a "cross-cultural" rather than a monocultural experience.[12] However, Georgetown in the 1940s was a city with strict social expectations of its inhabitants.[13] A young Creole or "coloured" man from a respectable family might be invited to The Woodbine House Club, a private club run by a prominent doctor's wife, Dorothy Taitt.[14] On Friday evenings until ten o'clock she would 'bring English culture within reach of the desirable young' and act as matchmaker to bring together couples of a similar social class.[15] Seymour was often a speaker at these events; reading his own poetry or speaking on English literature.

However, Carter was already proving that he would not follow the expected routes mapped out for talented men of the Empire. Unlike his brothers, he decided not to go to university in England nor to the newly founded University College in Jamaica. His first ambitions were for a career in journalism, but the Georgetown-based *Argosy* newspaper turned him down as an overqualified Queen's graduate.[16] When Carter left Queen's College he became a clerk at the local Sprostons foundry.[17] His first job introduced him to the labour conditions experienced by the Guyanese working class. However, Carter's father, Victor Emmanuel, believed that the civil service was the best career for a man to follow and told his sons that he did not want them to have a life of 'counter jumping' – his term for a career in business.[18] Carter followed his father's advice, and after leaving Sprostons foundry he joined the civil service, working initially at the Post Office and later for the Prison Service.[19]

Although political radicalism was not a determined route for the middle class Carter, Guyana's constitutional inequalities were clear: by the time Carter was 21 universal franchise had not been introduced in the colony.[20] Furthermore, the politicisation of the Creole middle class had been established in the 19th century; the Political Reform Club, led by journalists, lawyers, schoolteachers and merchants, helped to precipitate the political reform that would eventually lead to universal suffrage in 1953.[21] At home, Carter's father encouraged his children to consider their family as a democratic household; when the house needed painting the family would be gathered together and the job would be done collectively. Victor's children soon nicknamed their Anira Street home, 'the conference house', and its welcoming atmosphere of discussion made their house a popular base for family and friends.[22] Victor also encouraged his children to read, particularly philosophy. Ben Carter remembers his father attending house sales in order to buy books. The BBC news provided a powerful focal point for the family and Victor would unfailingly call his children to the radio to listen to the war- and peace-time speeches by Winston Churchill. Carter's mother, Violet, was also a dedicated reader; to the children she passed on her love of poetry and also her interest in the folk stories and Creole sayings of Guyana and the Caribbean.

Although Carter's paternal grandparents had emigrated to Guyana from Barbados, and although his maternal grandparents were from Grenada, Carter's parents were committed to a life in Guyana for themselves and their children. They rejected the future chosen by the 'Windrush' generations of the post-war period, and never considered emigration. If this was Guyanese nationalism, it was not consciously politicised. Ben Carter describes their older brother, Keith, as the person who 'converted Martin into Socialism and Communism'. Keith left Guyana to read Law at Oxford University in the late 1940s, and he would send home the latest Communist publications from the UK. Keith's passion and the constant flow of material, including *The Communist Manifesto* and issues of *The Daily Worker*, soon persuaded Carter that politics was as important as the literature that had already captured his attention.[23]

In the post-war period there were several Georgetown-based forums for political discussion. The Carnegie Library's weekly discussion circle was distinguished in its welcome reception of radical political opinion. Regular members of the circle were a couple who would play a crucial role in Carter's life and Guyana's history: Cheddi and Janet Jagan. In *The West on Trial: My Fight for Guyana's Freedom*, Cheddi Jagan writes of the post-war period: 'My wife and I began to make our impact and to gather around us a group of young radicals and intellectuals'.[24] In 1946 Cheddi Jagan, Janet Jagan, Jocelyn Hubbard and Ashton Chase formed the Political Affairs Committee, modelling their name on the American Political Action Committee of the Congress of Industrial Organisations of the USA. Their *PAC Bulletin* was circulated without charge to approximately 60 people, and included articles about working conditions on the sugar plantations, the stranglehold of the Booker group upon the economy of Guyana and the need for constitutional change. In a society in which the planter class sought to retain its control over the government and economy, the PAC quickly earned a reputation as a Communist organisation. Cheddi Jagan recalls demands from both the Guyanese Legislative Council and the British House of Commons for the banning of the *PAC Bulletin*.[25] By 1950 members of the PAC saw the need for a larger electable political party, and in January 1950 the People's Progressive Party (PPP) was formed with Cheddi Jagan as leader, Linden Forbes Burnham as Chairman and Janet Jagan as Secretary (*see page 22: Carter at a political meeting*). As a member of the civil service, Carter had to sit anonymously on the PPP's Executive Council.

Carter's membership of the PPP offered him a further forum for writing. Janet Jagan in her role as the editor of *Thunder* (a new publication to replace the *PAC Bulletin*) encouraged supporters to send in contributions, and Carter's first piece appeared in June 1950. This poem – titled 'The Indian Woman', attributed to M. Black – provides an early indication of Carter's commitment to a poetic that could incorporate political expression. The pseudonym, M. Black, served to retain Carter's anonymity and kept his career in the civil service secure; the choice of surname, at a time when 'Black' was not current in vocabularies of racial colour ('Negro' being the more usual term), is perhaps a politically provocative announcement of racial pride, and an indication to the 'White' powers in the colony of Carter's political allegiances. His pseudonym, however, was not intended to divide African-Guyanese and Indian-Guyanese; a unified, multi-racial party was one of the earliest goals stated by the PPP:

There is a need for a political party with its roots and strength in the mass of workers of this country and supported by all truly loyal Guianese – a party to weld together all progressive thinkers and groups – dedicated to the service of our society and not to the fulfilment of the selfish ambitions of individuals or separate groups.[26]

ABOVE: *Martin Carter with Cheddi and Janet Jagan at a PPP meeting.*

BELOW: *Martin Carter marries Phyllis Howard, 31 January 1953.*

There is a shift from Seymour's wish to create a public readership for cultural expression to the PPP's wish to represent politically the 'mass of workers' as well as 'progressive thinkers and groups'. Carter's 'The Indian Woman', is an attempt by a poet to write outside his own experience of gender, race and class, and to portray something of the 'present abyss of poverty, despair and frustration' [27] that was experienced by the mass of workers, and witnessed by all Guyanese people:

> Among the grass green lettuce which
> Grew round the rusted railway line,
> The Indian Woman bent and worked
> Beneath the sun the whole day long.

The working class of Guyana shared some of the labour conditions experienced in the highly industrialised areas of America and Europe, but as 'The Indian Woman' depicts, those employed on rice and sugar plantations also endured conditions of a pre-industrial age. As if in response to these experiences, the poems draw on a rural ballad tradition. Carter does not follow common metre, but reins the poem to an economy of narrative well-known in the ballad form. Then he shifts from narrative to prophetic lyric in an attempt to bring a political analysis to the poem: 'No! No! The misery of the years / Against time gives birth to flaming wrath.'

A belief in the inheritance of the workers was probably influenced by the socialist writing of William Morris. The motto to *Thunder* is a quotation from the chorus of Morris's poem, 'The March of the Workers': 'Hark the rolling of the thunder! / Lo the sun! and lo thereunder / Riseth wrath, and hope, and wonder.' Appearing in *Chants for Socialists* (1885), the poem tracks the rising collective consciousness of the 'workers' and their ultimate victory over 'ye rich men'. Although Raymond Williams describes Morris's 'romantic socialist songs' as weak and 'disabling', such songs offered a comparative example to Guyanese poets.[28] Whether 'The Indian Woman' and the other poems that appeared in *Thunder* were politically enabling in Guyana is difficult to determine; certainly most were never republished by Carter. For the PPP, Morris's poetry of wrath and hope offers a racially neutral motto, broad enough to appeal to the 'Guianese of all races and classes championing the cause of the oppressed and exploited' – the groups which the PPP identified as its supporters. Broad appeal (which Morris helped to generate in England with the founding of the Socialist League in 1884) was crucial to the PPP if it was ever to counter British received opinion about the ill-preparedness of Caribbean populations for independent governments. The 1945 Moyne Commission on working conditions in the West Indies reported that 'social reform in the West Indies has had to come from above, as the mass of the population have had insufficient experience of conditions elsewhere to be in a position to formulate demands'.[29] By contrast, the PPP worked to speak *with* the voice of all Guyanese people, not just *for* individuals or separate groups. Yet Carter's poetic aims were not so clear-cut: 'The Indian Woman' initiates a poetic that defines Carter's work, one that is socially driven but that still prioritises the subjectivity of the poet. His poems were not written in the service of his politics as was much other poetry published in *Thunder*. The poems of Sydney King (now Eusi Kwayana) provided clear promises, in rhyming verse, about the workers' future: 'Folks will waken, and their chains be shaken / And things will change in the slumyard'.[30] Carter's poetry, however, reveals a writer more equivocal about how creative forms could be devised to serve political ends.

'I will not still my voice'

By the 1950s socialist writing, particularly in its Soviet form, was losing appeal in Western Europe and the USA.[31] But for Carter and other members of the PPP the Communism set out in Marxian writing was still attractive. In Georgetown, Cheddi Jagan's dental practice became the unofficial bookshop for left-wing publications. Reviews in *Thunder* recommended publications such as Beatrice and Sidney Webb's *The Truth About Soviet Russia* (1942) and R. Palme Dutt's *Britain's Crisis of Empire* (1949). The links between exploitative systems of capitalism and empire are stated in these books, and the pairing of liberatory moves towards Communism and political independence suggests that colonised peoples had much to gain from Communism and little to lose from abandoning a capitalist system that had already made them colonial subjects.

The pages of *Thunder* offered numerous reports of anticolonial organisations. For example, George Padmore – a Trinidadian trade unionist based in London, and later a key member of the Pan-African movement – reported on the overwhelming electoral victory of Kwame Nkrumah's Convention People's Party in the Gold Coast (now Ghana). Padmore detailed that once in government Nkrumah used his platform to denounce 'African capitalists for exploiting their own people'.[32] News stories such as this, and the internationalist mandate to which *Thunder* subscribed, served to emphasise similarities in imperial and capitalist exploitation throughout the colonised world: articles on the monopoly in Guyana of the British sugar conglomerate, Booker, exposés on the substandard housing in which sugar estate workers lived, and statements voicing PPP demands for constitutional reform were bolstered by reports of similar experiences elsewhere in British colonies, and more importantly, political successes like those in the Gold Coast offered the PPP the hope that their political struggle would be the next to succeed.[33]

Carter's *The Hill of Fire Glows Red* (1951) is full of revolutionary promise for its readers. The collection stridently calls for social change and many poems are consistent with Leon Trotsky's maxim that 'revolutionary literature cannot but be imbued with a spirit of social hatred'.[34] Certainly, 'social hatred' can define some of the emotional import of 'Not I with This Torn Shirt' (the opening poem), 'Do Not Stare at Me', 'Three Years After This' and 'It Is for This That I Am Furious'. Nevertheless, the national liberation cause that Carter voices in this collection is rooted in the dynamics of community and ultimately Carter must address what kind of society he wishes to create. The colour-symbolism of the title points the way, suggestive of Communist victory. But that is not all. Although the collection is firmly written about the present, it draws on the history of the slave plantation in Guyana, and in 'The Blood of Quamina' Carter makes red the symbol of a past struggle against the inequities of plantation slavery.

Carter looks for ways to give his protest poetry a distinctly Guyanese context, and he finds in Guyanese history a revolutionary promise. Quamina, one of the actors in the failed Demerara Slave Rebellion of 1823, is a reminder of the Caribbean's violent past, and he is invoked by Carter as a revolutionary ancestor. As he writes in 'Not Hands Like Mine', 'mine was a pattern woven by a slave'. An understanding of Guyana's history of slave rebellion had obvious political appeal for an anticolonial activist. This historical understanding was also important in helping Carter to develop a poetic voice. In *To a Dead Slave* (1951) Carter had invoked the importance of Quamina, but even more so he had hoped to address the anonymous 'dead father' who was his direct ancestor. Carter wanted to confront not only his slave past – this had been done before in the Caribbean in poems like A.J. Seymour's 'Drums' and Vera Bell's 'Ancestor on an Auction Block' – but also wanted to understand how slavery was still part of his present life. Prose pieces such as 'The Lesson of August', 'Sensibility and the Search', 'A Question of Self-Contempt' and 'Sambo at Large' explore aspects of the present ramifications of slavery. In 'Sensibility and the Search' Carter puts it bluntly: 'the sensibility of the slave and the status of the colonial combine to make us what we are'. In *To a Dead Slave*, Carter recognised the dual importance of slavery and colonialism. If slavery had brought African culture to the Caribbean, his poem also understands that colonialism had enforced an earlier encounter between Amerindians and Europeans and a later meeting of Amerindians. Africans, Indians, Chinese and Europeans through the system of indentureship that replaced slave labour in the 19th century.

Given Carter's interest in colonial history in *To a Dead Slave* and *The Hill of Fire Glows Red*, it would have been understandable if he had continued to develop this historical imagination. However, it was not slavery, Amerindian presence or Indian indentureship, so much as the attendant idea of 'what we are' that was important in his next collections from 1952. The concerns of *The Kind Eagle (Poems of Prison)* and *The Hidden Man (Other Poems of Prison)* are particularly complemented by Carter's later essay 'A Question of Self-Contempt':

> Self was here in visible location, aware of the datum and exigence of land and community. But who was my? Who self? [...]
> Out of these swirling confusions I stepped into a world of action. I became a member of an organisation formed by Cheddi Jagan, a friend of great days. And every Sunday night a meeting in an unpainted hutch with grey dust like history's night-soil between the creases in the floor. Sometimes no more than five of us. Five bewildered creatures on a Sunday night repeating ourselves like desperate obeahmen. Outside the world. Dog dung in the street. A black man in South Africa. Love beneath the gay stars. Firelight in the cane-pieces. Degradation, absolute vomit. Bed. Same tomorrow. Tomorrow again. Tomorrow always.

Although Carter does not date this period, it is obviously the early days of the PPP, and the politics are represented as confusion. As Carter's prose fragments in this essay, it is painfully aware of the crises of that time. *The Kind Eagle* shares some of the repetitive desperation of 'A Question of Self-Contempt', and the tone of *The Hidden Man* is characterised by the social bewilderment described in the essay: the poet faces his 'world of action', unclear how to proceed in poetry or in this world. The challenge of the two collections can be pared down to two words: 'Who self?' Carter writes in 'Cartman of Dayclean' (included here within *Poems of Resistance from British Guiana*), 'Now to begin the road: / broken land ripped like a piece of cloth', and each poem of the collections arguably restates this assertion of uneasy beginnings. However, there are suggestions, although tentative, of a poetry that does not only compute 'the datum and exigence of land and community' but transforms them. 'Cartman of Dayclean' attempts to be both linguistically and socially transformational. It is a descriptive poem of labour at dawn, written in standard English, but the Creole title-word, 'dayclean' (meaning 'dawn'), is used transformationally not neutrally: cleansing the day and – by implication – the 'broken land' of Guyana, constitutes a revolutionary act. Carter's use of Creole proves that politically charged words and ideas can originate in Guyana and be absorbed into a global vocabulary of proletarian experience.

In these 'poems of prison' Carter moves away from the intimate, colloquial tone – at times fiercely accusing, at other times warmly inclusive – that characterises *The Hill of Fire Glows Red*, attempting instead to achieve a denser metaphorical range. These collections address the poet's necessary search to understand his place in the world. The collective pronouns of 'we', 'they' and 'you' – used dramatically in the 1951 collection – are often pared down to the poet's 'I', 'my' and 'me'. In 'Bare Night Without Comfort' Carter introduces the alienated and alienating world that provides the landscape of *The Kind Eagle*. Working at the time as Secretary to the Superintendent of Prisons in Camp Street Prison, Georgetown, Carter had ample opportunity to think through the implications of incarceration for his life and poetry. Each of these 'poems of prison' attempts to locate precisely what it means to live an imprisoned existence, and how it conditions an apparently un-imprisoned consciousness. Notably, in *The Kind Eagle* and *The Hidden Man*, Carter does not make any comparison between prison and colonial experience. But the comparison stands. Although the imagery is not as pronounced as the angrily drawn colony of *The Hill of Fire Glows Red* ('province of flood / Plantation – feudal coast!'), the nightmare of this 'bare night', 'the burnt earth of these years' and the 'slow slow time rotting the bone away' nonetheless evoke the incarcerating condition of colonialism.

By 1953 Carter had married Phyllis Howard and their first child was born later that year (*see page 22*). With Phyllis's support, Carter left the security of the Civil Service in order to play a larger role in politics. He stood for the PPP in the first universal suffrage election in 1953. He was not elected, but his party achieved a landslide victory – yet it was in government for only 133 days. The fear of a Communist takeover, intensified by a strike in the Guyanese sugar industry and the consolidation of the Cold War internationally (in Korea, Vietnam, Kenya, Malaya), persuaded the

Conservative British government that they needed to act swiftly to stamp out the threat of Communism in the British West Indies.

Although Carter's early political prose (here collected as 'Anti-colonialism and "race" in British Guiana') was written with the urgency of journalism, it reveals a sensitivity to the real crises of the 1950s. Carter was quick to argue for non-cooperation in the face of the Emergency; he protested against US involvement in the colony; he greatly feared the divisive "race" politics that were increasingly defining a Guyanese population descended from both the African continent and the Indian sub-continent; and he predicted the politics of personality that would eventually govern the Guyanese political arena. But this was all still to come; between April and October 1953 the PPP was getting on with the job of government and pro-independence campaigning. Carter travelled to Europe to attend the World Festival of Youth in Romania and to represent the PPP Peace Committee in Hungary, but on his return the political landscape of British Guiana and the British West Indies changed. Carter was banned from Trinidad as an 'undesirable visitor'. On 9 October the British government called a State of Emergency in British Guiana, the PPP government was dismissed, and British troops took control of Georgetown. Carter was arrested on 25 October 1953, and detained without charge at the US Airbase, Atkinson Field; the authorities claimed that he and four others were 'spreading dissension' on Plantation Blairmont in West Berbice. On 23 November, Carter and his comrades began a month-long hunger strike to complain about the diet in the internment camp; the fact of martial law in British Guiana; the injustice of indefinite detention; and the use of heavy bombers in the British government's fight against the Mau Mau in Kenya.

During this period of incarceration local newspapers reported that Carter was spending his time writing; at this time Carter's magnificent poem 'University of Hunger' was published in *Kyk-Over-Al*:

> is the university of hunger the wide waste
> is the pilgrimage of man the long march
> The print of hunger wanders in the land
> The green tree bends above the long forgotten

Those opening lines Carter insisted were to be voiced as Creole statements, not questions. But he is not so much interested in duplicating speech patterns for mimetic representation, as he is concerned to work with the rhythms afforded by Creole speech and to give these rhythms a poetic role.

Since the 1960s linguists have suggested that 'a creole continuum

28

can evolve in situations in which a creole exists with its lexical source language and there is social motivation for creole speakers to acquire the standard, so that the speech of individuals takes on features of the latter – or avoids features of the former – to varying degrees'.[35] As a middle-class, high-school-educated, Georgetown dweller, Carter's position on the Creole continuum spanned from the acrolect to the mesolect but not to the basilect. But there were social situations in which he would extend himself towards the basilect, notably in his political work. Between 1950 and 1953, Carter and his PPP comrades organised weekend classes in order to carry out educational work. Rupert Roopnaraine describes their activities: 'They worked along the coast. An important highlight of this was their study of the landlord system in the rice farming village of Golden Fleece, Essequibo. In this study and teaching, the young activist was getting down to the anatomy of the estate system on the Essequibo coast.'[36] As a PPP member, Carter was an educator but also a student; he would have to understand the basilect vocabularies and grammars of the plantations and the villages as well as those of the city, and as a poet, Carter would reinterpret these vocabularies and the values attached to them. It is key to his political and poetic thinking that Carter's 'University of Hunger' operates within an ultimately inclusive continuum of linguistic registers.

Released in January 1954, Carter was placed under restriction orders not to leave Georgetown. However, he was quickly rearrested and sentenced to six months' imprisonment at the Camp Street prison (his former workplace) for taking part in an illegal PPP procession. While Carter was restricted to Georgetown until the elections of 1957, his poetry was on the move. His work appeared in the US political journal, *Masses & Mainstream* and the West Indian Independence Party published a pamphlet of his work, titled *Songs of Freedom: Poems of Resistance*. His collection, *Poems of Resistance from British Guiana*, was published in London by the left-wing publishing house, Lawrence and Wishart, which heralded Carter as 'the foremost poet of the Caribbean'.[37] The collection would go through three editions. He became one of the first poets of his generation to be published outside the Caribbean. His work was recited at clandestine labour meetings in Guyana and across the Caribbean. However, the PPP, and Carter's involvement in it, did not survive the Emergency. Split between Cheddi Jagan's radical and Linden Forbes Burnham's moderate factions, in 1955 the PPP fragmented. Carter chose the radical Jagan side, only to leave the party a year later having been accused of 'ultra-leftism' by Jagan.

What was to become of the poet who had invested so much in the PPP? The answer can be found in Carter's poetry. In his introduction to *Poems of Resistance from British Guiana*, Eusi Kwayana reads Carter's poetry as a direct expression of the mood and experiences of anticolonialism in Guyana: 'When the people began to display their young vigour, Carter turned his attention to nurturing the forces of the radiant future, to sustaining the people in their struggle'.[38] But *Poems of Resistance from British Guiana* was not written wholly in response to the Emergency (over half the poems had been published in varying forms prior to 1954), nor for a political party. Translated into Chinese and Russian, *Poems of Resistance from British Guiana* certainly appealed to anticapitalist readers, but this should not obscure how any local poetry can be understood trans-nationally. Carter's wish to define 'the university of hunger' in which he studied, and the iconic raised fist of sugar worker on the front cover meant that Carter did not need a political party to continue to write his revolutionary poetry.

Lyric poetry and the uses of silence

Addressing the first Carifesta in Guyana in 1972, Gordon Rohlehr argued that in the later 1950s Carter moved from 'rhetoric to reticence'. Certainly Carter's poetic production slowed down: only three brief, but major series of poems were published between 1955 and 1977, compared to the five published between 1951 and 1954. For Rohlehr, Carter is the Caribbean poet whose work directly charts the disappointed political trajectory of the West Indies. In his estimation, Carter's 'retreat into reticence and doubt' is the direct result of political failure, of the 'inevitable shatter and waste of politics' that saw the split of the PPP and the divisions within Guyanese society.[39] 'In 1955 when it was clear that Guyana's future would for some years be fracture, fraud and frustration, hope, the kind eagle had lost its wings'.[40] It is worth thinking clearly about the implications of a reticent and doubtful poet. If we think of reticence, not as the uncritical lapse into silence, but as the critical use of silence, Carter's 'retreat' (as Rohlehr puts it) might not necessarily be seen as a retrograde step. The doubting that Carter expresses in his poetry from the 1950s and 1960s is interrogative. Hope, however submerged, did not disappear entirely and in 'Black Friday 1962', it just survives in this searching poem: 'in despair there is hope, but there is none in death. / now I repeat it here, feeling a waste of life, / in a market-place of doom, watching the human face'.

But politics and the pursuit of a poetic that deals with political hope or despair should not be our only frame of reference for Carter. A consideration of identity, place and vocation drives much of the work that he produced. His poetry always moves between the topical, the geographically locatable and the abstractly drawn, and as he became older it was clear that Carter's politics were part of a larger search to understand his individual and collective identity, and his vocation as a poet. 'Who am I?', 'where am I?', 'what am I doing and why?', are often the central questions of Carter's poetry. If this sounds too personal and subjective in its emphasis on the poet's feelings, we should remember that Carter's poetry is lyrical, as well as rhetorical, narrative and dialogic. Derek Walcott suggests that Carter's 'impulse is always lyrical' and Michael Gilkes has described Carter's poetic as a 'lyrical humanism'.[41] For Carter, what distinguished the lyric as a favoured form was its prioritisation of the voice in action (he calls it a 'verbal art'), its intuitive origins, and its hope to present feeling rather than represent it (he contrasts 'the soliloquial station' of the lyric with the 'representational intention' of narrative).[42] In his notebook Carter writes that 'lyric representation is understandable as the singular performance of reflected feeling'.[43] The performance of reflected feeling did not, however, let Carter abandon social responsibility in favour of the private, personal song of the poet. Lyric poetry offered him a way of locating himself emotionally within the social forces he criticises. The poetic 'I' can be understood as Carter groping to make sense of his world, but his located subjectivity also challenges his readers (who provisionally occupy his position while reading) to join him in this endeavour. In short, even in their most personal form, Carter's lyrics pursue the goal of collective feeling.

Three Poems Shape and Motion – A Sequence (1955) is a fine example of Carter's lyric poetry. The quality of the nouns is telling: they are a combination of the elemental, the emotional and the concrete, framed by the latent spirituality of the poet's 'passion':

> I was wondering if I could shape this passion
> just as I wanted in solid fire.
> I was wondering if the strange combustion of my days
> the tension of the world inside me
> and the strength of my heart were enough.

This voice in action is interested in recasting its emotion in order to achieve clarity of expression and feeling about its present and future. But although this is a poem that articulates the feelings of the poet, the longing that he expresses is not only personal. Clem Seecharan believes that this series of poems were borne out of Carter's political concern about the 'corrosive power of race, the death of reason' in colonial Guyana.[44] That may be so. Certainly, Carter's prose from this period reads that way. But this poetic voice is not written in the register of political expectation or disappointment. The poem is about identity but not about self (understood as the limits of one individual's personhood). The poem concludes, 'If all the population of stars / would be less than the things I could utter / And the challenge of space in my soul / be filled by the shape I become.' Here at the close of the poem Carter presses for an expanded understanding of human identity, recalling the words of Aimé Césaire in the essay 'Poetry and Knowledge': 'Man of every age is within us. All men are within us. The animal, the vegetable and the mineral are within us. Man is not only man. He is a universal humanity.'[45] Carter does not share Césaire's confidence, but his poems in this sequence contemplate the possibility of universal humanity. In the third and final poem Carter tempers this longing with an understanding of the limits of humanity: 'I walk slowly in the wind / I walk because I cannot crawl or fly'. Carter's lyric poetry understands the costs of acting and feeling in a world where failure of action (the collapse of politics) and failure of expression (the collapse of poetry) are too common.

In 'This Race Business' Carter writes, 'realising that the only profound solution is the creation of an equitable social order, we tend to repeat worn-out clichés, until even we ourselves stop believing in their value'. The suggestion is that when nobody will join the PPP in its attempts to create in deed an equitable social order, the party will be forced to repeat a now necessarily inferior demand in words for such an order. This tension is an identifiable Marxist concern. In *The German Ideology* Marx and Engels write against 'what men say' and in favour of 'real active men'.[46] Comparably, Carter recognises that the creation of an equitable social order is worthless (or impossible) if Guyanese anticolonial, socialist activists do not recognise racial division in Guyanese 'material life-process' and the threat posed by political dogma.

Carter's interest lies in the degeneration from political conviction to cliché, which is related to the delay in putting words into action, but he argues for a further stage: from cliché to the destruction of political belief ('until even we ourselves stop believing in their value'). It is not only failure of action that leads to political dis-illusionment, according to Carter, but failure of expression. Marx and Engels seek to avoid 'empty talk about consciousness' and institute a 'real, positive science' of 'the practical process of development of men'.[47] And through its relationship to cliché, Carter's poetry congruently aims to achieve a suitable vocabulary to describe and criticise material social process. It should be noted that Carter does not always avoid cliché; indeed for some poems it could be argued that their rhetorical stress relies upon it. From the rallying poems like 'I Clench My Fist', which are dependent on shared (and therefore possibly overworn) sentiments and expression, to the *Conversations* poems, which are positioned directly against unchanging preconceptions and oversimplification, Carter's poetry works inside and against cliché.

The first poem in *Conversations* questions the poet's duty to write for a particular readership:

> They say I am a poet write for them:
> Sometimes I laugh, sometimes I solemnly nod.
> [...]
> A poet cannot write for those who ask
> Hardly himself even, except he lies.

Carter's series of poems offers a set of arguments about the appropriateness of speaking: from the poet who refuses to write, to the poet who dare not keep too silent, to the poet who is forced into silence, to the poet who writes about silence. In a sequence of poems that deal with the role of the poet, the corruption of society and loss of faith, it is necessary to remember Carter's resignation from the PPP, the political party in which he placed his faith from 1950 to 1956. What is relevant here is that these poems prove Carter to be, not a poet who is silenced by the political failures of the anti-colonial movement in Guyana, but a poet who wishes to speak freely and truthfully in all spheres of human life, and one who is willing to interrogate the meaning of this desire. In the words of Pierre Naville, Carter turns to the 'organisation of pessimism', rather than giving in to it.[48] Conversation then becomes a series of demands, evasions and refusals, and Carter's snapshots of his local, interconnected, conversing nation are prophetic of the disputes and violence that would govern Guyana in the later 1960s.

In a *Thunder* editorial of January 1955, Carter wrote:

> The year that lies before us will be a year of heart searchings, a year of doubt and perplexity, a year in which each one of us will question himself in secret, studying whether the path of life we now tread is

the right one or whether a wrong one. In the midst of all the turmoil and confusion, there will be some whose convictions crumble, some who will repudiate past activities, some who will say in an hour of fear that the road they have been walking is the wrong one because at the given moment all is dark and dreary and apparently hopeless.

Between then and the 1960s Carter's convictions and fortunes had changed. After leaving the PPP, he worked as teacher, for the British Council, and then Booker. It might seem like an ideological U-turn for Carter to associate with institutions which represented cultural and economic imperialism. Certainly, the irony of working within these environments was not lost on Carter. His friend and one-time publisher, David de Caires remembers the early 1960s:

> I would hear him teasing other people. If you came back from England, let us say, with a reputation of being a member of the Communist Party or something of that kind, and he met you he would say, 'Have you thawed out yet?' Then if you made the mistake of saying you hadn't, he would look at Keith [Carter] and say, 'Can't help it, a young boy, you know, he don't know better'. Pouring scorn on idealism, but sort of tongue in cheek [...]. He just became against failure. I don't think he thought a solution was possible. Sometimes I would say 'but what about this, and isn't this possible?' and he would look at Keith and [say] 'can't help it you know, born here'. [...] It was really amusing in some ways, but the underlying theme was a bitterness at failure.[49]

Carter's friendship with de Caires developed into a literary relationship in 1964. Carter submitted an open letter and the series of poems, *Jail Me Quickly*, to de Caires' new Guyanese magazine, *New World Fortnightly*. It is possible to argue that Carter was offering readers of the magazine a manifesto on how to revolt. The five poems could be read as a guide for Guyanese people hoping to regain their revolutionary fervour. However, it is essential to consider the lesson of the poems, if indeed there is one, as tied to Carter's open letter, in which he calls for 'the serious examination of ideas'.

These were poems written 'against failure'. In his open letter Carter queried, 'What I do not know is why so few revolt, either by word or by deed against such acute spiritual discomfort'.[50] *Jail Me Quickly* is a set of poems that explores the city as the locus of revolt, but as he predicted in 1955, revolt would also be accompanied by doubt, perplexity, turmoil and confusion. Even in Carter's most politically insistent collections – *The Hill of Fire Glows Red* and *Poems of Resistance from British Guiana* – these four emotions are present. In *Jail Me Quickly*, Carter turns his own political autobiography on its head, now demanding imprisonment instead of liberty: 'clang the illiterate door / if freedom writes no happier alphabet'. Guyana was not yet independent, but the revolutionary vocabulary martialled against imperialism was no longer appropriate, for what Carter faced was an internal conflict of Guyanese against Guyanese. The 1960s saw the rise of violence not in the name of "anticolonialism" but in the name of "race", as Indian-Guyanese and African-Guyanese fought over the right to define a future independent Guyana. Later writers, such as Grace Nichols in *Whole of a Morning Sky* (1986) and Oonya Kempadoo in *Buxton Spice* (1998), have fictionalised these years, but Carter's poems – with their spare, impassioned analysis of celebration and citizenship – fully expose and reject the failings of the time.[51]

Nation Building and Speaking Again

In 1966 David de Caires and Miles Fitzpatrick invited George Lamming and Martin Carter to edit a special issue of *New World*, which would coincide with the formal declaration of political independence. On 26 May 1966, British Guiana was renamed Guyana and declared an independent nation-state and member of the Commonwealth. The *New World* publication offered its editors a unique opportunity to explore the links between Guyanese politics, national identity and cultural practices.

In the Foreword the Guyanese Prime Minister, Linden Forbes Burnham, demanded that thinkers 'address their minds to the need for cultural and artistic independence; to the need for formulating cultural and artistic goals for the new nations'.[52] In presenting Guyanese independence as a cultural condition, Burnham added his voice to the debate, begun by N.E. Cameron and A.J. Seymour in *Kyk-Over-Al*, about the distinctive nature of artistic and cultural expression in Guyana and its relationship to the political future of the country. Burnham's vision of the importance of cultural and artistic independence can also be analysed according to the framework that Frantz Fanon established in 'On National Culture'. Fanon outlines how (and how not) to use the root idea of 'nation' within the context of colonialism, defining a national culture as 'the whole body of efforts made by a people in the sphere of thought to describe, justify and praise the action through which that people has created itself and keeps itself in existence. A national culture in underdeveloped countries should therefore take its place at the very heart of the struggle for freedom which these countries are carrying on.'[53] The intellectual plays an important part in this struggle. Fanon claims that 'the continued cohesion of the people constitutes for the intellectual an invitation to go farther than his cry of protest. The lament first makes the indictment; then it makes an appeal.'[54] It is possible to argue that Carter never advanced beyond his cry of protest. Indeed in 1985, Carter said to his friend, the artist Stanley Greaves, that 'he was past his peak and that what he wrote when he was in his 20s has stood the test'.[55] However, Carter's work did not stall in the period after independence.

For Fanon, the ability of the intellectual 'to go farther than his cry of protest' is dependent on the cohesion of the people. Yet if their continued cohesion enables the intellectual to abandon negative 'indictment' in favour of positive 'appeal', an incohesive people (perhaps like the population of Guyana) arguably locks the intellectual into a constant cry of protest, with no opportunity for an alternative voice. Fanon's discussion of the role of the intellectual might be interpreted as a critique of the repetitious dead-end into which protest can fall when societies remain, or become, divided. Another interpretation is that Fanon simply does not address the possibility of *continued incohesion*. In Guyana political representation was a marker of the continued incohesion of the people. The progression to independence was particularly fraught: a move to proportional representation left the governing PPP with the conviction that it had been manoeuvred out of power.[56] After the 1964 elections Burnham's PNC formed a government with the conservative United Front, and this coalition led the colony to political independence.[57] To the UK and US governments, the Communist PPP had been rightly forced to face the consequences of the Cold War.[58]

As if in an attempt to break the political stalemate in Guyana, Burnham argued in his Foreword to the Independence issue that 'we must acknowledge the urgent and essential role of the intellectual worker in the process of transforming our societies and nations'.[59] However, by 1972 Gordon Rohlehr was demanding that the Caribbean ask 'how far the politics of independence has kept in tune with the wholeness of creative sensibility and enquiry, which one can feel in our artists and scholars'.[60] For Rohlehr, artists and scholars had become the true independents of the Caribbean, as politicians had not delivered the equitable future demanded by anti-colonialism. 'Wholeness' recalls Fanon's discussion of national culture as 'the whole body of efforts made by a people in the sphere of thought', but as Rohlehr uses it here, the word belongs to Wilson Harris. In 'The Writer and Society', Harris claims: 'the writer lays bare a fiction corresponding to a community whose wholeness in reality cannot exist except by confessing its own insubstantial limits'.[61] Carter's work supports Harris's belief in the wholeness of community, a wholeness which is not fatally undermined by social incohesion on what Harris calls 'the surfaces of life'.[62]

Where Carter and Harris diverge is in their comparative concern for addressing the importance of social incohesion on 'the surfaces'. For Harris the wholeness of community cannot be delimited, but it is always already existing, waiting to be unearthed or discovered. For Carter the wholeness of community must be created, and therefore social incohesion on 'the surfaces of life' is not just an obstacle to be transcended, but a clue to the nature of this potential wholeness. A concrete example of Carter's sense of the wholeness of community can be witnessed in one of the editorial decisions made for the Guyana Independence Issue of *New World*. As editors, Carter and Lamming agreed that the publication should 'cut across all the party lines'.[63] The decision to include both of the violently opposed politicians, Linden Forbes Burnham and Cheddi Jagan, is a Carterian move. Lamming holds that it was only through Carter's continuing relationship with the two men that the editors were able to unite, if only on paper, two politicians who were irreconcilable, and who would never again share a single platform.[64]

Carter had originally planned a retrospective publication in 1970. At that time he was working as Minister of Information and Culture in the Burnham government; he had joined in July 1967, after resigning from his position as Manager at Booker Group's Information Services Department.[65] It is unclear what brought Carter back into the political sphere. Eusi Kwayana has speculated that Carter simply wished to get involved in the country's affairs again, that perhaps he felt a duty to accept the responsibility when it was offered to him.[66] Burnham offered Carter a position as a technocrat, rather than as a party member of the PNC. This appealed to Carter: a technocrat was by definition non-political, and Carter might, therefore, consider his governmental role as non-partisan.[67] Employed for his technical expertise in poetry and experience in the information services, it was these qualifications, rather than shared political beliefs, that determined Carter's role in the government. In *A Georgetown Journal* Andrew Salkey describes the ministerial Carter:

> His words were tellingly chosen; his person, a gentle, tall, big man, a poet who may yet do a very serious injury to the sterile vocabulary and syntax of bureaucracy.
>
> I felt, then, that if he did succeed in giving something new to the style of his particular ministerial responsibility, not only would it sub-

vert the standard image of the other ministries, for the better, but he would have emerged as the pioneer re-discoverer of the long-lost beating heart in anybody's politics.[68]

Salkey suggests that Carter had the potential to alter Guyanese, and regional, politics. *A Georgetown Journal* was published in 1972, and by this time Salkey would have known the outcome of Carter's political career in Burnham's government. The poet who could injure the vocabulary and syntax of bureaucracy did not change it, and Carter's time in the PNC coincided with a period now defined by allegations that the government kept itself in power by rigging the 1968 election.[69]

Carter later admitted the general difficulties he faced:

> It was out of character, so to speak. I remained three years in the government, and I resigned after that. It was a question of incompatibility. I think that was the whole question: a question of incompatibility. I simply couldn't do it. [...] I expected that it was something that I could handle, you know – a pretty straightforward business. I had an idea how people would act. People don't act like that: it's not a straightforward business at all.[70]

As a Minister, Carter was involved in Guyana's transition from a monarchy to a Co-operative Republic, removing the final constitutional link between Britain and Guyana. In one information broadcast Carter linked this act of liberation from the British Crown to the 1763 Berbice slave revolution, as both were intended 'to liberate ourselves from our inherited economic, social and psychological bondage'.[71]

Carter's other high profile role concerned the organisation of the Caribbean Writers' and Artists' Convention, held in Georgetown at the same time as the Guyana Republic celebrations. A.J. Seymour was the official organiser of the event, with Burnham's support. The list of delegates was impressive: Kamau Brathwaite, Jan Carew, Michael Gilkes, Wilson Harris, John La Rose, Earl Lovelace, Philip Moore, V.S. Reid, Sam Selvon, Ivan Van Sertima, Aubrey Williams. Their brief was to discuss the shape of the proposed Caribbean Arts Festival of 1971 (Carifesta, as it became known, was eventually held in Guyana in 1972.) And there were other interests to pursue. Carter had invited John La Rose, a Trinidadian writer and founder of New Beacon publishers, now based in London. At the convention Carter discussed the possibility of New Beacon publishing a retrospective collection of poems. La Rose agreed and Carter gave him the provisional title, *Poems 1970-1950*, destabilising the standard chronological understanding of a writer's work.[72] Salkey remembers much of the convention as 'blissfully unhinged', but Wilson Harris expressed deep concern: 'This place [Guyana] turns everything into a comedy of the absurd. It's nihilistic without knowing it. It reduces ideas and people to simple disposable units. Take Martin singing *Where have all the flowers gone?* D'you know that since I arrived, I haven't been able to talk to him for *Where have all the flowers gone?* Everytime I see him, he's singing it.'[73]

Harris was probably right to draw attention to Carter's behaviour. However, we might notice that Carter had already expressed doubts about the intellectual value of writers' conferences. When he attended the Commonwealth Arts Festival Meeting in Cardiff in 1966, he returned disappointed at the lack of 'vitality' amongst his peers.[74] The emotional power and even 'divine wildness' that Carter had demanded from the Cardiff conference seems to have been delivered, to some extent, in Georgetown.[75] Carter's singing can be seen as at once an attempt to contribute to this 'wildness', an attempt to disrupt any sterility at the convention, and perhaps also a wry commentary on the contemporary development of Caribbean culture.[76] But Harris was perceptive in his concern for Carter. Carter was not happy in his government role and Burnham had repeatedly persuaded him not to leave, but in November 1970 Carter officially resigned.[77] Carter later revealed to Janet Jagan the particular circumstances that had led to his resignation. As he stepped off a plane returning from a state visit, he had seen a man with elephantiasis of the foot, and he knew that he could no longer square his own privileges with the man's suffering.[78]

Carter's return to Bookers made front-page news in the *Sunday Argosy*.[79] And it also marked a return to publishing poetry. In a 1969 letter, written while Carter was still Minister of Information and Culture, C.L.R. James wrote, 'I hope you have not entirely abandoned the writing of poetry'.[80] He had not, and the retrospective collection of poems expanded over the next seven years into *Poems of Succession*. Rather than emphasising earlier work, ultimately the collection was distinguished by its inclusion of new poems. *The When Time* – the name given to the newly published work – proved the continued poetic activity of Carter. It is tempting to understand 'The When Time' as a euphemism for social revolution; Marx can be read as fundamentally concerned about 'the when time', the moment when the development of historical forces reaches an appropriate time for revolution. But Carter does not use Marx's terms, nor write in the clarificatory register of political theory. As the syntactical structure of the phrase, 'The When Time', intimates,

Carter composes riddles for himself and his readers. The fact that Carter resigned from politics during the time in which he first conceived this collection may suggest that *The When Time* is defined by a certain kind of failure: a fulfilment of the disillusionment with politics to which the earlier poetry in *Jail Me Quickly* points. Instead, *The When Time* proved the range of Carter's poetic interests and successes. 'For Milton Williams' sees Carter address the concrete geography of Guyana and his particular Guyanese friendships. 'For Angela Davis' praises the revolutionary work of the African-American activist. Carter explicitly sees Davis's work as a sign of hope and here the concluding flood imagery of *Conversations* is replaced by another covenant: 'what I want to do / is to command the drying pools of rain / to wet your tired feet and / lift your face / to the gift of the roof of / clouds we owe you'. He revisits his childhood in 'As When I Was', writes of the longevity of love in 'My Hand in Yours', includes an elegy for the Trinidadian poet, Eric Roach, and meditates on the rivers, flora and fauna of Guyana. Rupert Roopnaraine rightly describes *Poems of Succession* as a collection of 'private wonder', but that is only part of its power.[81] *The When Time* is more importantly a series of poems defined by the affiliations that emerge from the privacies of poetic compostion. Hanging in Carter's study was a framed quotation from Friedrich Hölderlin: '...Never gladly the poet keeps his love unshared, but likes to join with others who help him understand it. But if he must, undaunted the man remains...'.[82] *The When Time* is a series of poems defined by the affiliations that emerge from the privacies of poetic composition.

Searching for Affinity

The titles of Carter's three longest collections – *Poems of Resistance*, *Poems of Succession*, *Poems of Affinity* – gesture to an overarching consistency in his work. The first repetition of 'Poems of' came in *Poems of Succession*, after a period of experimentation with both prose fiction and direct governmental action. The further repetition in *Poems of Affinity* (1980) can be read as a reaffirmation of Carter's loyalty to poetry. And the repeating title is part of a continually developing pattern. In the biographical statement that appears on the inside cover of *Poems of Affinity*, we read that 'Carter has already started on a new collection, *Poems of Mortality*'.[83] The titles of the four collections (one prospective) hint at an ordering principle for

Carter's entire corpus. Resistance, succession, affinity and mortality provide the markers of a forty-year career. In *Poems of Resistance* the political engagement of the poet forms an expansive base for his work. Even if the etymology of *resistance* demands that Carter "stand against" (colonialism, invasion, poverty, slavery), the poems prove that his poetics cannot be reduced to a narrowly reactive stance. *Poems of Succession*, from which *The When Time* is drawn, medially points forward and back to Carter's political and poetic 'successions'. After stressing firmness of position with resistance, it might seem that succession – with its emphasis on the passing from one state to another – denies this. But succession does not necessarily imply the supplanting of one thing at the expense of another. While Carter's use of 'succession' allows agonistic readings of the rhetorical poet versus the reticent poet, it is much more appealing to see Carter's poetic as cumulative, advancing temporally, but never abandoning the poetry of the past.

Like resistance and succession, the word *affinity* holds positional implications. Etymologically, its root lies in the Latin verb, *finire*, meaning 'to border, end, limit'. In its present usage, affinity describes structural resemblances, kinship and attraction. In an interview with Frank Birbalsingh, Carter explained the poetic importance of affinity: 'Everything borders with something else. When you speak to me about something, I usually see it one way, then in another in one flat second. And that is what I'm trying to do – to deal with two things simultaneously, not separately.'[84] The final poem of *The When Time* indicated the direction Carter's poetry might move, with its gnomic invocation of 'two in one', and the enigmatic opening of 'Our time' in *Poems of Affinity* re-establishes Carter's interest in simultaneity: 'The more the men of our time we are / the more our time is.' The rest of the poem acts as an unravelling of the implications of this proverbial statement:

> The more the men of our time we are
> the more our time is. But always
> we have been somewhere else. Muttering
> our mouths like holes in the mud
> at the bottom of trenches. Looking
> for what is not anywhere, or certain.

The demand for the production of 'men of our time' quickly appears to be a hollow rhetorical utterance. It is a tragic variation on affinity and on Carter's assertion that 'everything borders with something else', for the borders, if they exist, are here obscured. The hope of common belonging to a particular victorious historical moment is a powerful but impossible aspiration.

The imperative of 'our time' is not lost on Carter. 'Badly abused / we fail to curse. Our fury pleads. / Yet fury should be fire; if not light.' This vocabulary of abuse and fury and fire is reminiscent of Carter's lexicon of the 1950s, but its purchase in the 1970s was quite different. Criticism of the PNC government increased throughout the 1970s and fears about Burnham's increasingly dictatorial régime were voiced inside and outside Guyana. During this decade Carter's reflections on resistance had renewed relevance, and in his 'Open Letter to the Guyanese People', Carter itemised his objections to the PNC, calling for 'Resistance to the brute fact of degradation itself. Resistance to the exploitation of this degradation by the régime.'

In 1979, a year before *Poems of Affinity* was published, Carter's Guyanese publisher, Release, reissued *Poems of Resistance*. Earlier, in 1976 Rupert Roopnaraine had begun work on a film titled, *The Terror and the Time*, based on Carter's 1950s poems (the title having been taken from 'University of Hunger'). Carter narrated his poems, notably 'The Cartman of Dayclean' and 'I Come from the Nigger Yard', over sequences of film shot in contemporary Guyana. Roopnaraine comments on the impact of this artistic time-lag: 'To have the poet read, in 1976, the *Poems of Resistance*, a work deeply rooted in the conditions of 1953, and to have those words reverberate over images of 1953 shot in 1976, is to take account of and to emphasise the similarity in disparity between the two sets of conditions, the colonial and the neo-colonial.' [85] The film took its prompt from Carter's description of the cartman as 'consistent in the dark': 'we took the cartman's consistency in the dark to mean a kind of integration of man in his world, a moment of oneness and cohesion'.[86] And from this moment of 'cohesion' the filmmakers charted the 'fragmentation' of contemporary and colonial Guyana.[87] *The Terror and the Time* and Carter's poetry can be defined by their exploration of the dialectical opposites of cohesion and fragmentation, and although these ideas pull in antithetical directions, they form the key ideas of *Poems of Affinity*, a collection that atttempts to understand the disappointments and solaces to be found in Carter's postcolonial nation.

In 1978, Carter offered seven new poems to *The Georgetown Review*, a journal newly founded by Andaiye, Brian Rodway and Rupert Roopnaraine (all active members of the Working People's Alliance, a new political party that attempted to bridge Guyana's ethnic divisions and protest against the PNC government). Simply titled, 'New Poems by Martin Carter', the selection of seven poems included six poems that would later appear in *Poems of Affinity*: 'Our Number', 'Rice', 'Paying Fares', 'Rain Forest', 'Playing Militia' and 'Our Time'. Carter's work is ambiguous and complex enough to discourage any attempt to locate a narrative in these seven poems, but it is notable that Carter leads up to 'Our Time' here, whereas in *Poems of Affinity* it launches the collection. Given the journal's aims to understand the economic, social and political crisis in Guyana, Carter's sequence – with its material discussions of fishing ('Our Number'), rice growing ('Rice'), the buses ('Paying Fares'), the interior ('Rain Forest') and the militarisation of the Guyanese youth ('Playing Militia') – can be read as a checklist of these crises. 'Our Time' then becomes the summation of Carter's material concerns. Yet while Carter is insistently concerned with everyday life in this sequence, his poetry is not constrained by his materialism. 'Our Number' is at first a surreal snapshot of marine life – 'The fisherman's / wife, another seagull, leans on the sky / counting shrimp' – but like so much of Carter's work, its focus sharpens, the wordplay toughens and we are left with a poem of riddling significance: 'Shrimp is our number. Is so / we stay. Is a way / of counting born we'.[88]

Sidney Singh, boatman and Martin Carter, Mahaica River.

'A poet cannot truly speak to himself save in his own country'

Edward Said's formula that 'poetic calling develops out of a pact made between people and poet' is partially supported by a reading of Carter's work.[89] In 'For César Vallejo I', Carter initially adheres to this notion of 'calling', urging his fellow poet, 'Brother, let us now break / our bread together.' Yet Said's notion of a pact made between a set of 'people' and separated 'poets' provides an inadequate summary of the dynamics of Carter's poetry. Carter throughout his work resisted being summoned as a 'poet', and similarly resisted summoning 'people' to read his poetry in an authorially defined way. Yet the relationship between people and poet remains compelling. What needs to be reformulated is Said's distinction between 'people' and 'poet'. In 'For César Vallejo I' we find Carter's attempt at such a reformulation:

> César Vallejo. The parrots
> call your name, fertile as
> rain. My habit of utterance
> kneels down at the sound of it.
> I, who only wanted to be
> and to have a name.

Carter offers an intimate homage to the Peruvian poet. Here, Carter becomes reader and disciple, defining his own poetry humbly as 'my habit of utterance'. In the manuscript of the poem, though, Carter ends the poem thus: 'I, who wanted to be / a poet, and to have a name / like yours'.[90] The emphasis is placed on poetic reputation and emulation and the poet dreams of belonging to a poetic community. This statement might offer us a glimpse of the poetic ambition that Carter rarely expressed: a desire to belong to an international community of writers who ratify each other's identities as poets. In the published poem, however, this poetic ambition has either been suppressed or discarded, as Carter offers a more self-effacing and searching confession about personal identity, that is related but not limited to his status as a poet.

Carter continued to write poetry after the publication of *Poems of Affinity* in 1980, stopping only when he suffered a stroke in 1993 (after which he was unable to write with ease, and so never completed *Poems of Mortality*).[91] 'Four Poems and Demerara Nigger' was published in *Kyk-Over-Al* in 1984. In 'Two' Carter returned to the theme of the poet; the manuscript submitted to Seymour shows that the poem was first entitled 'On Reading a Young Poet'.[92] The opening lines mimic the young poet's hesitant process of writing, as well as hinting at the older poet's discriminating process of reading:

Not so is it done, O no
not so. It is done, so,
as I think I am doing it,
neither not, nor so, but only
just in a wait, in a
moment, in a year, in
and this moment, this
yester just so.

Carter's decision to change from a descriptive to a non-descriptive title helps to unite the younger and the older poets' expressions into one poetic voice. The hesitancy, the exacting eye and the compositional speed (which knows no difference between 'a moment' and 'a year') are Carter's scribal traits. So when Carter comes to write the next lines – 'Because a poet cannot truly speak / to himself save in his / own country' – we might expect to read the straightforward expression of his role in Guyanese society. While this is arguably Carter's most explicit statement in poetry about how 'his own country' enables the writing of poetry, he does not name Guyana nor a Guyanese body of readers. It was only in a later interview that Carter stated, 'I stayed in Guyana deliberately. I felt that to be a writer, especially a poet, I should.' [93]

In his poetry lyrical honesty can include national allegiance, but bare national allegiance cannot create poetry. In 'Two' that lyrical honesty is found in the implied conversation between Carter's younger and older poetic selves. A year later Carter contributed a poem to *Walter Rodney: Poetic Tributes*. Rodney, a leader of the Working People's Alliance, had been killed by a bomb, which many believe was an assassination ordered by the Burnham government. [93] Titled simply 'For Walter Rodney', Carter challenges 'Assassins of conversation', confronting and defying the consequences of Rodney's death: 'they bury the voice / they assassinate, in the beloved / grave of the voice, never to be silent'. If Carter sees Guyana as his 'own country', the only place within which he can 'truly speak', then we can track in his work the struggle to attain lyrical honesty in a country too often characterised by interment, graves and the silencing of the voice.

In his 1979 notebook, under the heading 'Guyanese Poetry', Carter wrote:

Guyana's analogies on a global scale are the prisons, madhouses, hospitals, slums, street pavements which all countries, developed or underdeveloped have. This is what makes it possible for Guyanese poetry to have universality, because it is the poetry of naked men and naked minds locked in cells.[95]

These bleak man-made places are identifiably Carter's Guyana and his poetry inhabits and dissects them throughout his career. Imagined and real cells gave him a theme for writing and 'naked' describes well the clarity of expression to which Carter aspired and the poverty he often wished to expose. But this striking analysis cannot register the other places from which Carter drew his poetry: the ocean, the river, the forest, the stars, the sea wall, the bridge, the house, the window. In this collection we find (in the words of Derek Walcott) a 'tenderness' that could make poetry out of a flower, a leaf, the rain, a bird or a fish as easily as it could address fury, fire and futility.[96] Writing in Georgetown, in the country where he spent his whole life, Carter's world was not small. Composing poetry on whatever was in front of him – cigarette cartons, envelopes, scrap paper – the urgency of his writing matched his need to understand himself and the world. If Carter's is 'the poetry of naked men', it is all the better for it. In his work nakedness revealed the vulnerabilities and strengths of human existence, and importantly, nakedness provoked truthfulness. This, for better or worse, is the testing lesson of his 'university of hunger'.

NOTES

1. 'Exit Carter with a poem', *Sunday Graphic*, 15 November 1970, p.1.
2. Ibid.
3. Quoted in Cameron, *Guianese Poetry*, p.2. Cameron includes work by 'Colonist', *Midnight Musings in Demerara* (Georgetown: Courier Office, 1832).
4. Kenneth Ramchand, *The West Indian Novel and its Background* (London: Faber & Faber, 1970), pp.32-38.
5. Although A.J. Seymour often uses the non-hyphenated spelling *Kykoveral* and also employs *Kyk-over-al* or *Kyk* within articles, I follow here the hyphenated, capitalised, *Kyk-Over-Al*, which appears on the majority of title-pages of the journal.
6. A.J. Seymour, 'Editorial Notes', *Kyk-Over-Al*, 1 (December 1945), p.7.
7. See A.J. Seymour, 'Editorial Note', *Kyk-Over-Al*, 8 (June 1949), p.3 for his hope that *Kyk-Over-Al* would act as a forum for cultural discussion.
8. Martin Carter, 'From "An Ode to Midnight"', *Kyk-Over-Al*, 6 (June 1948), p.5. The full text of this poem is no longer extant.
9. Ben Carter, Interview, 30 July 1999.
10. Rory Westmaas, Interview, 2 November 1999.
11. Ben Carter, Interview, 30 July 1999.
12. 'We read Shakespeare, Donne, Milton, Pope, Coleridge, Tennyson, Wordsworth, we also read Latin texts, Ovid, Caesar, Sallust. But that was

not all [...] Queen's College did not have actual courses that dealt with the Americas as a whole but there was no overt censorship of books in the college library'. Wilson Harris, 'Wilson Harris, 1921-', *Contemporary Authors Autobiography Series*, 16 (1992), 121-37 (p.131).

13. See Edgar Mittelholzer, *A Swarthy Boy* (London: Putnam, 1963), p.35, pp.155-56, for a description of the strict social and racial expectations within New Amsterdam.

14. Clem Seecharan writes that 'coloured' was the term used to describe Guyanese people of mixed race in colonial Guyana, and that the term is still used today. See 'The Shape of the Passion: The Historical Context of Martin Carter's Poetry of Protest (1951-1964)', in *All Are Involved: The Art of Martin Carter*, ed. by Stewart Brown (Leeds: Peepal Tree, 2000), pp.24-47 (p.24).

15. Richard Allsopp, Interview, 25 November 1998.

16. Ben Carter, Interview, 30 July 1999.

17. There is some confusion about the dates of Carter's school career: he remains on the Queen's College register until 1946/47. In the Introduction to Carter's *Selected Poems*, Ian McDonald states that Carter left school at 17, p.22. Carter was born in June 1927.

18. Ben Carter, Interview, 30 July 1999.

19. McDonald, Foreword, *Selected Poems*, p.22.

20. See Maurice St Pierre, *Anatomy of Resistance: Anti-Colonialism in Guyana 1823-1966*, Warwick University Caribbean Studies (London: Macmillan Education, 1999), p.51, p.74.

21. The Political Reform Club was established in 1887 and renamed as the Reform Association in 1889; see Walter Rodney, *A History of the Guyanese Working People* (Baltimore: The Johns Hopkins University Press, 1981), pp. 139-45. In 1945 there were franchise qualifications based on income, property and literacy.

22. Ben Carter, Interview, 30 July 1999. All the information in this paragraph about the Carter family was kindly passed on to me by Mr Ben Carter.

23. Carter never joined the Communist Party.

24. Cheddi Jagan, *The West on Trial: My Fight for Guyana's Freedom* (London: Michael Joseph, 1996; St Johns, Antigua: Hansib Caribbean, 1997), p.62.

25. Ibid, p.104.

26. PPP, 'Aims and Programme of People's Progressive Party', *Thunder*, 1.4 (April 1950), [n.p.].

27. Ibid.

28. Raymond Williams, *Culture and Society* (London: Chatto & Windus, 1958; London: Hogarth, 1993), p.155.

29. *West India Royal Commission Report Presented by the Secretary of State for the Colonies to Parliament by Command of His Majesty June 1945*, Cmd. 6607 (London: HMSO, 1945), p.305.

30. Sydney King, 'A Hymn of the Slumyard', *Thunder* 1.6 (June 1950), p.3. 'The Jobless Brothers' and '"Call to the Toilers"' appear in *Thunder*, 1.4 (April 1950), p.2.

31. See Richard Crossman, ed., *The God that Failed* (New York: Harper, 1949) including articles by Arthur Koestler, André Gide, Richard Wright.

32. George Padmore, 'Moral Leadership to Gold Coast People', *Thunder*, 2.5 (May 1951), p.3 (p.3). See also anon, 'People's Victory in Gold Coast Elections', *Thunder*, 2.3 (March 1951), p.10. The Gold Coast became independent as Ghana in 1957.

33. See anon, 'Pity the Poor Exploiters', *Thunder*, 1.11 (November 1950), p.9; anon, 'Housing on Sugar Estates', *Thunder*, 1.3 (March 1950), pp.6-7; anon, 'Unite to fight for a New Constitution', *Thunder*, 1.10 (October 1950), p.2.

34. Leon Trotsky, *Literature and Revolution* (1924), trans. by Rose Strunsky (Ann Arbor: University of Michigan Press, 1960), p.230.

35. John Holm, *Pidgins and Creoles*, 2 vols (Cambridge: Cambridge University Press, 1988; repr., 1995), *1: Theory and Structure*, pp.52-53. See also John R. Rickford, *Dimensions of a Creole Continuum: History, Texts, and Linguistic Analysis of Guyanese Creole* (Stanford: Stanford University Press, 1987).

36. Rupert Roopnaraine, 'Martin Carter and Politics', in *All Are Involved: The Art of Martin Carter*, ed. by Stewart Brown (Leeds: Peepal Tree, 2000), p.51.

37. *Lawrence & Wishart 1954 Catalogue* (London: Lawrence & Wishart, 1954), p.9.

38. Sydney King, 'Introduction', *Poems of Resistance from British Guiana* (London: Lawrence & Wishart, 1954), pp.i-iii (pp.i-ii). Other critics have followed King. Rayman Mandal in the Foreword to the third edition of *Poems of Resistance* (retitled *Poems of Resistance from Guyana*) writes, 'historically, the *Poems of Resistance* have grown out of a given period in Guyana's history'; see p.5. Bill Carr in the Foreword to *Poems of Affinity 1978-1980* writes of the 'significant political content of Carter's volume *Poems of Resistance*', p.vii. See also Clem Seecharan, 'The Shape of the Passion: The Historical Context of Martin Carter's Poetry of Protest (1951-1964)', in *All Are Involved: The Art of Martin Carter*, ed. by Stewart Brown (Leeds: Peepal Tree, 2000), pp.24-47 (p.25).

39. Gordon Rohlehr, 'The Creative Writer and West Indian Society', *Kaie: The Literary Vision of Carifesta '72*, 11 (August 1973), 48-77 (p.63).

40. Ibid, p.52.

41. Derek Walcott, '...His Impulse is Always Lyrical', in *All Are Involved: The Art of Martin Carter*, ed. by Stewart Brown (Leeds: Peepal Tree, 2000), pp.307-10 (p.310) and Michael Gilkes, 'The Poems Man: Lyrical Humanism in the Poetry of Martin Carter', in *All Are Involved: The Art of Martin Carter*, pp.237-44.

42. Martin Carter, *Lyric: A Sufficiency*, mss dated 24 October 1982, Martin Carter Private Papers. These papers are held by Mrs Phyllis Carter and I would like to thank her for allowing me to quote from the manuscript.

43. Untitled note, 11 January 1983, Brown Notebook, Carter Private Papers, held by Mrs Phyllis Carter.

44. Clem Seecharan, 'The Shape of the Passion: The Historical Context of Martin Carter's Poetry of Protest (1951-1964)', p.35.

45. Aimé Césaire, 'Poetry and Knowledge', *Refusal of the Shadow: Surrealism and the Caribbean*, pp.134-46 (p.139). This essay was first published in *Tropiques*, 12 (January 1945).

46. Karl Marx and Friedrich Engels, *The German Ideology* (London: Lawrence & Wishart, 1970), p.47.

47. Ibid, p.48.

48. Quoted in Walter Benjamin, 'Surrealism: The Last Snapshot of the European Intelligentsia' (1929), in *One-Way Street* (London: Verso, 1997), pp.225-39 (p.238).

49. De Caires, Interview, 20 July 1999.

50. Martin Carter, 'Letter', *New World Fortnightly*, 1 (30 October 1964), 2 (p.2).

51. For further discussion of Carter in the 1960s, see my '"If freedom writes no happier alphabet": Martin Carter and Poetic Silence', *Small Axe: A Caribbean Journal of Criticism*, 15 (March 2004), 43-62.

52. Linden Forbes Burnham, Foreword, *New World: Guyana Independence Issue*, in *On The Canvas of the World*, ed. by George Lamming (Port of Spain: The Trinidad and Tobago Institute of the West Indies, 1999), p.13.

53. Frantz Fanon, 'On National Culture', *The Wretched of the Earth*, trans. by Constance Farrington (Harmondsworth: Penguin, 1967; repr. 1990), p.188.

54. Ibid, p.193.

55. Stanley Greaves, unpublished diary, 29 September 1985, p.32. Greaves kindly sent me pages from his diary in which he records his meetings with Carter. The diary remains in Greaves's private possession.

56. There is a great deal of literature on the subject of Guyana's independence constitution. For further information, see Cheddi Jagan, *The West on Trial*; Cheddi Jagan, *The Role of the CIA in Guyana and its Activities Throughout the World* (Georgetown: PPP, 1967); Latin America Bureau, *Guyana: Fraudulent Revolution* (London: Latin America Bureau, 1984); Percy C. Hintzen, *The Costs of Régime Survival: Racial mobilisation, elite domination and control of the state in Guyana and Trinidad* (Cambridge: Cambridge University Press, 1989); Lily Ramcharan, *The Cold War in the Third World: Guyana 1953-1989* (Georgetown: Lily Ramcharan, 1997); Fr Andrew Morrison, SJ, *Justice* (Georgetown: Red Thread Women's Press, 1998).

57. Demographic projections of the increasing Indian-Guyanese population suggested that after 1961 the PPP would have a built-in electoral majority in a "first past the post" constituency system. The PNC and UF were in favour of a shift to proportional representation, while the PPP remained opposed. See David de Caires and Miles Fitzpatrick, 'Twenty Years of Politics in our Land', New World: Guyana Independence Issue, in *On The Canvas of the World*, ed. by George Lamming (Port of Spain: The Trinidad and Tobago Institute of the West Indies, 1999), pp.57-64 (p.62).

58. In 1996 the Guyanese *Stabroek News* published newly released US National Security files on British Guiana, revealing the influence of the US in Guyana's independence. One document quotes the US Secretary of State enjoining the British Foreign Secretary that 'I hope we can agree that Jagan should not accede to power again', *Sunday Stabroek*, 15 December 1996, p.18.

59. Burnham, Foreword, *New World: Guyana Independence Issue*, p.14.

60. Rohlehr, 'The Creative Writer and West Indian Society', p.52.

61. Wilson Harris, 'The Writer and Society', in *Tradition, the Writer and Society: Critical Essays* (London and Port of Spain: New Beacon, 1967), pp. 48-64 (p.49).

62. Ibid.

63. George Lamming, 'Martin Carter: A Poet of the Americas (in conversation with Stewart Brown)', in *All Are Involved: The Art of Martin Carter*, ed. by Stewart Brown (Leeds: Peepal Tree, 2000), pp.311-17 (p.312).

64. Ibid., pp.311-12.

65. Anon, 'Carter Back With Bookers', *Sunday Graphic*, 17 January 1971, p.1.

66. Eusi Kwayana, Interview, 30 July 1999. Kwayana was also a member of the PNC at this time. He resigned from the party in 1971. Kwayana founded the African Society for Cultural Relations with Independent Africa (ASCRIA) in 1968, and he became increasingly disillusioned with the Burnham régime.

67. When I spoke to Carter he pointed out that his position was that of a technocrat, not a politician. Martin Carter, Interview, 12 December 1995.

68. Andrew Salkey, *A Georgetown Journal: A Caribbean Writer's Journey from London via Port of Spain to Georgetown, Guyana, 1970* (London and Port of Spain: New Beacon, 1972), p.102.

69. It is alleged that in the December 1968 elections, the Burnham government falsified electoral ballot papers. See Latin America Bureau, *Guyana: Fraudulent Revolution* (London: Latin America Bureau, 1984), p.10.

70. Martin Carter, Interview, 12 December 1995.

71. Martin Carter, Broadcast Statement by Minister of Information, 1 August 1969. Transcript dated 23 June 1992 and filed in Ian McDonald's Martin Carter file (presumably the piece was considered for the *Kyk-Over-Al Martin Carter Prose Sampler*). Note that 1 August is Emancipation Day in the Caribbean, commemorating the abolition of slavery in the West Indies in 1838.

72. John La Rose, telephone conversation, 24 June 1998. See also John La Rose, 'Martin Carter 1927-1997: A Personal Memoir', in *All Are Involved*, pp. 319-23 (p.322).

73. Andrew Salkey, *Georgetown Journal*, p.104.

74. Martin Carter, 'A Guyanese Poet in Cardiff: Martin Carter reports in a radio interview', *Kaie*, 2 (May 1966), 18-21 (p.19). See also 'Sambo at Large' in this collection.

75. Ibid.

76. The lyrics to the song, or Carter's repetition of them, should not necessarily be interpreted in Harris's terms as absurdist or nihilist. The song asks:

Where have all the flowers gone?
The girls have picked them every one.
Oh, when will you ever learn?
Oh, when will you ever learn?

Carter's repetition of these lyrics might be considered as a concentrated effort to encourage his fellow delegates to 'learn' from past experience in their present and future conduct. *Where have all the flowers gone?* was played at Carter's funeral in December 1997.

77. Sonia Dolphin, Interview, 27 November 1998.

78. Janet Jagan, Interview, 29 October 1998. In his interview with me Carter contradicted this and said that there was no particular incident that had caused his resignation, but that 'it was brewing all the time'. Carter Interview, 12 December 1995.

79. Anon, 'Carter Back with Bookers', *Sunday Graphic*, 17 January 1971, p.1.

80. C.L.R. James, letter to Martin Carter, 14 October 1969, held in Carter's private papers.

81. Rupert Roopnaraine, Comment on the back cover of the first edition of *Selected Poems*.

82. Friedrich Hölderlin, 'The Poet's Vocation', *Poems and Fragments*, trans. by Michael Hamburger (London: Routledge and Kegan Paul, 1966), pp.173-77 (pp.175-77).

83. Martin Carter, *Poems of Affinity* (Georgetown: Release, 1980), inside front cover.

84. Frank Birbalsingh, 'Interview with Martin Carter' in *Kyk-Over-Al*, 46/47 (1995), 218-34 (p.228).

85. Rupert Roopnaraine, 'The Terror and the Time: interview with Monica Jardine and Andaiye', *The Georgetown Review*, 1.1 (August 1978), 102-26 (p.116).

86. Ibid.

87. Ibid, p.117.

88. For further discussion of *Poems of Affinity*, see my '"Me-riddle me-riddle": The Manuscripts of Martin Carter', *Moving Worlds: A Journal of Trancultural Writing*, 3.2 (2003), 34-49.

89. Edward Said, *Culture and Imperialism* (London: Chatto & Windus, 1993), p.282. Said's sentence is part of a discussion of W.B. Yeats and Pablo Neruda, but the formula remains pertinent to Carter.

90. Martin Carter, 'For César Vallejo', *Poems of Affinity* Manuscripts. These manuscripts are in the private possession of Mrs Phyllis Carter.

91. Carter, Interview, 12 December 1995.

92. Martin Carter, letter to A.J. Seymour including the manuscript of 'Four Poems and Demerara Nigger', 12 November 1984. I would like to thank Ian McDonald for letting me see the letter and manuscript; McDonald holds the originals in his *Kyk-Over-Al* file on Martin Carter.

93. Carter, Interview, 15 December 1995.

94. See Morrison, *Justice*, pp.151-59.

95. Martin Carter, Brown Notebook (1976 Diary), entry dated 28 October 1979.

96. Walcott, '...His Impulse Is Always Lyrical', p.310.

ACKNOWLEDGEMENTS

I am forever grateful to Phyllis Carter and her family for support-
ing this edition. In particular Phyllis has always welcomed me to
her home, allowing to me to work through Martin Carter's private
papers and patiently answering my persistent questions. I have also
benefited from discussions with Richard Allsopp, Andaiye, Ronald
Austin, Karin Barber, Edward Baugh, Kamau Brathwaite, Stewart
Brown, Jane Bryce, Ben Carter, Jerry Carter, Keith Carter, Hugh
Cholmondley, al creighton, Tim Cribb, Rowan Cruft, David Daby-
deen, Fred D'Aguiar, David and Doreen de Caires, Sonia and
Joseph Dolphin, Joan Fields, Miles Fitzpatrick, Gordon Forte,
Martin Goolsaran, Stanley Greaves, Wilson Harris, Alim Hosein,
Eric and Jessica Huntley, Rashleigh Jackson, Janet Jagan, Adeola
James, Louis James, Joyce Jonas, Dudley Kissoore, Eusi Kwayana,
John La Rose, Nicholas Laughlin, Janice Lowe Shinebourne, Ian
McDonald, Mark McWatt, Sheree Mack, Mervyn Morris, Jim
Murray, Moses Nagamootoo, Phillip Nanton, Grace Nichols, Ngugi
wa Thiong'o, Molara Ogundipe, Salvador Ortiz-Carboneres, Diana
Paton, Peter Patrick, Petamber Persaud, Francis Quamina-Farrier,
Vanda Radzik, Kenneth Ramchand, Gordon Rohlehr, Rupert Roop-
naraine, Terry Roopnaraine, Lloyd Searwar, Clem Seecharan, George
Simon, Clive Thomas, Anne Walmsley, Sarah White, Nigel West-
maas, Rory Westmaas. Thanks also to all my family.

This edition would not have been possible without the support
of the librarians at the University of Guyana, the University of the
West Indies, the National Libraries of Guyana, Trinidad, Barbados
and Jamaica, the National Archives of Guyana and the UK, and
the archivists at the Cheddi Jagan Research Centre, Rodney House,
Freedom House, *Stabroek News*, BBC Written Archives, the George
Padmore Institute, and Lawrence & Wishart. I am also grateful for
the support provided by the British Library, the University Library
in Cambridge and Newcastle University's Robinson Library. My
research has also benefited from the support of the British Academy
and the Arts and Humanities Research Council.

The study of Carter's work has been aided by several key pub-
lications in recent years. The *Selected Poems* (Georgetown: Demerara
Publishers, 1989) gives us Carter's choice of his work. The 1993
Kyk-Over-Al Martin Carter Prose Sampler and the 2000 *Kyk-Over-
Al Martin Carter Tribute* publish rarely seen prose and poetry. A
second edition of *Selected Poems* was published (Georgetown: Red

Thread Women's Press, 1997), followed by a new bilingual English-Spanish edition (Leeds: Peepal Tree, 1999). Stewart Brown's *All Are Involved: The Art of Martin Carter* (Leeds: Peepal Tree, 2000) gathers together the growing body of criticism on Carter's work. I owe a large debt to the editors of these and Carter's earlier works: Stewart Brown, David Dabydeen, Neville Dawes, David de Caires, Miles Fitzpatrick, Rayman Mandal, Ian McDonald, Vanda Radzik and A.J. Seymour.

NOTE ON THE TEXT

This edition brings together all of Carter's published poetry with
selections from his prose. It is the first edition of its kind, in that
it is the most comprehensive collection of Carter's poetry to date,
and includes previously unpublished work. Furthermore, it is the
first edition that consults and comments on the variant readings of
his work. The editing of Caribbean literature is at an important
crossroads. We have to ask ourselves the question: 'Why edit?' No
edition of Carter's poems and prose can unassailably claim to have
printed just what Carter wrote. Only some of Carter's own hand-
written drafts of his work survive, as do only a few fair copy manu-
scripts (that is, work copied out after composition), so in most cases
we cannot compare drafts and manuscripts to the printed versions.
When we turn to the editions of Carter's poetry, only the corrected
proofs of *Poems of Succession* survive. The 1989 *Selected Poems*
published Carter's chosen selection, and represents his final inten-
tions for the poetry. This work has been invaluable to the present
edition, but despite its almost definitive status, I could not use it
as my copy text. The loss of the proofs containing Carter's correc-
tions, and lack of a manuscript, mean that the printed edition of
Selected Poems may still stand at some remove from Carter's final
intentions.

I have edited these poems in order to understand how Carter's
work has descended to us. There was no feasible way to create a
compositional chronology of Carter's work; even on the manuscripts
that survive he seldom recorded the dates on which he wrote the
poems. Carter released his poetry carefully, both in terms of tim-
ing and place, and often in collections with small print runs or
journals with specific readerships. This interest in the significance
of public release has not been able to provide me with a clearcut
editorial principle. I have had to decide which public we should be
interested in and what kind of release is most important when there
exist multiple publications of what might normally be described as
one poem and one text. The editor I hope to be is one who enables
you to find the Carter that interests you most and to judge the text
before you.

In this edition I have used two working principles. The first is
to prioritise the poems as they appear in the large groupings that
Carter designated and that have increasingly defined his corpus
for many of his readers: *Poems of Resistance*, *Poems of Succession*

and *Poems of Affinity*. In particular, *Poems of Resistance* has become such a central document in Guyanese, Caribbean and postcolonial poetics that the decision to reproduce the first edition can help us to appreciate the contribution it made to anti-colonial politics and poetics in the 1950s. The same could equally be said of *Poems of Affinity* in relation to postcolonial politics and poetics in the 1970s and 1980s. My second principle is that for poems that did not appear in the three major collections, I have reproduced the text as it appears in its first publication in the shorter collections. In the notes I describe variations between the different publications, and whenever possible and helpful to a reading of the published poems I have drawn on the manuscripts. Readers wishing to reconstruct the original orderings of *The Hill of Fire Glows Red*, *The Kind Eagle* and *The Hidden Man* are advised in the notes.

Collected in this edition are 169 poems. This, however, is not the complete poetry of Carter – given the uncatalogued nature of his papers and his own often improvised working practices, the discovery of more work is likely. Only when we have a Martin Carter archive will we be able to compile the complete works.

Martin Carter, as Guyana's Minister of Information, late 1960s.

COLLECTED POEMS

TO A DEAD SLAVE (1951)

Believing that things like verse, painting or sculpture should need neither explanation nor directive, but should be both self-expressive and self-explanatory, I give here neither preface nor introduction.

How well what follows can do without either of these is one measurement of its worth − so much, no more.

GEORGETOWN, 28.5.51.

To a Dead Slave

To you
dead slave
from me, a living one:
I do not write these words
thinking that you will read,
I know your eyes are sightless in a grave,
your hands are still, your bones are lost away.
I only want
to heat these pages with my own heart's fire,
to touch these hearts that live beside me here,   10
to hasten birth, to drive the shadows back,
to free the memories shackled in the mind,
to raise a beacon in these smoky nights,
to follow rivers from the shore and creek
until this land is green and wide and free.
I am eager, dead father,
most eager,
for all the boughs are laden down with hours
whose minutes and whose moments filled with grief,
like sentinels are keeping us apart.   20
in all these years
that bridge of human making, words and tales
reach me, and I clench my teeth at night,
at a window by the dusty streets of care
I sit impatient, counting days and months.
but I have no more tears to weep:
even those that should not fall from eyes,

those that are made in the heart's most tender vault
have spilt from me, like groans mingled with words,
like dreams which have no language of their own.   30
Ah! land
and country
              not yet really mine!
ah! land
and rivers
              multitudinous!
I never knew such rivers here were flowing,
one time I stood I gazed the Pomeroon,
another time the Demerara course,
and thrice on Essequibo did I float   40
whose forest walls are green like living things,
how green those temples on those river banks!
at evening flies the heron over all
a prophecy that I would love to make
to you
dead slave
from me a living one:
today is not like any other time,
behind me come your children pressing on
they need more slates to write their destinies,   50
to draw the shore line and the river bend,
to copy names the Caribs give to us
like Wichabai and mountain Kanaku.
to learn that Ganges is an ancient word
and Quamina a brave and rebel slave.
I am humble, dead father
most humble with my brown and trembling hand,
for when I think of children and these names
I understand how human is the world,
how human is a rock with patterns carved,   60
or hut of trash which was a sanctuary,
or beating drum or dance & marriage feast,
or ship that moves between some different shores,
or cargoes listed in a museum
which show what names the slaves inherited;
or birth or death, or woman really loved
wide earth and sun and things growing between.
to you
dead slave
from me a living one: 70

60

I sometimes notice how the day begins
first,
slight
and soft
and barely
     in the East,
then
   creeping
      creeping
         like a little child,   80
then like some wakened sleeper getting up,
then
   brighter
      on the flowers
         and the leaves,
until at last
      the land is full of dawn.
until at last
      the land is full of day.
then men and women   90
bend and lift their cares,
some draw their water at artesian wells,
some tend new fires for the living day,
some lead the bullock to the iron plough,
some pelt ripe padi seeds into the soil,
some feed their babies weeping as they do,
some see no sun, they and their shadows one,
some blindly stare upon their very hands
as one may stare upon a brother's grave,
as one may stare into unlighted years,   100
as one may stare and see a barren place;
yet I believe and think
that all these hands which know the vein-filled womb,
and all these wombs which know of waking life
are toiling, toiling to a better dawn
when those who see no beauty in the sun
no greenness in the fields of lovely rice
will give their voices echoes reaching far,
till pause the birds that fly beneath the clouds,
till wheel the birds astounded at the gaze   110
of free land which a people call their own:
a people whose great hands stretch everywhere,
from estuary to forest hidden creeks,

from earnest footprint to some mighty book
of flaming spirits who are always young:
they grasp at life to live
they hold the brand of fire
they struggle on to find
that which is free or slave:
they crush what suffocates   120
they heal their bleeding wounds
they like the eagle's gaze
they choose their mountain peaks
they reason always how the slave should end
a day which rarely had a shaft of light.
to you
dead slave
from me a living one:
I do not write these words
thinking that you will read,   130
I know your eyes are sightless in a grave
your voice is done, your bones are lost away.
I only want
to kindle firelight,
to be the keeper of the coming flame,
to feed it with the power of itself
until it warms me like a father's care,
so that I live and call myself a man
one link in all the thousand million links
which make this earth the human world it is.   140
and seas and oceans with their currents go
by continents, the very old, the new
the cradle which is Asia old and great,
America, of Inca Cherokee,
now burdened with the black man's groaning heart.
yes, I have watched the sea,
the Caribbean with a sunny tide,
the Caribbean with an anxious tide,
the Caribbean of the corial
of kitchen midden at the very shore;   150
the Caribbean cut by Europe keels
which sailed the Afric and the Indian seas;
and though my hand is brown as mother earth
yet moves my tongue in English syllables
beside a Hindu in her white ramal –
that tongue I took, but as the falling rain

drops clear yet flows deep brown on river beds
so do I fill the words with different things,
and give them number tone a meaning too,
like drum beats throbbing with a jungle noise   160
telling of how a slave might be reborn,
a slave who struggles till the birth is done
until the pain of birth is fully done.
to you
dead slave
from me a living one:
six hands enclose me in my citadel,
and black and brown are those nearest to grief,
nearest to grief which is their constant guide,
which seeps & soaks through every human thing   170
looking for age to be its weary house –
for nothing young can always suffer pain
yes nothing young can always suffer pain,
and here is pain, a liquid mass of pain,
a liquid mass of pain beneath a crust,
a brittle crust like thin but opaque glass,
a passive wording in a book of laws –
and yet I know the boiling of a pot
the boiling of a pot upon a fire
in benab village and the city house,   180
in everywhere the people make their homes,
in everywhere two humans make a child:
as beat my heart in spite of deadening things,
stamp hard my feet and shake these wooden walls,
these walls enclose me in a darkened room
as if my country were a little house,
with not a fire burning anywhere!
with not a fire burning anywhere!
my spirit flame and go over the land –
that I compare the year with other years,   190
that I compare new deeds with older deeds,
till I compare the present with the past
the gripping past with things that liberate.
to you
dead slave
from me a living one:
I purge my heart in all these heavy words,
I see my life in all these things I write,
and I because I know them how they be

am learning how to bear them as they are,   200
for who can fight when darkness blinds the eye
and throws a shadow on the enemy?
yes, flash bright lightning in my southern sky!
roll thunder roll, vibrate and shake the air!
I can point out any beam of light
what bends the knee and bows the human face.
does not the soul who lives in misery
say hunger leads into a helpless grave?
I
   must bend down   210
   and take up in my hand
the soil that saw you father die a slave,
and never must I let it fall to earth,
until these chains that bruise our children's necks,
until the tears that blind our children's eyes,
until the groan, this groaning misery,
this bleeding in the mighty heart of man,
this traitor to the noble heart of man
sinks with most foul oppression in the pit and swamp of time.
to you   220
dead slave
from me a living one:
along our coasts do Hebo dances pound,
Mosambos, Ochus beat their goat skin drums,
and to some bride the kurtaed magi reads
the Koran in a green leafed bamboo tent;
and I have seen the gray haired pandit weep
when his black brother told of India;
and still my sisters weep for Africa
but if they knew how blood stained is the land   230
how dim the white man keeps the village street,
then they would wait and rock in agony,
for in these days the old world sucks away
the power of our blood to keep alive:
those ancient things we made to guide our hands
they now discover, and they grasp at them
to store away and keep like curios
in museum to flatter Philistines.
they take our dances and our rhythmic drums
and sell their pulsing in their gambling dens.   240
I heed them father with an angry heart,
first was a ship, then toil and razor whips

and now a poisoning of the very blood.
to you
dead slave
from me a living one:
they say they freed us and they let us go,
they say they took their chains and let us go,
but how is it the mourning cemetery
the grave without a headboard or a mark   250
the place you lived and sang of love & life
is yet unknown in any crowded school?
to you
dead slave
from me a living one:
I do not write these words
thinking that you will read,
I know your voice is muted in the ground,
your heart is earth your bones are lost away.
I only want   260
to heat these pages with a fire stick,
to make my pen into a fire stick,
to send some light where bitter darkness is,
to pierce the dark clouds hanging on the land,
to free the new, the germinating spark,
to give it warmth and let it come to life
in this
my land
of rivers in the sun,
in this   270
my land
of people in the sun,
in this
my land,
my own Guiana land,
my land of rivers on the Carib sea.

THE HILL OF FIRE GLOWS RED (1951)

Not I with This Torn Shirt

They call here,
            – Magnificent Province!
Province of mud!
Province of flood!
Plantation – feudal coast!

Who are the magnificent here?
Not I with this torn shirt
but they, in their white mansions
by the trench of blood!

I tell you
this is no magnificent province
no El Dorado for me
no streets paved with gold
but a bruising and a battering for self preservation
in the white dust and the grey mud.

I tell you and I tell no secret –
now is long past time for worship
long past time for kneeling
with clasped hands at altars of poverty.

How are the mighty slain?
by this hammer of my hand!
by this anger in my life!
by this new science of men alive
everywhere in this province!
thus are the mighty slain!

Do Not Stare at Me

Do not stare at me from your window, lady
do not stare and wonder where I came from –
born in this city was I, lady
hearing the beetles at six o'clock
and the noisy cocks in the morning
when your hands rumple the bed sheet
and night is locked up in the wardrobe.

My hand is full of lines
like your breast with veins, lady –
so do not stare and wonder where I came from –
my hand is full of lines,
like your breast with veins, lady –
and one must rear, while one must suckle life....

do not stare at me from your window, lady
stare at the waggon of prisoners!
stare at the hearse passing by your gate!
stare at the slums in the south of the city!
stare hard and reason lady where I came from
and where I go.

My hand is full of lines
like your breast with veins, lady
and one must rear, while one must suckle life.

Old Higue

Old higue in the kitchen
peel off her skin –
mammy took up old higue skin
and pound it in the mortar
with pepper and vinegar.

> 'Cool um water cool um
> cool um water cool um'

Old higue come back in the kitchen
        'Cool um water cool um'
She grab the skin out of the mortar
        'Cool um water cool um'

She danced meringue when the pepper
burn up her skin –
dance meringue when the pepper
burn up her skin.

            'skin skin you na know me
            skin skin you na know me'
she dance meringue when the pepper
burn up her skin.

Like the Blood of Quamina

Across the night face of the river
whenever cane is ripe
there is deep red flame –
flame like a smouldering hill of fire
across the dark face of the river.

from the edge of this city
the hill of fire across the river
is like sunset arrested on the edge of the world
like sunset of day without end
long day of grieving without end.

O Jesus Christ man!
it is as if the soul of slavery
crouching like a tiger on the edge of the world
waits for the slave to leave his house!

across the dark face of the river
the hill of fire glows red like fresh blood
like the blood of Quamina
flowing through the green forest
the green green forest.

Shines the Beauty of My Darling

If I wanted
I could make pictures of night
the map of stars above the mass of water
the mass of water underneath the stars
the beauty of my beloved
like a flower bringing down the light into dark.

Yes, if I wanted
I could close my eyes right now
And bring these things like life into my brain.

but new are these times
and no matter where I turn
the fierce revolt goes with me
like a kiss –
the revolt of Malaya
and Vietnam –
the revolt of India
and Africa –
like guardian.

like guardian at my side
is the fight for freedom –
and like the whole world dancing
for liberation from the slave maker
shines the beauty of my darling in her laughing eyes.

Three Years After This

Enmore!
twenty miles beyond the city
down the long red road.

Enmore!
twenty miles beyond the city
a lorry rolls –

steel helmets rifles bullets bayonets blood
and five men bleeding on the innocent grass!

Three years after this
I walked behind a memory of flowers
a memory of flowers red and white
and yet, and yet my city had no shame
my city with a prison for a heart
city of dust and silent streets
city of street preachers........

Looking at Your Hands

No!
I will not still my voice!
I have
too much to claim –
if you see me
looking at books
or coming to your house
or walking in the sun
know that I look for fire!

I have learnt
from books dear friend
of men dreaming and living
and hungering in a room without a light
who could not die since death was far too poor
who did not sleep to dream, but dreamed to change the world.

and so
if you see me
looking at your hands
listening when you speak
marching in your ranks
you must know
I do not sleep to dream, but dream to change the world.

Tomorrow and the World

I am most happy
as I walk the seller of sweets says 'Friend'
and the shoemaker with his awl and waxen thread
reminds me of tomorrow and the world.

happy is it to shake your hand
and to sing with you, my friend
smoke rises from the furnace of life
red red red the flame!

green grass and yellow flowers
smell of mist the sun's light
everywhere the light of the day
everywhere the songs of life are floating
like new ships on a new river sailing, sailing.

Tomorrow and the world
and the songs of life and all my friends –
Ah yes, tomorrow and the whole world
awake and full of good life.

It Is for This That I Am Furious

We all came naked here
naked as the new born
the new born in the light of day.

we all came naked here
we brought nothing with us in this world
and yet easy it is for me to hear the coughing infant
to see idle men in the bawdy house
and to know the madness of hunger in this world.

we all came naked here
and yet easy is it for me to be like wood
like ant or roach in any dusty crevice –
empire of some loathsome spider's web.

it is for this that I am furious, my brothers
if I am not furious my brothers
I will be nothing more than a cow
and I will die like a cow
if I am not furious –
like a cow with a nose ring
after years in the byre.

Run Shouting Through the Town

Oh! wake and give to me
the flames, the red flames!

see me? I would rip off my clothes
run shouting through the town
'wake up houses – open windows
I want flames, red flames!'

a black child in a kitchen
searching in a black pot
smoke-hanging on his head
naked! naked! naked!

O wake and give to me
the flames! the red flames!

Listening to the Land

That night when I left you on the bridge
I bent down
Kneeling on my knee
and pressed my ear to listen to the land.

I bent down
listening to the land
but all I heard was tongueless whispering.

On my right hand was the sea behind the wall
the sea that has no business in the forest
and I bent down
listening to the land
but all I heard was tongueless whispering

the old brick chimney barring out the city
the lantern posts like bottles full of fire
and I bent down
listening to the land
and all I heard was tongueless whispering
as if some buried slave wanted to speak again.

A Banner for the Revolution

This is my hand
for the revolution........

that night there will be thousands of torches
from the hospitals the lame will come
the mad will be sane again
for the revolution.

those who cannot read
will learn to read
for the revolution –
those who despair not
will be glad
for the revolution –
those who are eager to be men
will be glad
for the revolution –
I myself shall be so fiercely happy
that I will make my shirt
a banner
for the revolution,
a banner
for the revolution.

THE KIND EAGLE (POEMS OF PRISON) (1952)

Bare Night Without Comfort

In a bare night without comfort
stood like an infant hearing a drum:
Shadows and green grass spinning
but clutched at a world without nearing.

Like dark ball rising from nothing
hurling curse at me and full of scorn:
Bare night without comfort
stood like an infant hearing a drum.

Who Walks a Pavement

Iron gate, the terrible hands of a clock
a calendar with days scratched off and buried,
slant roof of slate black as the floor of tight cell
is not a prison, nor a convict shelter.

A prison is go back, go back, go back,
lash of two things, shell which is the heart
and heart which is the shell – the hollow tear:
The man of time whose look can stain a sky
who walks a pavement, walks and disappears.

O Where to Hide

These lumps of hardened air
invisible drums are beating at my head:
I hear drum drum drum
loud drops of wax falling from time's black candle.

O drum beat drum beat terrifying night air!
O drum beat drum beat let me tear away!
O drum beat! dark night! stamp foot!
                          A-a-a-h!
O God! the face of earth is moving!
O where to hide? O where to hide? O where to hide?

All of a Man

O strike kind eagle, strike!
Grip at this prison and this prison wall!
Scream and accuse the guilty cage of heaven
Hurling me here, hurling me here.

O strike kind eagle, strike!
All of a man is heart is hope
All of a man can fly like a bird
O strike kind eagle, strike!

O Human Guide

In the burnt earth of these years
I dip my hand, I dip my hand:
I plunge it in the furies of this world.
I splash the pool that feeds my painful flowers
I find the lake whose source leaks from a river.

So near so near the rampart spiked with pain
so near so near the sharp stone and the flint.
The eager window looking from a prison –
The guilty heaven promising a star.

O beauty of air like a glad woman!
O fringe of grass always so ever green!
O sloping ocean, sloping bed of love!
O trophy of my search! O human guide,
Each day I ride a wild black horse of terror
but every night I lock him in my bosom....

The Discovery of Companion

I

This tower of movement bending on the world
is shocked to motion
crumbling knee and face
in the strange sands of discovery.
A gasp of fear is the first farewell to death
the first wave of a hand, the first heart beat.
But the return of arrival is merciless
is a pool of dark water, a terrible mirror.
To bend on a planet of misery
is revelation like apocalypse.
No longer the trunk of a palm, the trunk of a tree
but pillar of endurance.
Yes, to be born again, astonished and made bare
is awareness of companion.
While the blue swords of lightning kill
knowledge is intense and scorching fire.
And only when a man is clad in flame
can he be made to know companion.

II

This is his first companion valuable fear
a beacon on the sea, a lane of light.
This matron of the trembling loin of man
becomes companion at the precipice.
His human hands are brittle and will crack
like the wall of his heart.
In the ladder from the cave the rungs of time
bend like the working roots that eat the soil.
But fear of losing all is strong like life
losing but not lost.
Fear of inhuman movement is the curse
or blessing, guide of traveller.

III

While time is measured in the stretch of years
night can be measureless.
The veinless womb of darkness breeds a bird,

the flying child of fear or curse or blessing
to soar in the blue gables of the world's imprisonment.
And this too is companion
mother of life and motion.
The stranded cables loosen bit by bit
and sink in the flood of a river.
The brittle heart expands a moistened flower.
And the kind eagle soars again
but in the tension of his wing and shadow
moves a man.
Now this is the completion of discovery
the life of the world.
So man is wrapped or clad in gowns of fire
each human clutches at companion
in an original sequence, no desire of death.

IV

The arrival in the camp of broken glass
is full of wounding points.
And the streets of life are set about with knives
to cut the travelling feet.
Merciless and bare the moving world revolves
like a circling star.
Only men of fire will survive
all else will move to ashes and to air.

THE HIDDEN MAN (OTHER POEMS OF PRISON)
(1952)

I Stretch My Hand

I stretch my hand to a night of barking dogs
feeling for rain or any dropping water:
But the wind is dark and has no shower for me
and the street is strange and has no pathway for me
and the sky is old and keeps no comet for me.

I stretch my hand to a night of weary branches
feeling for leaves or any twig of blossom:
But the branch is withered with no green leaf for me
and the stalk is brown and has no petal for me
and the root is tap root boring in equator.

I stretch my hand to a night of clinging distress
feeling for sleep or any rest to heal me:
But dreams are things that never come at calling
and sleep is time that hides me from my labour
and rest is death that rids me of my panting
and dogs and branches and dim rooms of distress
are living worlds that populate my dark.

Sunday Night

This night is me
I walk the wall of life:
Sand is out there and little crabs that hide.
Sky is up there and yellow piece of moon
City's down yonder like a shabby church.

This night is me
I walk the wall of life:
The congregation only hears the priest
but more I hear – the clicking of the rat
gnawing that holy altar comes to me.

There is no human laughter in these streets
no sheets of comfort on these beds in prison
no warmth in blood to melt the ice of death
but slow slow time rotting the bone away.

This night is me
I walk the wall of life:
This wall is mud and bitter bitter rain
make pools and gutters which like stagnant swamps
drain out my heart and husk it into shell.

This night is me
I walk the wall of life:
This wall is stone and iron heels of anger
kick sparks into my husk and shell of darkness
till flesh ignite and burn in black and red.

Looking Again

Looking again I see the old mad house
All within are saner when they rave
More human in their inhumanity
More free and calm when bound like maniac.

So has it been O sky dark as a yard!
What looks like fire is no more than ice
What looks like stone is sand blown up by air
What looks like air is suffocating space.

Looking again I glimpse the old mad house
no doorway out – O many doorways in!
And only burning in the constant ember
Will heal this cripple of reality.

I Walk and Walk

Then, when I close my mouth
I taste the bitter world upon my tongue.
Then, when I spit upon the grass
the smear is blood! is blood! is black! is coal!

O streets like coffins lidded with glass!
O time like air that neither ebbs nor flows!
O ugly hour ugly hour face!
O wound wound wound that will not bleed at all!
I lacerate myself! I walk and walk!

No Madness Like This Sanity

Now to absorb and be absorbed again
and in such fashion marry to the world.

Sky blue, grass green, glittering noon.
Dust white, bones naked, hopes barren – beautiful world!
No mark, no madness like this sanity.

At a bright day's end the dark sky will hide us
dream time will guard us, night will mend our being
yet wind will wake us, rain drench every doorway.

*

Now to absorb and be absorbed again
and in such fashion marry to the world.

City moon clad, black tree domestic, dreary doormouth gaping
earth no mother, sky no father, space no home in comfort:
No mark, no madness like this sanity.

At a dark day's end a darker night will choke us
night claws will rend us, gloom lay bare our being
and smoke engulf us, swirling in our faces.

*

How to absorb or be absorbed again?
How in such fashion marry to the world?

TWO FRAGMENTS OF 'RETURNING' (1953)

Two Fragments of 'Returning'

1

From heavy iron
from twisted leather
from wet cord stung with cruelty
through the hot jungle thrusting to a mountain
and into rivers leaning on a stone
he ran exhausted, spitting out his tongue
drumming his belly tearing out his throat.

Tattered white singlet
three quarter trousers underneath both knees
one roasted green plantain, a drink of the creek   10
the edge of sand, the pad of skin and nerve.

Rocks explode and scatter in his head
then settle down a lizard and a man
a frog a ship a leaf another hand
another heart another flow of blood.

This hidden mark among the centuries
confusion birds who speak like squat brown men
the stretch of Asia over Africa
the black man's leap, the alphabet of stone.

Between his vast surprise of sleep and wake   20
between the whip and then between the wind
between the wind, between the pain of wind
between the gap of footprints and the coin
the trembling nerve the lake of crystal sweat.

From things unseen
to things forever watched.
From hidden stone
to naked delicate heart.
From works forgotten and from works to be
these waters ripple shaking up the sky.   30

2

The wet convulsions striking everywhere
and the fling of passion turning on itself
renew the light to cleanse the pure sun witness.

I lay back on the blue walls of heaven
I count the fine lines of morning etched out before me
I dissolve like mist and turn myself to air
golden as liquid fire green as a bunch of grass.

The father of wind stands howling on the roof
sea waters crumble, goats and sheep in pens
and fowls in feathers wood around my head   40
earth bending nearer like a tree.

The cold foot moves silently in the midst of rain
fires awaken and blown ash goes whirling in the world
a touch commands, a voice is mingling
all things commingle rivers rise and ebb.

The point of life in strict suspension vibrant
the blazing seed but no blue smoke nor fume
the rich dark earth and heavy smell of air
no thunder and no lightning and no sound
no visible looming only conscious strife.   50

Behind morning, behind the drawn lines of morning
behind the gold fires and the green fires
and behind myself and behind the light and behind the wood
        around my head

and behind the crumbling sea waters behind the regions of daylight
to the place of the mountain the big big mountain
the high sky of humanity lifted by a child.

POEMS OF RESISTANCE FROM BRITISH GUIANA
(1954)

University of Hunger

is the university of hunger the wide waste
is the pilgrimage of man the long march
The print of hunger wanders in the land
The green tree bends above the long forgotten
The plains of life rise up and fall in spasms
The roofs of men are fused in misery.

They come treading in the hoof marks of the mule
passing the ancient bridge
the grave of pride
the sudden flight   10
the terror and the time.

They come from the distant village of the flood
passing from middle air to middle earth
in the common hours of nakedness.

Twin bars of hunger mark their metal brows
twin seasons mock them
parching drought and flood.

is the dark ones
the half sunken in the land
is they who had no voice in the emptiness   20
in the unbelievable
in the shadowless.

They come treading on the mud floor of the year
mingling with dark heavy water
And the sea sound of the eyeless flitting bat,
O long is the march of men and long is the life
And wide is the span.

is air dust and the long distance of memory
is the hour of rain when sleepless toads are silent
is broken chimneys smokeless in the wind   30
is brown trash huts and jagged mounds of iron.

They come in long lines
toward the broad city.
is the golden moon like a big coin in the sky
is the floor of bone beneath the floor of flesh
is the beak of sickness breaking on the stone
O long is the march of men and long is the life
And wide is the span.
O cold is the cruel wind blowing
O cold is the hoe in the ground.   40

They come like sea birds
flapping in the wake of a boat.
is the torture of sunset in purple bandages
is the powder of fire spread like dust in the twilight
is the water melodies of white foam on wrinkled sand.

The long streets of night move up and down
baring the thighs of a woman
and the cavern of generation.
The beating drum returns and dies away
the bearded men fall down and go to sleep   50
the cocks of dawn stand up and crow like bugles.

is they who rose early in the morning
watching the moon die in the dawn
is they who heard the shell blow and the iron clang
is they who had no voice in the emptiness
in the unbelievable
in the shadowless
O long is the march of men and long is the life
And wide is the span.

I Am No Soldier

Wherever you fall comrade I shall arise
Wherever and whenever the sun vanishes into an arctic night
there will I come.
I am no soldier with a cold gun on my shoulder
no hunter of men, no human dog of death.
I am my poem, I come to you in particular gladness
In this hopeful dawn of earth I rise with you dear friend.

O comrade unknown to me falling somewhere in blood.
In the insurgent geography of my life
the latitudes of anguish   10
pass through the poles of my frozen agonies, my regions of grief.
O my heart is a magnet
electrified by passion emitting sparks of love
Swinging in me around the burning compass of tomorrow
and pointing at my grandfather's continent, unhappy Africa
unhappy lake of sunlight
moon of terror...

But now the huge noise of night surrounds me for a moment
I clutch the iron bars of my nocturnal cell
peeping at daylight.   20
There is a dark island in a dark river
O forest of torture
O current of pain and channel of endurance
The nausea of a deep sorrow hardens in my bowels
And the sky's black paint cracks falling into fragments
Cold rain is mist! is air, is all my breath!

There is a nightmare bandaged on my brow
A long hempen pendulum marks the hour of courage
Swinging over the bloody dust of a comrade
one minute and one hour and one year   30
O life's mapmaker chart me now an ocean
Vast ship go sailing, keel and metal rudder.

It began when the sun was younger, when the moon was dull
But wherever you fall comrade I shall arise.
If it is in Malaya where new barbarians eat your flesh, like beasts
I shall arise.

If it is in Kenya, where your skin is dark with the stain of famine
I shall arise.
If it is in Korea of my tears where land is desolate
I shall wipe my eyes and see you   40
Comrade unknown to me...

I will come to the brave when they dream of the red and yellow
          flowers blooming in the tall mountains of their nobility...
I will come to each and to every comrade led by my heart
Led by thy magnet of freedom which draws me far and wide
over the sun's acres of children and of mornings....

O wherever you fall comrade I shall arise.
In the whirling cosmos of my soul there are galaxies of happiness
Stalin's people and the brothers of Mao Tse-tung
And Accabreh's breed, my mother's powerful loin
And my father's song and my people's deathless drum.   50
O come astronomer of freedom
Come comrade stargazer
Look at the sky I told you I had seen
The glittering seeds that germinate in darkness
And the planet in my hand's revolving wheel
and the planet in my breast and in my head
and in my dream and in my furious blood.
Let me rise up wherever he may fall
I am no soldier hunting in a jungle
I am this poem like a sacrifice.   60

Death of a Slave

Above green cane arrow
is blue sky –
Beneath green arrow
is brown earth –
Dark is the shroud of slavery
over the river
over the forest
over the field.

Aie! black is the skin!
Aie! red is heart!
as round it looks
over the world
over the forest
over the sun.

In the dark earth
in cold dark earth
time plants the seeds of anger.

This is another world
but above is the same blue sky
the same sun
Below is the same deep heart of agony.

The cane field is green, dark green
green with a life of its own.
The heart of a slave is red deep red
red with a life of its own.

Day passes like a long whip
over the back of a slave.
Day is a burning whip
Biting the neck of a slave.

But the sun falls down like an old man
beyond the dim line of the River.
and white birds
come flying, flying flapping at the wind
white birds like dreams come settling down,

Night comes from down river
Like a thief –
Night comes from deep forest
in a boat of silence –
Dark is the shroud
the shroud of night
over the river
over the forest.

The slave staggers and falls
his face is on the earth
his dream is silent
silent like night
hollow like boat
between the tides of sorrow.
In the dark floor
In the cold dark earth
time plants the seeds of anger.

Death of a Comrade

Death must not find us thinking that we die.

Too soon, too soon
Our banner draped for you.
I would prefer
the banner in the wind
not bound so tightly
in a scarlet fold –
not sodden sodden
with your people's tears
but flashing on the pole
we bear aloft
down and beyond this dark dark lane of rags.

Dear Comrade,
if it must be
you speak no more with me
nor smile no more with me
nor march no more with me
then let me take
a patience and a calm –
for even now the greener leaf explodes
sun brightens stone
and all the river burns.

Now from the mourning vanguard moving on
dear Comrade I salute you and I say
Death will not find us thinking that we die.

Not Hands Like Mine

Not hands
like mine
these Carib altars knew –
nameless and quite forgotten are the gods
and mute
mute and alone
their silent people spend
a ring of vacant days
not like more human years
as aged and brown their rivers flow away.

Yes
pressing on my land
there is an ocean's flood –
it is a muttering sea.

Here, right at my feet
my strangled city lies
my father's city and my mother's heart
hoarse groaning tongues
children without love
mothers without blood
all cold as dust nights dim there is no rest.
Ah!
Mine was a pattern woven by a slave
Dull as a dream encompassed in a tomb.

Now still are the fields
Covered by the flood
and those rivers roll
over altars gone.
Naked naked loins
Throbbing deep with life
rich with birth indeed
rouse turning to the sun.

and more fierce rain will come again tonight
new day must clean have floods not drowned the fields
killing my rice and stirring up my wrath?

Letter 1

This is what they do with me
Put me in prison, hide me away
cut off the world, cut out the sun
darken the land, blacken the flower
Stifle my breath and hope that I die!

But I laugh at them –
I laugh because I know they cannot kill me
nor kill my thoughts, nor murder what I write.
I am a man living among my people
Proud as the tree the axeman cannot tumble –
So if my people live I too must live
And they will live, I tell you they will live!
But these...
I laugh at them
I do not know what thoughts pass through their minds
Perhaps they do not know to think at all –
tigers don't think, nor toads nor rooting swine
but only man, just listen and you know.

In Kenya today they drink the blood of black women.
In Malaya the hero is hunted and shot like a dog.
Here, they watch us and lick their tongues like beasts
who crouch to prey upon some little child.

But I tell you
Like a tide from the heart of things
Inexorably and inevitably
A day will come.

If I do not live to see that day
My son will see it.
If he does not see that day
His son will see it.
And it will come circling the world like fire
It will come to this land and every land
and when it comes I'll come alive again
and laugh again and walk out of this prison.

Letter 2

After twenty days and twenty nights in prison
You wake and you search for birds and sunlight
You wait for rain and thunder
and you think of home with pain inside your heart
and your laugh has scorn more bitter than a curse.

You think of green mornings
Naked children playing in the rain
And even fishes swimming in a pool –
A shop in a street and women passing by
Walking from home to market in the morning –
a blind old man now tapping with his stick
Seeing no one, no light, no golden flower
But wandering through that night wrapped on his face.

O my darling!
O my dear wife whose voice I cannot hear
Tell me, the young one, is he creeping now
And is he well and mischievous as ever?
Or is the cloud so heavy on the land
Too deep for him to see the wonderful sky?
I send a kiss to tell you everything
about today the twentieth in the distance.

And you comrade, you know
I cannot come to the city in myself
Where a garden should be green in the light
They have planted sharp vines of barbed wire
and every footstep is a soldier's bootstep
marching me down the corridors of silence.

O comrade, if I should try to come now to the struggle,
Perhaps their iron garden then will bloom!
The scarlet flower bleeding on the vine
Will be my corpse and you will never see me.

But let our red banner fly in the city, comrade
Let the wild wind strike it ringing like a bell
And sing a song for me comrade let the sun be made to echo
Will I not hear no matter where I be?

Letter 3

It is not easy to go to sleep
When the tramp of a soldier marches in your brain.
You do not know whether to sleep or wake
When a rifle crashes on the metal road ...

This is all they want me to hear
A soldier marching with a long black rifle
A guard commander lining up his squad
The stamp of feet upon the floors of sunset
The yawn of darkness swallowing up the world....

It is not easy to go to sleep
When the tramp of a soldier marches in your brain.
You do not know whether to sleep or wake
When the long night comes and takes you in its arms....

Let Freedom Wake Him

Give me your hand comrade
Do not cry little one, do not cry.
This is the bond we make in the dark gloom about us
Hand in hand! heart in heart! strength in strength!

If you see a smile of bitterness on my mouth
You must not think some joke amuses me
It is only the fury of my heart changing to scorn
At the sight of a soldier searching for me.

Comrade the wind is sweet with eucalyptus
Early at morn green grass reflects the sun
Here in my home my little child lies sleeping
Let freedom wake him – not a bayonet point.

Comrade the world is loud with songs of freedom
Mankind is breeding heroes every day
On high the scarlet banner flies aloft
Below the earth re-echoes liberty!

Till I Collect

Over the shining mud the moon is blood
falling on ocean at the fence of lights.
My mast of love will sail and come to port
leaving a trail beneath the world, a track
cut by my rudder tempered out of anguish.

The fisherman will set his tray of hooks
and ease them one by one into the flood.
His net of twine will strain the liquid billow
and take the silver fishes from the deep.
But my own hand I dare not plunge too far
lest only sand and shells I bring to air
lest only bones I resurrect to light.

Over the shining mud the moon is blood
falling on ocean at the fence of lights –
My course I set, I give my sail the wind
to navigate the islands of the stars
till I collect my scattered skeleton
till I collect...

Cartman of Dayclean

Now to begin the road:
broken land ripped like a piece of cloth
iron cartwheel rumbling in the night
hidden man consistent in the dark
sea of day clean washing on the shore
heart of orphan seeking orphanage.

Now to begin the road:
the bleeding music of appellant man
starts like a song but fades into a groan.
the cupric star will burn as blue as death
his hopes are whitened starched with grief and pain
yet questing man is heavy laden cart
whose iron wheels will rumble in the night
whose iron wheel will spark against the stone
or granite burden of the universe.

Now to begin the road:
hidden cartman fumbling for a star
brooding city like a mound of coal
till journey done, till prostrate coughing hour
with sudden welcome take him to his dream
with sudden farewell send him to his grave.

Weroon Weroon

I came to a benab
sharpening my arrow of stone
knitting my hammock of air
tying my feathers all around my head.

Then I drank from the calabash of my ancestors
and danced my dance of fire
Weroon Weroon –
Land of the waters flowing over me
Weroon Weroon.

And I prayed to the blue ocean of heaven
dreaming of the voyage of death
and my corial of paradise paddling forever.

Now I climb toward the hole of heaven
and my hands are stretched to the altar of god
O wonder of all the stars departed
Weroon Weroon Weroon...

The Knife of Dawn

I make my dance right here!
Right here on the wall of prison I dance
This world's hope is a blade of fury
and we who are sweepers of an ancient sky,
discoverers of new planets, sudden stars
we are the world's hope.
And so therefore I rise again I rise again
freedom is a white road with green grass like love.

Out of my time I carve a monument
out of a jagged block of convict years I carve it.
The sharp knife of dawn glitters in my hand
but how bare is everything – tall tall tree
infinite air, the unrelaxing tension of the world
and only hope, hope only, the kind eagle soars and wheels in flight.

I dance on the wall of prison
it is not easy to be free and bold
it is not easy to be poised and bound
it is not easy to endure the spike –
so river flood, drench not my pillar feet
So river flood collapse to estuary
only the heart's life the kind eagle soars and wheels in flight.

This Is the Dark Time My Love

This is the dark time, my love
all round the land brown beetles crawl about.
The shining sun is hidden in the sky
Red flowers bend their heads in awful sorrow.

This is the dark time my love.
It is the season of oppression, dark metal, and tears.
It is the festival of guns, the carnival of misery.
Everywhere the faces of men are strained and anxious.

Who comes walking in the dark night time?
Whose boot of steel tramps down the slender grass?
It is the man of death, my love, the strange invader
watching you sleep and aiming at your dream.

I Clench My Fist

You come in warships terrible with death
I know your hands are red with Korean blood
I know your finger trembles on a trigger
And yet I curse you – Stranger khaki clad.

> British soldier, man in khaki
> careful how you walk
> My dead ancestor Accabreh
> is groaning in his grave
> At night he wakes and watches
> With fire in his eyes
> Because you march upon his breast
> and stamp upon his heart.

Although you come in thousands from the sea
Although you walk like locusts in the street
Although you point your gun straight at my heart
I clench my fist above my head; I sing my song of FREEDOM!

I Come from the Nigger Yard

I come from the nigger yard of yesterday
leaping from the oppressor's hate
and the scorn of myself;
from the agony of the dark hut in the shadow
and the hurt of things;
from the long days of cruelty and the long nights of pain
down to the wide streets of tomorrow, of the next day
leaping I come, who cannot see will hear.

In the nigger yard I was naked like the new born
naked like a stone or a star.   10
It was a cradle of blind days rocking in time
torn like the skin from the back of a slave.
It was an aching floor on which I crept
on my hands and my knees
searching the dust for the trace of a root
or the mark of a leaf or the shape of a flower.

It was me always walking with bare feet,
meeting strange faces like those in dreams or fever
when the whole world turns upside down
and no one knows which is the sky or the land   20
which heart is his among the torn or wounded
which face is his among the strange and terrible
walking about, groaning between the wind.

And there was always sad music somewhere in the land
like a bugle and a drum between the houses
voices of women singing far away
pauses of silence, then a flood of sound.
But these were things like ghosts or spirits of wind.
It was only a big world spinning outside
and men, born in agony, torn in torture, twisted and broken like
        a leaf,   30
and the uncomfortable morning, the beds of hunger stained and sordid
like the world, big and cruel, spinning outside.

Sitting sometimes in the twilight near the forest
where all the light is gone and every bird
I notice a tiny star neighbouring a leaf

a little drop of light a piece of glass
straining over heaven tiny bright
like a spark seed in the destiny of gloom.
O it was the heart like this tiny star near to the sorrows
straining against the whole world and the long twilight   40
spark of man's dream conquering the night
moving in darkness stubborn and fierce
till leaves of sunset change from green to blue
and shadows grow like giants everywhere.

So was I born again stubborn and fierce
screaming in a slum.
It was a city and a coffin space for home
a river running, prisons, hospitals
men drunk and dying, judges full of scorn
priests and parsons fooling gods with words   50
and me, like a dog tangled in rags
spotted with sores powdered with dust
screaming with hunger, angry with life and men.

It was a child born from a mother full of her blood
weaving her features bleeding her life in clots
It was pain lasting from hours to months and to years
weaving a pattern telling a tale leaving a mark
on the face and the brow.
Until there came the iron days cast in a foundry
Where men make hammers things that cannot break   60
and anvils heavy hard and cold like ice.

And so again I became one of the ten thousands
one of the uncountable miseries owning the land
When the moon rose up only the whores could dance
the brazen jazz of music throbbed and groaned
filling the night air full of rhythmic questions
It was the husk and the seed challenging fire
birth and the grave challenging life.

Until today in the middle of the tumult
when the land changes and the world's all convulsed   70
when different voices join to say the same
and different hearts beat out in unison
where on the aching floor of where I live
the shifting earth is twisting into shape

I take again my nigger life, my scorn
and fling it in the face of those who hate me
It is me the nigger boy turning to manhood
Linking my fingers, welding my flesh to freedom.

I come from the nigger yard of yesterday
leaping from the oppressor's hate   80
and the scorn of myself.
I come to the world with scars upon my soul
wounds on my body, fury in my hands
I turn to the histories of men and the lives of the peoples
I examine the shower of sparks the wealth of the dreams
I am pleased with the glories and sad with the sorrows
rich with the riches, poor with the loss
From the nigger yard of yesterday I come with my burden.
To the world of tomorrow I turn with my strength.

On the Fourth Night of Hunger Strike

I have not eaten for four days.
My legs are paining, my blood runs slowly
It is cold tonight, the rain is silent and sudden
And yet there is something warm inside of me.

At my side my comrade lies in his bed watching the dark
A cold wind presses chilly on the world.
It is the night of a Christmas day, a night in December
We watch each other noting how time passes.

Today my wife brought me a letter from a comrade
I hid it in my bosom from the soldiers.
They could not know my heart was reading 'Courage'!
They could not dream my skin was touching 'Struggle'!

But comrade now I can hardly write at all
My legs are paining, my eyes are getting dark.
It is the fourth night of a hunger strike, a night in December
I hold your letter tightly in my hand...

You Are Involved

This I have learnt:
today a speck
tomorrow a hero
hero or monster
you are consumed!

Like a jig
shakes the loom.
Like a web
is spun the pattern
all are involved!
all are consumed!

THREE POEMS OF SHAPE AND MOTION
– A SEQUENCE (1955)

Number One

I was wondering if I could shape this passion
just as I wanted in solid fire.
I was wondering if the strange combustion of my days
the tension of the world inside of me
and the strength of my heart were enough.

I was wondering if I could stand as tall
while the tide of the sea rose and fell
If the sky would recede as I went
or the earth would emerge as I came
to the door of morning locked against the sun.

I was wondering if I could make myself
nothing but fire, pure and incorruptible.
If the wound of the wind on my face
would be healed by the work of my life
Or the growth of the pain in my sleep
would be stopped in the strife of my days.

I was wondering if the agony of years
could be traced to the seed of an hour.
If the roots that spread out in the swamp
ran too deep for the issuing flower.

I was wondering if I could find myself
all that I am in all I could be.
If all the population of stars
would be less than the things I could utter
And the challenge of space in my soul
be filled by the shape I become.

Number Two

Pull off yuh shirt and throw 'way your hat
Kick off yuh shoe and stamp down the spot
Tear off yuh dress and open yuhself
And dance like you mad
Far   far.

Oh left foot, right foot, left – Ah boy!
Right foot, left foot, right – Ah boy!
Run down the road
Run up the sky
But run like you mad
Far   far.

Jump off the ground
Pull down a star
Burn till you bleed
Far   far.

Oh right foot, left foot, right – Ah boy!
Left foot, right foot, left – Ah boy!
Oh right foot, right foot
Left foot, left foot
Dance like you mad
Far   far.

Number Three

I

I walk slowly in the wind
watching myself in things I did not make
in jumping shadows and in limping cripples
dust on the earth and houses tight with sickness
deep constant pain, the dream without the sleep.

I walk slowly in the wind
hearing myself in the loneliness of a child
in woman's grief which is not understood
in coughing dogs when midnight lingers long
on stones, on streets and then on echoing stars.
that burn all night and suddenly go out.

I walk slowly in the wind
knowing myself in every moving thing
in years and days and words that mean so much
strong hands that shake, long roads that walk and deeds that do
        themselves.
and all this world and all these lives to live.

II

I walk slowly in the wind
remembering scorn and naked men in darkness
and huts of iron riveted to earth.

Cold huts of iron stand upon this earth
like rusting prisons.
Each wall is marked and each wide roof is spread
like some dark wing
casting a shadow or a living curse.

I walk slowly in the wind
to lifted sunset red and gold and dim
a long brown river slanting to an ocean
a fishing boat, a man who cannot drown.

I walk slowly in the wind
remembering me amid the surging river
amid the drought and all the merciless flood
and all the growth and all the life of man.

III

I walk slowly in the wind.
and birds are swift, the sky is blue like silk.

From the big sweeping ocean of water
an iron ship rusted and brown anchors itself.
And the long river runs like a snake
silent and smooth.

I walk slowly in the wind.
I hear my footsteps echoing down the tide
echoing like a wave on the sand or a wing on the wind
echoing echoing
a voice in the soul, a laugh in the funny silence.

IV

I walk slowly in the wind
I walk because I cannot crawl or fly.

CONVERSATIONS (1961)

[They say I am a poet write for them]

They say I am a poet write for them:
Sometimes I laugh, sometimes I solemnly nod.
I do not want to look them in the eye
Lest they should squeal and scamper far away.

A poet cannot write for those who ask
Hardly himself even, except he lies:
Poems are written either for the dying
Or for the unborn, no matter what we say.

That does not mean his audience lies remote
Inside a womb or some cold bed of agony
It only means that we who want true poems
Must all be born again, and die to do so.

[I dare not keep too silent, face averted]

I dare not keep too silent, face averted
That tells too much, it gives the heart away
Quick words distract attention from the eyes
And smiling lips are most acceptable.

In any case it is not good to show
The nature of the silence of the heart
To talk is just as easy as to walk
And laughter can be one of a thousand kinds.

I must be casual even over death
This fools the fool whose triumph is a coffin
Shallow as grave pit is the mock concern
Which murders men as surely as a knife.

To cherish silence in the memory
Is to be full of utter loneliness.
It must be right when born with such a curse
To laugh and talk and drink like any boor.

[The wild men in prisons, they who rot like rust!]

The wild men in prisons, they who rot like rust!
The loud men who cry freedom and are so full of lies!
The drunk men who go dancing like shadows down the street!
These all surround me, shouting to God for help!

I really do not see how God can help them.
For each one wants the same thing – who can share
To prisoners, politicians and drunk men
What only souls that blaze and burn can win?

[Trying with words to purify disgust]

Trying with words to purify disgust
I made a line I simply can't remember:
For hours now I've poked through memory
A desperate child in a jam-packed garbage can.

It should have been a line with nouns and verbs
Like truth and love and hope and happiness
But looking round it seems I was mistaken
To substitute a temple for a shop.

To see a shop and dream of holy temples
Is to expect a toad to sing a song
And yet, who knows, someone may turn translator
When all these biped reptiles crawl again.

[Now there was one whom I knew long ago]

Now there was one whom I knew long ago
And then another to whom I paid respect:
The first I would salute, the second praise
But all is gone, all gone, the murderer cried.

Along what road they went he cannot say
So many roads there are, so many bends.
There is no short cut to integrity
All, all is gone, all gone, the murderer cried.

They did not mean to kill only to burn
But then one act can transform everything
A brother into charcoal, love to crime
Yes, all is gone, all gone, the murderer cried.

[Groaning, in this wilderness of silence]

Groaning, in this wilderness of silence
Where voices hardly human shout at me
I imitate the most obscure of insects
And burrow in the soil and hide from light.

Speaking with one on a pavement in the city
I watched the greedy mouth, the cunning eye
I reeled and nearly fell in frantic terror
Seeing a human turn into a dog.

Recovering, I studied this illusion
And made a stupid effort to be strong:
I nodded and agreed and listened close.
But when I tried to utter words – I barked!

[In a great silence I hear approaching rain]

In a great silence I hear approaching rain:
There is a sound of conflict in the sky
The frightened lizard darts behind a stone
First was the wind, now is the wild assault.

I wish this world would sink and drown again
So that we build another Noah's ark
And send another little dove to find
What we have lost in floods of misery.

JAIL ME QUICKLY (1964)

Black Friday 1962

were some who ran one way.
were some who ran another way.
were some who did not run at all.
were some who will not run again.
and I was with them all,
when the sun and streets exploded,
and a city of clerks
turned a city of men!
Was a day that had to come,
ever since the whole of a morning sky,
glowed red like glory,
over the tops of houses.

I would never have believed it.
I would have made a telling repudiation.
But I saw it myself
and hair was a mass of fire!
So now obsessed I celebrate in words
all origins of creation, whores and virgins!
I do it with a hand upon a groin,
swearing this way, since other ways are false!

For is only one way, one path, one road.
And nothing downward bends, but upward goes,
like leaves to sunlight, trees to the sun itself.
All, all who are human fail,
like bullets aimed at life,
or the dead who shoot and think themselves alive!

Behind a wall of stone beside this city,
mud is blue-grey when ocean waves are gone,
in the midday sun!
And I have seen some creatures rise from holes,
and claw a triumph like a citizen,
and reign until the tide!

Atop the iron roof tops of this city
I see the vultures practising to wait.
And everytime, and anytime,
in sleep or sudden wake, nightmare, dream,
always for me the same vision of cemeteries, slow funerals,
broken tombs, and death designing all.

True, was with them all,
and told them more than once:
in despair there is hope, but there is none in death.
Now I repeat it here, feeling a waste of life,
in a market-place of doom, watching the human face!

After One Year

After today, how shall I speak with you?
Those miseries I know you cultivate
are mine as well as yours, or do you think
the impartial bullock cares whose land is ploughed?

I know this city much as well as you do,
the ways leading to brothels and those dooms
dwelling in them, as in our lives they dwell.
So jail me quickly, clang the illiterate door
if freedom writes no happier alphabet.

Old hanging ground is still green playing field –
Smooth cemetery proud garden of tall flowers –
But in your secret gables real bats fly
mocking great dreams that give the soul no peace,
and everywhere wrong deeds are being done.

Rude citizen! think you I do not know
that love is stammered, hate is shouted out
in every human city in this world?
Men murder men, as men must murder men,
to build their shining governments of the damned.

What Can a Man Do More

O rain and fire, hopeful origins!
O rust and smoke, only enduring end!
I almost stumble underneath the waste
While squandered daylight mocks my deep remorse
for seeds that rot, for interrupted love
and hours spent measuring footsteps to the grave.

From birth to death what can a man do more
than want to dwell beside a flowering tree
and pick the blossoms if he fears the fruit
will fall like hatred to insult the earth.

And how to leap these sharp entanglements
or skirt this village of the angry streets?
How utter truth when falsehood is the truth?
How welcome dreams how flee the newest lie?

With you I search through nights of frightened stars
and weep by gateways of the bleeding houses:
With you I live to offer up to time
The sacrifice this god demands of us.

O rain and fire, hopeful origins!
O rust and smoke, only enduring end!

Where Are Free Men

O we have endured such absurd times
and waited so long, so weary with time.
Over the city our souls will fly like birds
crying in the night.

There will be wild cries in the still night.
Over the city they will sound like the cries
of the ghosts of homeless birds
flying to the forest
flying from the sea.

And what in dreams we do in life we attempt.
But where are free men, where the endless streets?
Since we were born our wings have had no rest
Our prison of air is worse than one of iron!

Childhood of a Voice

The light oppresses and the darkness frees
a man like me, who never cared at all:
Imagine it, the childhood of a voice
and voice of childhood telling me my name.

But if only the rain would fall,
and the sky we have not seen so long
come blue again.

The familiar white street
is tired of always running east,
The sky, of always arching over.
The tree, of always reaching up.

Even the round earth is tired of being round
and spinning round the sun.

THE WHEN TIME (1977)

Proem

Not, in the saying of you, are you
said. Baffled and like a root
stopped by a stone you turn back questioning
the tree you feed. But what the leaves hear
is not what the roots ask. Inexhaustibly,
being at one time what was to be said
and at another time what has been said
the saying of you remains the living of you
never to be said. But, enduring,
you change with the change that changes
and yet are not of the changing of any of you.
Ever yourself, you are always about
to be yourself in something else ever with me.

Fragment of Memory

We have a sea on this shore
Whole waves of foam groan out perpetually.
In the ships coming, in the black slaves dying
in the hot sun burning down –
We bear a mark no shower of tears can shift.
On the bed of the ocean bones alone remain
rolling like pebbles drowned in many years.

From the beginning of ships
there was always someone who wept when sails were lost.

Perhaps the brown Phoenician woman cried
and cried again because a ship went down....

Or then some Grecian boy with swollen eyes
looked for his father only saw the sea....

There must be some tale telling of a wife
who bred a son upon the Spanish coast
then died before her sailor husband came....

From the beginnings of ships
the sea was always making misery
water and wave, water and wave again.

On life the ocean stained with memory
where are the ships?
But none can say today.

The ships are gone and men remain to show
with a strong black skin what course those keels had cut.

[1956]

118

Voices

Behind a green tree the whole sky is dying
in a sunset of rain in an absence of birds.
The large pools of water lie down in the street
like oceans of memory sinking in sand.
The sun has committed itself far too soon
in the trials of conquest where triumph is rain –
O flower of fire in a wide vase of air
come back, come back to the house of the world.

Scarlet stone is a jewel of death
to be found in the sand when the ocean is dry.
And the life of the light will stay somewhere else
near the rain and the tree when these are alone.
O first sprouting leaf and last falling fruit
your roots came before you were given to air.

Sky only blossomed because man grew tall
from the edge of the water where stones fell and sank.
And that strange dissolution of shape into spirit
was traced from a snail and was found in a word:
O flower of fire in a wide vase of air
come back, come back to the house of the world.

[1957]

Words

These poet words, nuggets out of corruption
or jewels dug from dung or speech from flesh
still bloody red, still half afraid to plunge
in the ceaseless waters foaming over death.

These poet words, nuggets no jeweller sells
across the counter of the world's confusion
but far and near, internal or external
burning the agony of earth's complaint.

These poet words have secrets locked in them
like nuggets laden with the younger sun.
Who will unlock must first himself be locked.
Who will be locked must first himself unlock.

[1957]

Under a Near Sky

A near sky, no stars, another night.
Without warning I think of you,
and the blown away spatter
of rain, on a window sill.

Unable to learn what dreams are storing up.
Closing my eyes that sleep might suddenly fall
like rain or visions, I, in urgent mood
know certain things are certain in one life.

The beat of water on the faraway sand
comes, bringing to me all your woman figure
dress blown away, and hair alive as foam
or rioting leaves or blossoms without peace.

You have not lost what I have taken from you
and cherish in my violent memory.
Come. Let us race across the ocean, ebbing
under a near sky.

[1961]

What We Call Wings

Just as you come sometimes, unheralded,
Kind shower from an unexpected cloud:
So now your presence I do re-invoke
As you offered, I have welcomed it.

It is that sadness in your face I brood on
Rapt student in a dream with strange new speech:
Yourself you are as unaware as I
And fertile is the silence we endure.

Ineffable the vastness of the heart
Whether we die as children or as men:
Embodying both bright flower and live seed
The fruit of passion ripens where it wants.

If these are riddles, riddles write themselves
And where we end no starting indicates:
Your eyes that sparkle teach me how to mourn
For all our deaths are certain as our births.

And making this today I test the burden
Then free myself, but not to weigh you down.
What we call wings the birds can give no name.
To heaven is their flight, on earth our sin.

[1964]

All to Endure

Strong memory, bright pressure of a hand
more eloquent than any broken phrase:
I contemplate love's furious argument
knowing for certain no one ever wins.

Counting the days since last I spoke with you
I wonder whether words out of a mouth
are less than silence, or if silences
tell more than declarations make obscure.

And how a question such as this is answered
I merely ponder, since the heart of passion
can summon dreams, abolish conundrums
all to endure the dark length of a day.

[1965]

Rain Falls Upward

Someone, somewhere, shall know one day
more than I read of what I do:
Dog and a bird may bark or whistle
but human talk will tell me what.

My drought began before I knew
the meaning of a lack of water:
And grass is dry, and heart is cinder
and rain falls upward and away.

A carrion time, dead eye of sheep.
No serious hand is steady ever.
No serious lip, uncracked, undried.
One day, somewhere, someone, will know.

[1966]

In the Asylum

Nearby, in the silence
the abrupt runnel
mocking all the augurs
is piss not rain.
What an end to one season!
What a beginning of another!

The door key latches laughter.
The futile street lamp is an O,
open bocca della verita,
historic space in a crowded city.

Meanwhile, in the asylum
it is a woman's intelligent nerve
makes sense of all the waste
as her spread flank leaps
for the always first time.

[1969]

A Mouth Is Always Muzzled

In the premises of the tongue
dwells the anarchy of the ear;
in the chaos of the vision
resolution of the purpose.

And would shout it out differently
if it could be sounded plain;
But a mouth is always muzzled
by the food it eats to live.

Rain was the cause of roofs.
Birth was the cause of beds.
But life is the question asking
what is the way to die.

[1969]

Even as the Ants Are

In the beginning, if there was,
not of things I mean but of the way
in which are seen, are known,
and ends by offering just a bare hold
tenuous as the air-gripping nails of bird's feet
or the slipping claws of useless mortality.

In such a beginning if there was I say.
In such a beginning was our conspiracy.
And no one will ever know how we came to possess
and possessing are not allowed to speak
not even as the ants are, crossing from my cup
to your spoon.

[1969]

For Milton Williams

The map I study has one continent
though many seas and just as many skies.
And so before the final murder is done
let me locate the country of the act.

Places I barely thought of you know well.
Rivers that flow up mountains are to you
what streets are there, inevitable pathways
inviting naked feet to run away.

Milton, you are a splinter in my mind
a flint of glass lodged in a closed eyelid.
You make the trigger images reset
old time-bombs fused with memory and tears.

And the last to mend the shoes to fit your feet
was thrown away as rubbish, it was lost
as other things are in the normal fashion:
a map, a ring, a letter or a man.

[1969]

Endless Moment World

Would have turned to anyone
to say that my tongue was ready.
Would even have turned to silence
if speech had permitted it.
But finding out I had to tell
to all what my intention was
learnt wherefore certain things are done
and just for so put in my name.

Yes, would have turned to anyone
and worked with a different hand.
Would even have tried with a grammar
for the language of the unspeakable.
But knowing now I need not tell
at all what my intention is
I romp this endless moment world
returning, reshaping, rejoicing.

And would not have turned to myself
if language were only sound.
Nor would have made use of the breath
if the wind itself were voice.
So living where to breathe is hard
I fly like a fish in the air
and swim like a bird in the water
and gill stays gill, and lung stays lung
and my fin and my wing help each other.

[1970]

On a Pavement

I did not know the pavements of cities
were so willing to be soiled.
Thus, when I met you
the least I could do was take
the lighted cigarette from my mouth
and place it gently between your mind-torn lips.

And if in so doing I passed on
my madness, then let the pavements pay the toll.
Let those minds which are as the minds of concrete posts
blinking out red for stop, amber for slow, green for go
go mad too and gain a blessed unconsciousness.

Because I am convinced that death is of little help.
Only imagine what it is to be destined to become a tadpole
swimming in some original form of obscenity
since the forces of nature had no choice but to divide us.

But whatever we are, dust on a voiceless pavement
or men loaded with the love of men and women
the love I say, of men who love for the life of their spirits,
or the love of women who love for the life
of their own and other bodies and other spirits:
whatever we are, let us never forget to wrap
a tender hand upon the all-seeing brow of a child.
The longer we take to do so, the longer will nature divide.

[1971]

If It Were Given

If it were given to me
I would have had a serious conversation
with the fertile dial of the clock of the sun.
But then, I admit, I would have had to change the language
of the dead.

I would have had to haunt the cemetery where the living
believe they put away the varnished coffins
which mock them into making
wreaths for themselves and graveyards for their passions
and victories that mean nothing to them
though they win the trophy of life:
that cupped hand of anguish
open for love (but scattering pain
like seeds of padi) in the murdering drought.

[1971]

For Angela Davis

Rain blazes in that hemisphere
of my mind
where little else happens
neither sunshine nor cloudburst
and certainly not the blossoming of the
power of love you cherish
which so much overwhelms my tongue
given to speech
in the necessary workplaces
where freedom is obscene.

And from a drab window falls the
happy consequence of clouds
which the roots of passionate trees
receive with splendid gratitude
and which may return to us all in
their time

and in their special ways,
linking hand to fruit
and fruit to the promise of our
prayerful hope and love
and the triumph of the effort of
the always beating pulse
in the wrist and temple of the architect
who wars.

I am thinking about you,
Angela Davis
I am thinking about you and
what I want to do
is to command the drying pools
of rain
to wet your tired feet and
lift your face
to the gift of the roof of
clouds we owe you.

[1971]

Cuyuni

Inside my listening sleep
a roar of water on stubborn rock
was the whisper of blood in the womb of my mother.
And when I awoke
I began listening again.

Why does water
ever running water of the river
never pause to take a rest on the back of rocks?
Or even on that place God has designed for it
out of the violent marriage of sun and rain and wind
and the birth and death of trees, labour of roots
growing beneath the seeking upward face
of the ever yielding water
which hide the testicles of seasons
in its own and my groin.

It is for this reason and certain others
I have decided to have only an acquaintance
with this ever dropping, ever racing river
and to speak of it in a code
few can measure nearly;
and the unbelievable conclusion is not an ending
but a closing of lips
and to talk about it openly in common places
may well provoke its fury, and in that fury
liberate one of its many demons
and send his anger roaming the void for me.

So then if perhaps in some stupid fit of arrogance
I said something any fool can understand
and this river heard me, and decided on vengeance,
where is one who could give me
weapons I shall be able to use?

If any of you can I shall be willing to take the risk.
But I must warn you if good advices
prove as useless as a paddle in the falls
you will be happy to be transformed as much as I will have to
by the side of this menacing, sullen river
at the mercy of the swing of hawk sight
and far from the noise of language
where gods still live and brood on thrones of rock.

[1972]

How Come?

So now
how come
the treason
of the spirit?

The beggar man
pretends his tongue
is heavy;
and yet his crutch
his wooden limb
is light!

And he can fling it up
like any hat
and sail it in the air
just like a bird.

So now
how come
the treason
of the spirit?

So now
how come
the bafflement of speech?

So now
how come
the long delight of air
the sense of power
and the sense of passion
created by the dead and wooden
crutch of the spirit
and tongue?

[1972]

In a Small City at Dusk

In a small city at dusk
it is difficult to distinguish
bird from bat. Both fly fast:
one away from the dark
and one toward the dark.
The bird to a nest in the tree
The bat to a feast in its branches.

Stranger to each other they seek
planted by beak or claw or hand
the same tree that grows out of the great soil.
And I know, even before I came to live here,
before the city had so many houses,
dusk did the same to bird and bat and does
the same to man.

[1972]

And I Grope

Light waves like a field of grains of hair.
In the quick life of a flying bird
wings are hollow bones, where wind penetrates.
The eyes of statues blink, in stony unbelief.

Where I wanted to walk I could not.
The native and otherways merge as destiny
steeps. Rain drips like tears from the sudden eyes
of a blind child. And I grope
with the delicate touch of a god or a ghost.

[1972]

My Hand in Yours

As in sleep, my hand in yours, yours
in mine. Your voice in my hearing
and memory, like the sound of stars
as they shine, not content with light
only. My fingertips walk on your face
gently. They tiptoe as a dream does
away from sleep into waking. In a tree
somewhere a bird calls out. And I wake up
my hand still in yours, in the midst
of the sound of stars and a far bird.

[1972]

The Leaves of the Canna Lily

The leaves of the canna lily near the pavement
tremble like my own fingers.
And the torn edges of the cloud in the sky
are ragged like the lips of an idiot child.
To walk the street, that man whose heart is whole,
must never care, must never try to wonder
why the leaves of the canna lily
or the edges of the cloud
tremble like his own fingers
or stay ragged like the lips of his own mouth.

And it would be so good if we could learn
that while death is a final thing,
it is most likely a worse destiny
to be damned to live forever.
For it came to me once in a sudden enlightenment
that all of us, having once been born
can never die, can never choose the kind of sleep
we dream of, or recognise awake.

So this is partly why every day the chance comes
to jump over the bridge, or watch the carcass of the sun.

[1972]

As When I Was

Once, many years ago
decision all my own
and truant in the rain
regretting a cheated freedom
frightened but not like this
by what was strange yet near me
I tried to speak and could not.

Now, frightened into speech
by what you could not mean:
I said 'I will!' I told you;
and fever came as sudden
as when I was a boy
and smell of asphalt burning
made grass seem magical.

[1973]

Before the Question

Lightning clips the far night
like a pair of blue-steel scissors.
Thunder rolls in the throat of a toad
glad for the wild rain.
And the answer comes before the question.
And all I want to do is kneel down,
kneel down before you, hearing it.

[1973]

O My Companion

This afternoon white sea-birds
were quiet, very quiet, until
a cloud over the sun fooled them
it was sunset. The fishes laughed
at the hook in the bait. The cork danced.

Where you are, I am. Lost and seeking
I question the waste. The wind
is blue smoke. From the fires
no flame sprouts. In the distance
day is a foreigner. If a child drowns
it is the sky's fault. If sea-birds stray
the sun's. O my companion.

[1973]

Only Where Our Footprints End

Colliding universes like our lips
must meet and part and join and separate
and in their meeting and their parting fuse
what in their juncture, separation change
collision into crisis, speech resurgent.

Love eats itself to rob death of the feast
where the choice titbit is the tongue that speaks no more.
Where the bleeding heart, the tear-bruised eye is nothing,
or the ruptured ear, deaf even of the silence.

And only where our footprints end can tell
whether the journey was an old advance
or a new retreat; or whether in the dust
our heel marks and our toe marks are confused.

[1973]

The Great Dark

Orbiting, the sun itself has a sun
as the moon an earth, a man a mind.
And life is not a matter of a mother only.
It is also a question of the probability of the spirit,
strength of the web of the ever weaving weaver
I know not how to speak of, caught as I am
in the great dark of the bright connection of words.

And the linked power of love holds the restless wind
even though the sky shudders, and life orbits
around time, around death, it holds the restless wind
as each might hold each other, as each might hold each other.

[1973]

What for Now?

What for now we want to go
with thunder, behind the mountain?
The echo of the went jaguar's roar
is barely distinguishable.
In my hand the crushed pebble was a lizard's egg
and though I say farewell dragon, never to lurch
I am still fearful of those who left you here
and who perhaps are now, with the thunder,
behind the mountain.

[1973]

In the When Time

In the when time of the lost search
behind the treasure of the tree's rooted
and abstract past of a dead seed:
in that time is the discovery.
Remembrance in the sea, or under it,
or in a buried casket of drowned flowers.

It remains possible to glimpse morning
before the sun; possible to see too early
where sunset might stain anticipated
night. So sudden, and so hurting
is the bitten tongue of memory.

[1973]

No Consolation

Outraged, there is no consolation
in outraging the outrageous. Both
shrivel; and the inquisitive candle fly
competes with a bulb of vacuum power;
is soon dead by the blow of an ordinary hand;
ordinary hand to turn the total switch
of the bulb of vacuum power to kill
the light of the candle fly wanting to blink.
The outrageous outrages; remains outraged
in the rubbish wings of the inquisitive candle fly
for whom is no consolation.

[1973]

On a Child Killed by a Motor Car

Child, a moment of love ago
you danced in the eye of the woman
who made you. Within another moment
like the innocent wheat that made the loaf
of bread she sent you for
in this field of the heart's ploughed land
you were threshed!

[1974]

The Child Ran into the Sea

The child ran into the sea
but ran back from the waves, because
the child did not know the sea
on the horizon, is not the same sea
ravishing the shore.

What every child wants is always
in the distance; like the sea
on the horizon. While, on the shore
nearby, at the feet of every child
shallow water, eating the edges
of islands and continents does little more,
little more than foam like spittle
at the corners of the inarticulate mouth
of some other child who wants to run
into the sea, into the horizon.

[1974]

On the Death by Drowning of the Poet, Eric Roach

It is better to drown in the sea
than die in the unfortunate air
which stifles. I heard the rattle
in the river; it was the paddle stroke
scraping the gunwale of a corial.
Memory at least is kind; the lips of death
curse life. And the window in the front of my house
by the gate my children enter by, that window
lets in the perfume of the white waxen glory
of the frangipani, and pain.

[1974]

I Do Not Yet Know

Both sunrise and sunset have often been scarlet
and returning noontime so blue and so white.
I do not yet know the name men have given
that fluttering yellow and ubiquitous butterfly
whose life is not long but whose beauty is so startling.

[1974]

About to Pass Me

From your house through the night streets
I walked easily in the rain
between the drops of it. Behind window panes
faces that never lived stared at me
as I walked away from your house through the rain.
Street lights were averted glances.
Then, suddenly I knew,
what I thought was someone walking
toward me, coming through the rain, casting
his own shadow, was really myself
about to pass me on his way
to your house.

[1974]

Confound Deliberate Chaos

Stark and stay dance in mineral air
master in the sky. From the plantation earth I cry!
And it is futile trying to find out now
from a house-top or a clock
why canal beside a convent
was Amazon to a boy. Besides,
just facing about will make
what led follow; and what followed, lead.
And that is again as saying
a rain drop can be a flood
and an ant can be a nation.
Stark, and stay dance in mineral air
master of the master. Confound
deliberate chaos, all calculations!

[1974]

For a Man Who Walked Sideways

Proudful and barefoot I stride the street
who wants my shirt can have it.
Only the giver gets. The unwanted
unwants the world. The bruised heel of his foot
kicks like a meteor. And the dim dark behind
the blue illusion stands like an altar in a temple
in a forsaken land. Having failed to learn
how to die, they all perish ungracefully.
Laocoon, for all the snakes, struggled well.

[1974]

We Walk the Streets

All through the supine hours
I heard thunder. And lightning a flick-knife
in my mind's awkward hand. The blade
sharpens the wing of a mosquito; clear and swift
it cuts hours into pieces, and they pile up into history
like a bundle of dreams discarded
and waiting to be burnt. If you are a beggar
so am I. We walk the streets.

[1974]

Whence Come They

Whence come they, these urgent visitants
who do not warn of their coming?
How long has each been waiting
outside this door, this house, this room
silent and invisible, always waiting,
always there, impatient and enduring
the deaf ear, blind eye, idle hand
and distracted heart? I hardly know
how to say thanks. But I am grateful
to be so glad they never went away.

[1975]

There Is No Riot

Even that desperate gaiety is gone.
Empty bottles, no longer trophies
are weapons now. Even the cunning
grumble. 'If is talk you want,' she said,
'you wasting time with me. Try the church.'
One time, it was because rain fell
there was no riot. Another time,
it was because the terrorist forgot
to bring the bomb. Now, in these days
though no rain falls, and bombs are well remembered
there is no riot. But everywhere
empty and broken bottles gleam like ruin.

[1975]

Two in One

So different
from the snails,
no matter
two in one:
the wise men
of the mountains,
the immortals,
the hsien.

To wise men
of the mountains,
the immortals,
the hsien:
a season
is a midday,
a voyage
but a stroll!

[1975]

POEMS OF AFFINITY 1978-1980 (1980)

*These poems are dedicated to all children, flowers and dogs
in that order.*

*'language, the field of the most innocent of all occupations,
is the "most dangerous of possessions".'*
Heidegger on Hölderlin

Our time

The more the men of our time we are
the more our time is. But always
we have been somewhere else. Muttering
our mouths like holes in the mud
at the bottom of trenches. Looking
for what is not anywhere, or certain.
Is it only just a misfortune
to be as we are; bad luck
carefully chosen? In parallel seasons
if rain is any hour; if trees abandon
wind, what of the others? Badly abused
we fail to curse. Our fury pleads.
Yet fury should be fire; if not light.
And what is the mother of fury
if not ours. For any man
and for any time, one dream
is enough. This is true.

Playing Militia

Even in that place of final exile
among tombs, and mechanical inscriptions,
each leaf is a different green;
flower a different kind
of red and yellow; also, each ripe fruit
tumult of a really different seed
there, in that place.

Outside in the traffic
between the city's indifferent wheels and feet,
amid a hatred of trees,
the phalloid needles of sewing machines
have sown a new drill. The sleeves
of uniforms droop
like the wet feathers of a crow's wing
over secret carrion. Girls, unbreasted,
wear guns like earrings. Boys, ungamed,
grip them like tickets. The spree
is a wake. Admission is free.

I still stare

Beyond a pattern of stars, reserved
for sundown; beyond and through slats
once closed, now open, I still stare.
Time's fabulous fall down is
the slope of a strange mountain,
a shelf of books. Our hands have
written. They will continue to write
always the same. Title different.
Signature equal. Both are reserved
for the time beyond sundown, through
which, once closed, now open, I still stare.

In a world

In a purple world, I walked
among virgins and trees. Between
the thighs of time, I measured the swing
of a dead clock. Beating is
my heart. The sun of our own
sky's miserable convocation
of the finger of my bare and restless
forehead; memory of hair; climate
of the weather of the fork of virgins
and uprooted trees, through which
I walk again.

As new and as old I

Every day is as old
as a new day is. Time
represents itself. Night fakes
the rule of stars; as we fake
light's good pencil. A child's
chalk ridden black board. Alphabet
of hope in a season of insects. Crawl
of the beast in a season of days. I
unapologetic, remember why every
day was once a new day. As new
and as old as my childhood roaming
among grass. The world is a cold
wind. It is a glass of sweet water
in a grim place of thirst.
Farewell rain. When again shall I
taste your high cloud? Having betrayed
old gods in an old day, we seek
now to betray new ones
in a new day.

As new and as old II

This morning is new, but the sun
that made it is old. New and old
is the face of the world's great grief,
a kind of music we listen to and hear
when the toil of silence builds
our house of language in this wind's
throat, the grim larynx. A green leaf
on the branch of a tree fingers
our time's disgraceful space. We
are its measure.

In a certain time

Suddenly, air is very much colder
and so determined the world's accordion
throbs like music in my very weary
wrist. In a certain time, I have lingered.
But as an owl hoots
to startle the vile eye of a toad
and initiate its own defiance of dark:
I also speak. Having despised
all fangs, I neither have nor want
a time to bite. Ugly is the weak
coward mouth which having advantaged
advances. Old jaws and a toothless snarl. A
peeping of finger tips, a beggar man's rich
inquisition of my own and determined
but not sudden destiny.

Our number

The pins of the slack pin seine
irregular the horizon; the tide
has gone them bare. A most disturbed
seagull proportions a catch. The fisherman's
wife, another seagull, leans on the sky
counting shrimp.

Surrendering ourselves
we denizen an epoch of abuse
trying to defy with the seagull's
or seawife's similar desperation
the tide that naked skins us.
Shrimp is our number. Is so
we stay. Is a way
of counting born we.

With that loan

A tick on the flank
of a beast is also
a beast; as every answer
creature of a question. In
this world time is a snare
and I am masticated
by its jaw. All I could have
and have done was to borrow
its tongue. With that loan
I have gained a mastery
of the language of our negative yes.

Paying fares

Waiting for the bus
they see him, the powerful crab
edging sideways through the silt
of their lives. What, they wonder
does he eat, and who
his obeahman? Behind the window panes
of his hard house, they mark his new
window blinds, flags that rob their eyes
yet let him peep. But cloth
can burn they mutter, paying fares.

Rain forest

Every clear raindrop helps to obscure
the green towers; every grain
of white sand the specks
of bright gold. These are of memory
as nights of love are, inside
our human forest of loss.

It is the same everywhere.
Ants lay waste ants.
Peril lurks ambiguously
as it always does
in the least or most fertile
purposes of the works
of human courage. The swamps
are treacherous. The hustling creeks
of identical water are beautiful
and still, one cry, one however begun
human cry, contains all.

Rice

What is rain for, if not rice
for an empty pot; and pot for
in a hungry village? The son
succeeds his father in a line,
to count as he did, waiting,
adding the latest to the first
of his losses; his harvests
of quick wind padi. For him
the new moon was dry like the full moon
that promised. The sea always
as salt as wet. In his calculation
his yield was the share that he would reap
when he cheated, like the moon and the sea.

Beans of God

Sunlight and dreams
disunderstand. And
in the sky which has not
yet released the sun, the moon
pales, like the anaeming
of the sky, blue once, white
now, like a lone and laugh
world. On the pavements
of the feet of cripples I plant
the green pods of the beans of God.

Bent

On the street, the sun
rages. The bent back of
an old woman resurrects
the brimmed bucket of this world's
light and insupportable
agony. A damage of years.

Her bent back, time's bad
step, and the creeping out
is ash; is the crushed cloud
of an incredible want.

The last time I saw her
she was far more truthful
than the damage of the years
carried on her back. The
sky, blue and ever,
imitates her. Bent.

Ground doves

Vile, with exhalations
our time's new wind
terrifies the timid ground
doves, in a swamp of vapours.
They seek refuge
as you and I do, above
that wind. On electric wires
which stretch from nowhere
to somewhere, they perch to perish
with singed feathers. They
fall. We shall have
to pick them up. And burn our hands.

Our voice betrays

Show me a little freedom, different
from this. Time's tick tock
is our doom's astronomy. Caring
too little our voice betrays the hours
we tread upon. Only last night
I dreamed a stray dog eagerly,
as we would, devoured a kitten. Similarly,
in the firmament's disgrace Orion
the great sky hunter fled in front
of us. Yet I keep watch. Not
only their bad hands but worse
eyes I see. Everything blindfolds. Rain
and meteors want now in this season
to surrender their arts of falling.

Being always

Being, always to arrange
myself in the world, and the world
in myself, I try to do both. How
both are done is difficult. Why,
I have to ask, do I have to
arrange anything, when every
thing is already arranged
by love's and death's inscrutable
laws, mortal judiciary, time's
doll house of replaceable heads,
arms and legs? In another
house, not time's, time itself arranges
mine and the world's replacement.

Too much waiting

The jumbie umbrella cones
the lost dark into an early
morning's bright assault. If
trees die, what happens to
caterpillars? There is
much too much waiting
in this last of a lost world.
When an owl hoots, it warns
midnight, the fearing lost
and dark advice of a jumbie
umbrella, the gone sun's
wild memory of a parasol
sky.

As well is

Who walks as well is a man
seeing identical flaws
in the space between light
of lost long ago lamps
in the black outs of bright
hopes; tails of candle flies
are bright finger nails, cutexed
with an arrogant despair. Near
a leaf, a rain drop pauses
over a dead land. A land
which can be as much and as bold
as an error confused with a cause.

Some kind of fury

On the lintel of my hard mind's
and sky's opaque but apparent
window, the world's open book
the less green Bible, the insufficient
posture which reminds our great God
of his function. South western
of my long ago childhood are
the clouds, which when I was even
younger, were North eastern.
In this foul age of a new
and recurring despair, I
keep working for a storm, some
kind of fury to write new dates
in our vile calendar and book.

Inventor

In a yawning gun world I
am more criminal than any
of them. I, inventor of the law
I break, am more criminal, in
the world's definition. The
slipper on my foot does not
slip. The lace world is
a tie thing. I knot interruptions. I
start insurgencies. But our world
is a bowl or a bowel. I shit
it out, without castor oil, as
when, in people's grim
childhood, I was evacuated.

Rag of wonder

Your hair in my hand is a rag
of wonder. I keep searching to find
which one of my many selves has found out
why in my hand your hair is a rag
of wonder. A dog barks sometimes
because it is surprised. Some other times
because it is afraid. But whether surprised,
or afraid, our vile selves refuse to search
and to find out why love's hair
is a rag of wonder, since fear and surprise
are foreign to every vile self.

Anywhere

I have learnt how to dance
with eyes. The waist of the navel
is a kind of dance. The waste
I tried to war about, I,
an air starer at, smoke a cigarette.
I am so severely one
that I want to be somebody else
having learnt how to dance with these eyes.

The Sun's accordion

Fingered by a leaf, wind
begins a discussion to which
answering affirmatively, I
make every visible to me star
a chrysalis: the images
are light years, refusing
to be held in our dirty hands
by daylight comparisoned; as,
in a night long with waiting
only our love remains for a morning
comparable with the sun's work.

For César Vallejo I

Brother, let us now break
our bread together. My
plate is a small world. My
world a small plate. From
a place in which plates
and worlds are utensils
we have reconstructed our
selves, with a power of difference.
César Vallejo. The parrots
call your name, fertile as
rain. My habit of utterance
kneels down at the sound of it.
I, who only wanted to be
and to have a name.

For César Vallejo II

Proud of being coarse, we
coarsen pride, making
the act an issue. Even
cockroaches have begun
to flee from some
of our very dirty houses.
They, knowing better
their inevitable destination
better than many of us do,
flaunt their insect
pride, less coarse than ours.
They scorn us, which, I
think, is why they flee
so many of our dirty houses.

Bastille Day – Georgetown

Not wanting to deny, I
believed it. Not wanting
to believe it, I denied
our Bastille day. This,
is nothing to storm. This
fourteenth of July. With
my own eyes, I saw the fierce
criminal passing for citizen
with a weapon, a piece of wood
and five for one. We laugh
Bastille laughter. These are
not men of death. A pot
of rice is their foul reward.

I have at last started
to understand the origin
of our vileness, and being
unable to deny it, I suggest
its nativity.
In the shame of knowledge
of our vileness, we shall fight.

Let every child run wild

No need to throw a flower, throw
a petal. Rain is a cousin
of air, the blood of parents.
Let every child run wild, or stop,
or stop the way men journey
through the earth's loop, the freedom
of a guitar. As much or much more
delicate is the freedom
of a such instrument. This day
is an old one. It is as old
as a petal or a flower
or the rain or the still air
of a child's wild guitar
shuddering in the silence
of parents.

I tremble

Accursed, I curse, with
a green lip for a new mouth.
A green and wilder pencil
for a finger. And a freer
and much more dreadful
season for a climate. Almost
everywhere, I have wandered. Often
died and dreamed myself
back to mortality. Still
everything remains a peculiar
yet. Death and dreams are
warm. But also as cold as
the curses I utter about
myself. Often, I repeat, I
have died and dreamed. And
when I see a green tree, I
tremble.

Faces

The faces of my mother and wife
who is herself the mother of my mother's
random and old love; whose faces
make necessary my memory of the sea
as it leaps; as it lunges and plunges
in the mud of time and mind; in the blood
of the one season responsible
for every pointing finger that stares
like a star from nowhere. Thus I began
to learn when I discovered why
every tree is as green as the reason
of the land on my holy hand
which keeps pointing forever inward,
but not beyond the veil of the lace
of tears of these faces.

Watch my language

A world is fondled, when I fondle
you. From the tiptoe of shame
to the richness of the inside fondling
comb, I, having once touched
always the anywhere sculpture
of the freedom of a piece
of your sweet indecent hair.
As when, as out, and as when as
in, I walk decidingly about
disappear. Watch my language.

For Michael Aarons

At the foot of the stair
I stare. The spit of a star
invents the sky. The sky invents
the reflection of the world's
plurability of the principality
of mind. I, with as you do,
raise a great glass
new year of a new time.

He (for Farro)

Always wanting with ripe
magic his childhood planted
he, thought more than thinker
waits, ever in want of a signal
season flash in his stubborn dim.

He has to be what all
have been. And will be.
Mortality includes the feather
and the mind. And though both
are familiar with flying
it cares not how different
they be. Living flash is not thought flash,
nor either of them morning flash
mortality includes in him
in its casual arrogance.

Census

Use the true mathematic
in a real counting.
Indite about strays
and such as those them.
Include the new others.
The big ones. The not so big
ones. That very big one
too. Then indict. Then add up.
Smaller count. Ampler measure.
True mathematic.

Is why

Same only ghost come to suffice
all lost in air, ground, house
incomparable city
of false directions. Was real.
Was true. Is why. Not as these
undead. And about time too. Same
walk about ghost. About time to.

FOUR POEMS AND DEMERARA NIGGER (1984)

One

Trees are arranged like mourners by a sadness.
Root, stem, and wreath, and high above, the crown.
And a lizard upside down walks on the moon.
Futile rebuke of mourning. It will fall.
Balance was never. The spindle warps the thread.
The spin the spindle. And a work the work.
Body of soul, which world is like this one
if not this one? Which waywardness as right
as this scale leaning? The thing to be before
must be the thing again. More is that which was first
and stays the first. Again because before.
Apart because between. All is dominion.
The beach it breaks on is what makes it ocean.

Two

Not so is it done, O no
not so. It is done, so,
as I think I am doing it,
neither not, nor so, but only
just in a wait, in a
moment, in a year, in
and this moment, this
yester just so. Because
a poet cannot truly speak
to himself save in his
own country: even among
the fearers of joy, enviers
of pride. Standard-bearers
of his and their defeat. Just
so. And the sly drum.

Three

Withholding rain, I identify
myself with the withholden. But
no more ever cosmos. Mud
is the lacing of the boot
of a bird's wild whistle. Or
flute, the very same one I
imagined in the journey
of the flute's music, before
and after loss. When
rain becomes water the triumph
of a horse's hoof is
the sling shot of the pelt
of stars; imitating the drops
of the never to be withholding
rain of the world's blind
destiny. For what is rain
but delta? And delta
what but the immortal river
of rain? A thing falling
ever from these mortal
dripping fingers.

Four

The spared are not the saved. The living
but the unhanged. When that stair
of the gallows collapsed, no one was treading
on it. All had been hanged already.
Hangman gone home. No wood ants
in his house. So I was told and saw, but
still, not seeing, doubt. Because
everywhere something betokened
and previous is always to happen.
And everywhere something ordained
and mortal is rightly to method.

Hangman himself to bereave
wood ants their trade to accomplish
in stair of house and of gallows,
nor confidence betrayed,
truth such as this recovered
and famous justice made.

Demerara Nigger

In right accordance, and demandingly
because what withstands, stands,
Farinata, the Ghibelline,
'entertained great scorn of hell
and asked about ancestors'. So
be it. 'Demerera nigger. Downward
through the horse.' Hells are comparable
but mind stays in advance of dispensation.
This foot for instance. This shoe.
Step. Floor. Book for instance. Lamp.
From one to the other; and words
tortured out like a turd. Until the sudden
fumble of the premonitory wing
of the bat in the roof. I held
mortality a thing to be endured;
human fact deliverable. What
when fear is hope; if no messenger rode;
way and cause as right if not
an ending? Therefore found it just
often to barter talk for sight
and turn a bat and confuse clocks. At
any cost I had to go; went scorning
and demanding. Mortality put to question.
Cosmic justice reckoned in confirming
a horse of hell as likely as the riding
companion mind; mind in advance of mind,
the mind requiting and mind singular,
enabled mind, mind minded to suppose
nigger and Ghibelline.

BITTER WOOD (1988) and FOUR POEMS FROM *KYK-OVER-AL* (1993)

Bitter Wood

Here be dragons, and bitter
cups made of wood; and the hooves
of horses where they should not
sound. Yet on the roofs of houses
walk the carpenters, as once did
cartographers on the spoil
of splendid maps. Here is where
I am, in a great geometry, between
a raft of ants and the green sight
of the freedom of a tree, made
of that same bitter wood

[1988]

The Conjunction

Very sudden is the sought conjunction.
Sought once over and found once over
and again, in the same sudden place.

It is where the hair grows.
It is where the hand goes.
It is the conjunction
of loin and the rare
possibility of a head
on the cushion of hair and love.

Indeed, I have always wanted
to climb upon a window sill
to climb and compete with the rain
falling down, and rising up.
And staying still, in the promissory
hope of passion's signature
and the returned wealth of a conjunction.

[1989]

Horses

My shoe has fallen off
And the sole of the foot pleads.
As both of my hands.
Why is it I do love horses?
And their hooves
And their very free flanks.
It is because they climb the sky
And are at one with God.

[1989]

No Easy Thing

I must repeat that which I have declared
even to hide it from your urgent heart:
No easy thing is it to speak of love
Nor to be silent when it all consumes!

You do not know how everywhere I go
You go with me clasped in my memory:
One night I dreamed we walked beside the sea
And tasted freedom underneath the moon.

Do not be late needed and wanted love
What's withheld blights both love itself and us:
As well as blame your hair for blowing wind
As me for breathing, living, loving you.

[*circa* 1970s]

The Poems Man

Look, look, she cried, the poems man,
running across the frail bridge
of her innocence. Into what house
will she go? Into what guilt will
that bridge lead? I
the man she called out at
and she, hardly twelve
meet in the middle, she going
her way; I coming from mine:
The middle where we meet
is not the place to stop.

[*circa* 1960s]

169

SUITE OF FIVE POEMS (2000)

*This is the marvel of the play of forces
That they must sense, they move not otherwise
They grow in roots and dwindle in the tree trunk
And in the crown like resurrection rise!*

RAINER MARIA RILKE

1

Unwritten histories of human hearts:
Who knows, one day the books will write themselves
in a magic language soon transforming us
to image, symbol and the ultimate silence.

My hand grows weary on a truthful page
and stops at last in total resignation.
Shall it be told? I seek the quiet answer
To this first question which began it all!

2

For thousands of miles the sky is all the same
Just like the sea or time or loneliness.
It was the heart that noticed all of this
When it computed distance into loss.

The sky bends with the earth and earth with space
And those who navigate are full of hope:
But the compass that they need is far more kind
Than love's magnetic north pole of desire.

3

I will walk across the floor through tables, through voices
like a man who is very drunk I will think only of the moment
Abolishing time's furniture I will make myself my own
A high roof with rafters whereon I'll hang like a bat.

Flitting through twilight by trees that are going to sleep
I will disappear into the flame of sunset by the rim of the sea:
Plunging myself into depths that are always dark
I will see all things and return to tell you all.

Using the speech of men I will whisper to you
Of dreams that change to ghosts and haunt a life;
And prayers in the heart that mutilate
I will repeat, until your eyes are streaming.

4

I will always be speaking with you. And if I falter,
and if I stop, I will still be speaking with you, in
words that are not uttered, are never uttered, never
made into the green sky, the green earth, the
green, green love...
    And I was bathing by the sea and there was a
gull, a white gull, so far, so far...
    I saw the weak wing flutter long before it did,
and the webbed foot dip, long before it did; and
the sudden wave, and the scarlet tinted foam of
a sunset burning like fire already gold in flames.

5

Wanting to write another poem for you
I searched the world for something beautiful
The green crown of a tree offered itself
Because its leaves were combed just like your hair.

The sea wind brushes and the light rains wash
And crystal jewels cling to every twig
While tender are the tears in lovers' eyes
Sleep all those tiny blossoms yet to bloom!

Outside my window, law unto itself
This tall green crown confirms an oath I swore
with mighty roots invisible in earth
and amongst seeds that war with God and die.

UNCOLLECTED POEMS

From 'An Ode to Midnight'

O, midnight hour, why must thy time be sad?
Art thou not like the other hours of night?
E'en though the day and all its hours had
The smile of sunbeams, thou too has thy light.
For every even when the sun declines
And takes its couch beyond the western world
The stars awake and Venus first doth glow
Why, darkened hour, must all joy be furled
      Or sorrow show?

Hark! now I hear a wind's quick tongue outpour
A tale of grief into the listening leaves
No! 'tis not like a saddened lover's poor
And stammering voice while as he grieves
He speaks, and burdens every ear and heart.
No, it is like defiance 'gainst black fate
And it is like the spirit's mighty quest
Of Truth and Life which never shall abate
      Or seek for rest.

Indeed, indeed I gave ear to the winds
And listened with the leaves unto the voice
But vain alas were all the stolen gains
And nought the sweet for though it spoke of joys
Its grief, my fears, its lament and my thoughts
Did both complain that joy flies with the life
When Death the fiend comes with cruel wrath.
Ah, midnight voice, thou tellest this earth's strife
      The weary path!

The Indian Woman

Among the grass green lettuce which
Grew round the rusted railway line,
The Indian Woman bent and worked
Beneath the sun the whole day long.

Her dress down at the hem was wet
With water from her water can,
And as she worked she coughed and spat
Upon the grass green lettuce there.

When daily noon with burning sun
Came with the smoking midday train,
That Indian Woman was not there.
For home from school her children were.

With hands as rough as the rusted edge
Of some old spade left in the rain,
She worked beside a fire now
To feed her children and herself.

Her man came not from his rice field –
He could not spare the walking hour –
His wife and children ate at home –
He, from his saucepan in the sun.

At six o'clock the bees of night
All pierce with whistlings twilight's haze,
And darkness falling on the land
Makes man and woman look to home.

He, dead beat with day's murderous toil;
She, wearied out with weeding come
To their dim hovel and the rags –
Those rags called bed by slavery.

Now as they lie in bed, he feels
Her warm womb rising with a child,
And he remembers how she said
'Another child is live in me.'

Yes, like the new against the old
One passing and one springing up
Within her living body grows
Another child – one toiler more.

And she will work until her womb
Full pregnant makes her strength to fail,
But must she only work and dare
With this the misery of the year?

No! No! The misery of the years
Against time gives birth to flaming wrath
And wrath like fire, life's demands
Makes misery's fuel, freedom's flame.

And they whose eyes are dim with this
Which passes by the name of life
Will raise their faces to the world
And struggle on with different eyes.
So that those whose confounded wealth
Bloats up through all this death in life
Will only vainly struggle on
Against the victors of the world.
For like the dawn the struggle is;
The dawn's first witness is a gleam;
But like white noon to black midnight
Will what was dark face what seemed bright.

Poem of Prison

I

Now I go back to night
O dark slab of iron
wall of brick
o lonely window
face me not with heaven:
I go back, I return, I sink into the floor.

II

Life, wherever you are I hail you.
When my heart is ready shall blaze away.
This prison will be a mound of ashes.
I will be born, I will be born my love.

If Today

If today our city is like a house of stone
rigid and cold, silent and still
It is because a soldier walks with a gun
Not even a friend of the stars
Not even a friend of the dogs.

And if today the sound of the ocean on our shore
comes like a rumble of terror
It is because death rides at anchor in the sea
Watching until they sleep
waiting for hope to fade.

And even if today they try to stamp us down
flesh into mud, heart into stone
Are we not still a great generation of struggle
Strong and uncountable
born to be free?

Where Are Those Human Hands?

O prison cot in a prison cell
and prison food in a prison plate!
O heart of man! O tender heart!
O wall of prison! O wall of stone!

I am lying here in a quiet night
and the blue star of silence shines above me
From afar comes the muted voice of a convict
murmuring in a dream of freedom......

In every cell there is a day locked up
like a man I know.
In every heart there is a hope locked up
like a wingless bird.
And when the lights go out in every cell
the bird of hope will stumble in the darkness......
O wall of prison, iron, stone and sorrow
where are those human hands that built you up?

Immortal Like the Earth

They cannot lock a poet in a prison
The Keys they have are made of steel and iron
His heart is made of fire furious fire
bred from the flame that changes everything.

They cannot close a gate upon his dream
The gates they have are made of blood and sorrow
His dream is made of hope and man's triumph
over our night and all our screams of terror.

They cannot make a poet turn a beast
Either they kill him or they kill mankind
He is the bird flying above their heads
He is the drum beating their doom like music

They cannot kill a poet with a gun
nor choke his life with rope upon a beam
He is mankind immortal like a kiss
He is mankind immortal like the earth.

For My Son

The street is in darkness
Children are sleeping
Mankind is dreaming
It is midnight.

It is midnight
The sun is away
Stars peep at cradles
Far seems the day.

Who will awaken
One little flower
Sleeping and growing
Hour and hour?

Light will awaken
All the young flowers
Sleeping and growing
Hour and hour.

Dew is awake
Morning is soon
Mankind is risen
Flowers will bloom.

For Morton Sobell in Alcatraz

It could have been my name instead of yours
It could have been my wife and not your wife
They could have been my children, Morton Sobell,
Thinking of me locked up in Alcatraz

I too live in a prison Morton Sobell
In prison where a night is black and solid
Where day is made of hours each one numbered
by blows of courage on a brittle sky!

We all live in a prison, Morton Sobell,
But only what stays clean will reach to honour.
You said you will not soil those hands of yours,
I promise you – I will not soil mine either!

Cane Cutter

Cane cutter, cane cutter
Your cutlass is covered with mud.
In the chill wind of the bitter season
You walk against a wet and shivering sky

The silent labour of your dream must burn
beside the ocean where you go to sleep.
While blackened fragments of green cane stalks float
and fall on you like rain or endless sweat.

From those deep shadows in the field of roots
I see you looming in your weariness.
Your invisible feet sink down below the night
In your dark face two stars I make your eyes.

Cane cutter, cane cutter
The mud on your cutlass is wet
And in this world of dreams and shapes and shadows
I long to see you flash it at the sun.

In the Shadow of a Soldier

Two long years
in the shadow of a soldier.
Those long months have left us like a tree
in naked growth above its buried roots.

We never danced when cold wind made us shudder
and ocean was our road and hope our pain
in ships and fields where time was like a shroud.
But even that was cleaned sometimes with fire
in other years by other men than we
and all of us who see them all about.

They stay and cast a shadow on our life.
Our land goes dark with stain as from a blight.
We do not even tremble in the gloom
for all our flesh is burning into ash.

Two long years
in the shadow of a soldier,
These long months are ashes of our pain
heaped on the roots we cannot grow without.

Wind of Life

Birds of endurance
weary of flying
drop to the ground.

Feathers of hope
torn from the bone
lie in the dust.

Altar of earth
heavy with sacrifice
spins round forever.

Wind of life
is willing to bear
wings born again.

To be born
is to fly
from a nest
in the light
and go near
to the egg
in the dark.

Ancestor Accabreh

Was ancestor Accabreh
was ancestor himself
he stand up like a palm tree
his head touch the sky.

Was ancestor Accabreh.
He said no more the grey chimney no more
no more the cold wind no more no more.

He said, when I come back
O green shelter of long grass
hide me forever and ever.   10

He said, O woman face of earth
when I come back
let me lie down
kiss me to sleep.

He said when I come back
in the green shelter of darkness
let me lie down in peace.

Then he turned around
and he called them.
He pointed to the red sun   20
and said that is the field.

And the white birds over yonder
that is the chimney.
And the terrible cloud up there
that is our life
Not now but tonight
tonight in the darkness.

Then Accabreh sat down
and they sat down around him
and he told them   30
he said, when we go the night will divide
like the sea for Moses.

And all chanted
like the sea for Moses
like the sea for Moses.

But suddenly night fell down from the green roof
and earth rose up like a young woman
and took off her clothes
to go to sleep.
And Accabreh murmured   40
O woman face of earth moving side by side
O green shelter of long grass hide me forever and ever.

Then Accabreh rose up and crept softly through the jungle.
He walked with his bare feet on the bed of Wikki
on the cold bed of Wikki the black creek.
And all of them crouched down behind him
And crept softly over the bed of Wikki the black creek.
And the wall of the jungle
and the green wall of the night
opened for them, for all of them.   50

The great rough cayman with red eyes
and the shy agouti and the wild tapir
plunged in the scowl of the jungle
and dived in the soft banks of Wikki the black creek.

And down in the dark tunnel went Accabreh
down the dark tunnel of his time.
And behind him crept all of them
down the long tunnel of the dark.

Down in the tunnel
there is no star in the roof to follow
but only the sound of a foot like a drum.

Then they came to a hill of white sand
and searched the green darkness of the world
and the white moon was cold with rain
but nothing shifted in the green dream below them.

Then down in the jungle went again
and over the calm brown of the woman face of earth.
And when they came to the voiceless wail of freedom
Accabreh spoke and they listened to him.
He said, I come I come in the manner of a man
I shake darkness from my brow
with the fires of rebellion.

And night opened like a gate for him
and he went into the darkness of his doom.
And he took the parcel of night in his hands
and he loosened the knots that bound it
and held it up against the useless stars
and broke it into pieces
and scattered the lumps in the burning wall of his life.

But those who engender the bleak night
they caught him they caught him
and tied a chain around his hands and feet
and took him to the far white god of grief.
But there was no darkness on his brow
only a laugh of scorn deep in his mouth.

When Accabreh laughed
his scorn was like thunder.
And when he cried
his tears were like rain.

Was ancestor Accabreh
ancestor himself.
At the door of his death
he looked far away
his heart it was beating
like high wind on fire.

185

Was ancestor Accabreh
His laughter is scorn
He stand up like a palm tree
His head touch the sky.

Then they took him and broke him on a wheel. ₁₀₀
But before he died he laughed.
He said, O green shelter of long grass
O woman face of earth moving side to side
be naked for my children as for me
Accabreh! Accabreh!

[Let my greatnesses transcend my indecencies]

Let my greatnesses transcend my indecencies
and let the sun that nature fashioned to make trees green
be as nothing to the light I fashion to make myself nothingness.
Because I have discovered the secret of death
which has nothing to do with the end of a life
or a soul or a heart or an ignorant brutal mouth,
can be revealed in a moment of supreme love
and pain, the origin and birth of a face.

I have seen the rain fall in so many places
that I have ceased caring where the drops come from
whether from clouds or tree tops or the eyes of monkeys
who would like to cry but have to howl instead.

And so I look through the savage window of the world
sitting perilously on the sills of the shoulders of the clock
While a sweet child smiling with innocence
still wonders why a frown is not so ugly.

[Having, as I do, a profound hatred for humans and alcohol]

Having, as I do, a profound hatred for humans and alcohol
I welcome both as dear friends to my bosom.
For while the former enrages the instincts of love buried in my skin
the latter makes release of what I should not want.

On the pavement of the street near to my house
I saw a man kill nearly for a love
which like a beetle he knew would soon escape
and vanish in the yellow pool of moonlight.

Human moonlight, alcohol of beetle and murder of love is one
As everything is in my futile benab
where the tribesman's poison arrow is the rain
that makes the greenest leaf turn yellow brown.

And yet I want you seriously to know
that the poison on the arrow's bark is food
as a curse is, or a moan is, when a man and woman soar,
as all of us have soared beneath the ocean's drowning.

[Star code and tree fruit. Shout]

Star code and tree fruit. Shout
in the throat of the music of my loss.
Rain. The nymph of a grasshopper
laughs. Flood surrounds the fence
of the heron's knotted ankle. Cattle
man or beast of water. When I tried
I touched. When I touched
I found myself. The frail udder
of love waits for strong fingers.
This code of stars has been a long time waiting
and when my feet scuffle, the leaves of trees talk.

[As the eyes move and her hands]

As the eyes move and her hands
like the wings of the eyelids
            of her hair. I see you
child of the sun, the flambuoyant
            is flambuoying out
and the tiles of your fingernails have
            always built cities
Wait! Is it true
that the long canoe is full of water
and the sea is open
            like your lips

Talking Names

Sometimes a shout will do. Sometimes
a whisper. Sometimes to say nothing
is more than either. Sometimes enough.
Before you lead me out to dance
on the red coals like hot eyes
which follow everywhere; in front,
and behind, here the flames have gone out
or newly flicker: then, of your own feet,
and of the feet of those who danced before
and will dance after, judge
and name every man his crime.

For Walter Rodney

Assassins of conversation
they bury the voice
they assassinate, in the beloved
grave of the voice, never to be silent.

I sit in the presence of rain
in the sky's wild noise
of the feet of some who
not only, but also, kill
the origin of rain, the ankle
of the whore, as fastidious
as the great fight, the wife
of water. Risker, risk.
I intend to turn a sky
of tears, for you.

For the Students of St Rose's

Green must come the wind; trees are clouds
and a bosomful of rain a clutch of tears.
But life is not a uniform; nor do the socks
of a humming bird
fall down for a want of garters.
Every pavement is a hard salute
to a hand raised; the city a cell
and God a jail-bird. Hence
God lives in the prison of every human heart.
And for a green wind, a world waits.

2 October 1974

[My hand shadows my page]

My hand shadows my page.
If it were only the switch it
would be enough I mean my hand
not my page. Is this my last new
clock time of joy, sound
of a generation's despair? I
have heard other bells. I

189

have tried often to interpret
the wisdoms of silence; the holy
messages of rain in required
nights, in black sheets
of my father's waste of a city.
Also I have seen ghosts flitting
between paling staves, through,
when a boy, I shoved my wrists
as bats or candle flies do their bright
and compassing eyes. Precious as flour
are we but raw in air as the loaf
time's oven refuses to cook.

[The sweet memory of]

The sweet memory of
myself, like the ratoon
of an innocent cane,
must await the cutting
and not the suspect
sugar of the day

A green wave
of fissure sweets
from the kisses
of the moon. As the sun
licks, the crystals, every
callous day brings
me, memory
of burdened skins.

Savaged men sprinkle
the green parcelled
soil. Chrysalised
like dark worms
with a never light
edging a day of scars
with breaths of dead hopes.

SELECTED PROSE

The Lesson of August

Imagine for yourself a scene, somewhere in a dim land where hundreds of half-naked black men and women leap in the air shouting for joy. Make the picture with a background of tall chimneys, fields of green sugar cane and nigger yards sprawling close to dust. And think about a whip, hot as fire, posed in the raised hand of a slave driver. For this is August month, the month of emancipation in the year 1833, when hundreds of thousands of black slaves were released from the kennels into which the colonisers had locked them.

Today, August month succeeds ten months of darkness in an occupied country. Driven back upon themselves by the bayonets of imperialists who are direct inheritors of the traditions of slave traders, slave makers and slave owners, the people of Guiana stand like trees at midday, rooted in their own shadows. Where the wretched slave lived in fear of the whip and the stocks, the people now live in expectancy of bullets. And the hand that wielded the whip, and the hand that now holds the gun is the very same hand – the hand of the British overlord, rank with cruelty.

Not so long ago when the head of the statue of Queen Victoria was found peacefully nestling among grass and weeds one early morning, the local press bewailed the indignity and tried to make out to everybody that Victoria had freed the slaves out of the sheer goodness of her heart. But Eric Williams, the Trinidadian historian, in his book *Capitalism and Slavery* has shown that emancipation came fundamentally from economic developments in Britain itself, together with the rising militancy of the slaves in the colonies. Dr Williams points out how emancipation suited the interests of the expanding industrial capitalists in Britain and how it was only one point in a whole series of events. As for the militancy of the slaves, we have only to think about the insurrection of 1823 when thousands of slaves rose in rebellion at La Ressouvenir on the East Coast of Demerara. This is the insurrection in which John Smith was involved. And this is only one of the many that flamed up and down the land in that period of our history. It is good to note here too, that a Guianese writer, Mr P.H. Daly in his book, *West Indian Freedom and West Indian Literature* published here in 1951, not only acknowledged this aspect of our historical background, but also bases his main argument on these very premises. Thus, in stressing the outstanding significance of the slave revolts in relation to emancipation, Mr Daly writes: 'One can trace a pattern of concerted action from the Great Slave Rebellion in Berbice under the Dutch from February 1763 to March 1764, down to the La Ressouvenir Rebellion. It was the beginning of a sort of people's movement, a people struggling for their freedom and relying on their power to set them free.'

Everybody knows that it was after Emancipation, when the sugar estate owners, faced with the fact that the majority of ex-slaves no longer wanted to have anything to do with sugar plantations, initiated what we know as the indenture system. And after trying out the Portuguese and Chinese, to put it down in the sequence of their arrival here, they finally got down to India. From then until 1917 they brought Indians to Guiana to toil and make profit for them in the blistering sun and chilly rains. And so we have here, Negroes and Indians making up the bulk of the population, living and working in the face of a common enemy, hammering out a common destiny and creating a common will. Until now they stand like a human barricade against the insidious racialism of those that rule and seek to maintain power by using servants to foster Negro-India antipathy, in order to bring about the destruction of the unity of the whole people.

COMMON DESTINY

And by a happy chance it happens that while we here in Guiana celebrate August as emancipation month, Indians, not only in Guiana but also in India, celebrate August 15th as the day in 1946 when India made a great leap forward on the road to National Independence. So to us, August is a month of considerable significance.

When in the opening days of our misfortune, Comrades Jagan and Burnham went to India, the workers and people of that great country gave them a magnificent welcome, a welcome which we prize as a manifestation of profound friendship and solidarity going beyond the accidental limits of race and nationality. And in turn, they expect from us internal unity, internal brotherhood based on the knowledge that whether our ancestors came from Africa or from India, we are one community in this land. The hand the people of India held out to Comrades Jagan and Burnham was held out to all the people in Guiana. For they were not thinking about Indians or Africans, but only about a people, an unfortunate people tangled in the coils of a crushing serpent.

And now as we think about emancipation and India's leap, we look in front of us to see a future full of struggle. We see with our own eyes what the imperialist butchers keep in store for any people who dare to show that they want and intend to win freedom for themselves. We have seen how vile actions are accomplished by viler lies and slanders and distortion. We have seen how easily local editors of newspapers became fulltime prostitutes, betraying the honour of a noble profession without the slightest sign of shame. And we decide in the face of all these things, that the unity we have created among us, and the strength we sustain within us must always remain about us as we march against the crumbling ramparts of oppression, calumny and gloom. This, for us, is the lesson of August.

[1954]

Time of Crisis

The year that lies before us will be a year of heart searchings, a year of doubt and perplexity, a year in which each one of us will question himself in secret, studying whether the path of life we now tread is the right one or whether a wrong one. In the midst of all the turmoil and confusion, there will be some whose convictions will crumble, some who will repudiate past activities, some who will say in an hour of fear that the road they have been walking is the wrong one because at the given moment all is dark and dreary and apparently hopeless.

In such times it becomes necessary for us to understand ourselves, the world we live in, the people we live among and the problems we must solve. At such times, ideas and emotion become inflammable. And it is at such times that our fundamental outlook on life, the means we employ of measuring and assessing events and occurrences, either assist us or betray us.

In order to understand this better let us take the idea and processes of religion. One of the main reasons why people are usually so touchy about their relious beliefs and convictions is simply because religion for them provides a body of truths and principles which act as guide and leading light in the world's reality. And the range of human experience encompassed by religious systems gives weight

195

and convincingness to the systems. The attitudes sanctified by religion to such things as murder, theft, adultery, oppression etc., testify to the amount of experience involved, although the modern world has seen most of these attitudes challenged and in some cases refuted.

But to return to ourselves. We have seen that religion plays such an important role in the lives of the people precisely because it provides an outlook, a way of appreciating reality. In the same way too we can see how important it is for us to grasp a fundamental political understanding of our own experience in life and living. For every day brings some new event, some new development in the life of the community. And every new event or development requires an adjustment in thought. So from day to day ideas must change, old feelings must die away, new feelings must emerge, new ideas must be born. And to keep the mind clear and sharp in the swarm of things becomes difficult. It is then that a basic truth becomes a flame, burning away the rust from resolution.

What is the basic truth we can claim for ourselves? It is that here in Guiana we have a movement of the people dedicated to the winning of liberation from a foreign country. Around this central flame revolves all our hope and courage. And because this is the central truth of our lives, we must measure anything we do in the warmth of its heat. We can only tell whether we are acting correctly when we can be sure that all our actions are as fuel to the flame, making it burn brighter and better in the world. Our best deeds will be to those that assist in the movement, that strengthen it, that guarantees its ultimate success. Our bad deeds will be to those that hinder the movement; that weaken it, that prevent its ultimate success. So we must measure ourselves.

Against us, however, comes the attack of our rulers, the attack of those who have made our movement so necessary for human dignity. And this attack has a history of its own.

For the first time it showed itself in primitive form. Crude abuse, personal slander and all the vile muck flung in the face of those who led us, then came the tactic of splitting, the tactic of fomenting disunity on racial antagonism, on personal ambition, on anything low enough for the purpose. Then the guns, and then after the guns, more abuse, more slander, more muck-raking. But now after all this, and in addition to all this, something more subtle. Ideological challenge, moral sermons, call for change of heart, warnings and threats, and perhaps if we don't look out, in keeping with the farce, even the creation of an S.P.C.C. (Society for the Prevention of Cruelty to Colonials) run by a committee made up of the worried wives of imperialists.

But this is a time for crisis. When a man is seriously ill, the doctor does not say very much until the crisis is over. But for us however, 'the thing is now', as the saying goes. We must be able to see what can happen to us and to prevent it happening before it is too late. For just as bad housing and bad food reduces the human body's power of resisting disease, so too can conditions of emergency such as we now live under, make the mind a breeding place of corrupt ideas. Ordinary colonial conditions are bad enough as it is, but under a state of emergency, anything rotten is possible.

Thus, within the last few weeks a series of rumours have been flying around, and growing in intensity as the days pass by. Some people have been saying that one set of leaders are planning to throw another set out of the party leadership. Others have it that the East Indians want to dominate those of African descent and thus gain power to run the party in their own interests. But of all the rumours, the most absurd one is one which has it that if certain leaders are removed from leadership, Guiana would see elections next year. With regard to the first two of the rumours set down here, we should not be surprised to find them enjoying repetition. Both of those are somewhat shopworn, having been peddled in the past not only by the semi-official propagandist of reaction, but also by some of the less mature and less developed members of our party, who apparently do not want to see further than their noses. The third one of the rumours mentioned above, that is, the one about elections is a deliberate piece of Sabotage, a deliberate piece of lying. Who ever originated this trash is not only attempting to fool those who may not know better, but also attempting, barefacedly, to break the movement of the people. The motive behind such acting cannot be viewed without grave suspicion. It is the duty of all honest party members to forestall these attempts.

Let the people have a care. Let them know that imperialism is like Polyphemus that one-eyed maneater, who would as soon eat fools as wise men. Let them know that attack will come from every quarter and that the test of life in these times is the test of struggle, of truth and of staunch loyalty to the movement in this time of crisis.

[1955]

A Dark Foundation

Following in the wake of our political confusion, what can be described as a general bad-talking of black people has become quite a regular feature of street corner gossip. Statements like 'black people can never lead anything' and so on are quite popular. People of African descent are sinners in this respect just as much as anybody else. We know of course that this sort of thing has a long history in Guiana, deriving in part from slave psychology and in part from the disgraceful behaviour of some of our own leaders in the past.

On the other hand among some sections of the middle-class community like school teachers, civil servants (lower bracket type) of African descent a peculiar tendency is developing. Some time ago for instance a member of this section was heard saying that the black race is a master race. Since there is nothing in Guiana's history to show that anybody other than the European ruling caste and class has ever been master here, this statement can serve either only to expose the fantastic complexes resident among some of us, complexes which seek to mask themselves in their opposites, or to lay bare the secret wishes of some people, whose class interests find reflection in such utterances.

For it is quite likely that the person who made the statement quoted above is really wishing the class to which she belongs will some day become the master class in Guiana. By deliberately confusing race with class this person seeks to give all people of African descent a middle-class identity and ambition. By using racial argument a given class attempts to masquerade as a racial champion while low down in reality only the sordid selfish intention is the motive power behind everything. This applies to every racial grouping in this country.

Apart from all this however, it is high time for us to wrest from history what history has for us. Having been brought here like cattle bereft of the significant relations of our cultural patterns, we had to face a hostile and alien world without any weapon other than sheer physical life and strength. We were born in slavery raw and wounded, and we grew in it, raw and wounded, borrowing everything from the very culture that tortured the Light out of our life. Our position then and now is somewhat similar to that of a prisoner who on entering prison has to fit the clothes handed to him by a prison warden, consequently there is still a lot of space between skin and garment, space which only self knowledge can fill out and round off. And all that we have to work with is that which we have created right here in this country. The history of our existence from the first days of slavery is the very earth on which we stand in this world. Dark is our foundation.

Instead of abusing each other therefore, instead of giving ear to absurd claims of racial superiority, let us rather examine our background and pick some sense out of it. The two passages quoted hereunder should be useful as a start. This is from John Smith who saw slavery with his own eyes.

> The plantation slaves, are of course employed in the cultivation of the ground. The field then, is their place of work. At about six o'clock in the morning the ringing of a bell, or the sound of a horn is the signal for them to turn out to work. No sooner is the signal made, than the black drivers, loudly smacking their whips, visit the negro houses to turn out the reluctant inmates, much in the same manner as you would drive out a number of horses from a stable yard, now and then giving a lash or two to any that are tardy in their movements. Issuing from their kennels, nearly naked, with their instruments on their shoulders, they stay not to muster, but immediately proceed to the field accompanied by the drivers and a white overseer.
>
> When a slave commits anything worthy of punishment, he is ordered to lie down with his face to the ground. Should he show the least reluctance, a couple or four negroes are called to throw him down, and hold his hands and legs, stretched out at full length. In this posture a driver flogs him on his bare buttocks till his superior tells him to desist. In punishment no distinction is made between the men and the women; the latter being forced to strip naked are held prostrate on the ground by the men.

Against this let us place the achievement of 1763 when the slaves in Berbice rose up in rebellion and drove all the slave owners and overseers and rulers clean out of the county of Berbice. The Governor of Berbice wrote thus of this matter:

> Today now the 4th of October and we see no appearance of our deliverers as yet; nor do we receive word or sign your honour; what will become of us all, should your honours have entirely forgotten us? We have come to the end of our tether here, and are at our last gasp. If within a short time there is no deliverance, I will be forced according to the advice of the Court and the Sentences of the War Council, to make arrangements to abandon this post and again return to the extreme boundaries of the sea coast.
> (Hoogenheim)

These words indicate the position of the Dutch rulers in Berbice at that time, and illustrate the power wielded by the slaves in unity. The heroes of these years were Accabreh, Atta, Coffy and Accara who were the leaders of the insurrection. Needless to say when the insurrection was put down they were all executed.

From these two very brief quotations covering the misery and revolt of the slaves at different times, we can see how very much there is for us to learn about ourselves, how very much there is that requires attention if we are ever to stand erect in this world.

And the present state of things makes such attention an urgent necessity for all of us.

[1955]

This Race Business

Imagine a community of people, in which everybody is of the same racial stock. Everybody let us say has a green skin, purple hair and lilac eyes. Let us say that this community lives in the Western world, the world in which we live. Now if this imaginary community is like all the communities we know about, then we will find in it people who are greedy, envious, rich, poor, employed, unemployed etc. There will be also distinctions of class, occupational and educational differences and the rest of it. So then, in spite of the racial sameness in our imaginary community, there will be a whole network of conflicts, a network of antagonism between everybody, those in the ranks of the unemployed, those in the ranks of the employed, those in the ranks of the rich and those in every single rank. This is given.

We can see that even without introducing the elements of racial dissimilarity, all human beings who live as we live, are always in conflict.

If what we are saying is true, then the racial richness in our particular Guianese community makes our story a very complicated one. Because if in our community where everybody is of the same racial stock there is already cause enough for conflict, what is to happen when in addition to this the quarrelling parties are of different racial origin?

Take an example. A man of Indian descent was driving his car down one of the streets of Georgetown one morning. A little child of African descent ran across the road in front of the oncoming vehicle. The driver pulled hard on his brakes and barely saved the child. Immediately from a yard the child's mother and neighbours poured out into the street.

'Al you want to kill out black people nuh?' shouted the child's mother. 'You all coolie b____ want to kill out black people nuh?'

'You black a____ ' the driver shouted back, 'why al you black people don't keep your children off the road? Like you don't live nowhere, always got your children on the road.'

In this case, it can be seen that the incident only served to release attitudes, to provide symbols whereby each of the two persons involved fell back upon a system of belief. This system of belief has its origin, not in the barely avoided incident, as is obvious, but in the whole social, economic, cultural reality of the life lived by both the car driver and the mother of the child.

Now take the child's mother. Terrified by the danger her child was in, she immediately sought to give protection. But to protect her child in this instance meant to attack the source of danger, as she understood it. Thus, picking out the most obvious thing – the racial origin of the car driver – she blames everything on that. Had the car driver been a man of African descent, she would most likely have said, that because he could afford to drive a car, he (the driver) believes he could do whatever he likes, putting the blame in this case on economic fact.

As for the car driver, his knowledge of the conditions under which most of the people of Guiana live, whether Indian or African, gives him a defence, which although economic in origin, ends up in expression as racial abuse.

This very much over simplified example gives an idea of the complexity of the problem we are dealing with. What we can very easily see however, is that the racial antagonism usually expressed is not just due to what is sometimes called bad-mindedness. This instance cited above is only an accident that nearly occurred. How much worse must it be when things like property or jobs are involved?

With all this burden in front of us, we tend to become pessimistic and retreat into silence. On the other hand, realising that the only profound solution is the creation of an equitable social order, we tend to repeat wornout clichés, until even we ourselves stop believing in their value. Preaching is not going to help us very much, when all the raw causes remain. Be that as it may however, one thing we must remember. Without racial cooperation in the face of imperialist menace, we go nowhere. And that is the most significant point at this moment in our history.

[1955]

Wanted – A Great Obeah Man

From time to time over the past two years we have been hearing laments over the absence of great leaders in this country. These laments have come for the most part from the editors of certain newspapers, visitors from Britain and America and various others who either do not understand what is really going on around here or in the world at large, or who deliberately shut their eyes to facts.

On Sunday, the *Argosy* published an Editorial under the caption 'Wanted Now: Leaders', as though leaders were things like stamps or coins, only waiting to be collected. Written in round Victorian style, this Editorial contains the following interesting statement: 'There is as yet in British Guiana no one – at least we do not know him – who speaks with the voice of the people, whose words find an echoing thrill in the hearts of the people, whose leadership and magic personality are acknowledged by the people.'

If by the word 'people' the writer of the *Argosy*'s editorial means everyone in Guiana, that is to say, from the most humble fisher-man to the most arrogant Police Inspector, then the search will never end. For the words that bring hope to the unhappy cane-cutter are words that terrify estate managers. And ideas that lodge in the hearts of the weary masses are ideas considered subversive by those who conspire and intrigue to suspend constitutions, victimise fathers of children and hold the whip of starvation over their heads like a curse. Can any man who understands all this and takes his place among the little men, the wretched and the poverty-stricken, be a great leader in the eyes of the privileged or in the eyes of one who occupies the position of editor in a local capitalist newspaper? Quite obviously not.

All this argument has appeared in *Thunder* before. It's necessary to repeat it now so as to prevent ourselves being taken in by myths.

The history of the human race is full of great men. But these men had a very hard time of it in their own lives, and some of them were even crucified as Jesus Christ was. One of them, Giordano Bruno, a scientist in feudal Europe was burnt at the stake as a heretic. Another one, John Brown, the friend of the slaves in America, ended up with a rope around his neck. John Smith, the Demerara Martyr, was imprisoned right here in Guiana. And the great slave rebels like Accabreh, Accra and the others were burnt to death in Berbice. For the truth of the matter is that it is a dangerous thing to be great in this world. Those who are great are loved by some and hunted by others. Unfortunately for our generation at the present moment in the Western World, the hunters occupy powerful positions. And that is why they bark so coldly and bite so savagely.

The Editor of the *Argosy* can continue calling for great leaders but none will rise to fit his measurements. Because what the Editor and others who think like him really want is not a great leader, but a great obeahman, one who can defend the interest of the people without affecting the lords of the land, Messrs Sugar, Bauxite and Chamber of Commerce, the strangers of freedom, the authors of misery and despair. And we have not even mentioned the imperialists!

[1955]

Sensibility and the Search

There being no such thing as society in general, or a reader in general, I propose to introduce our subject by dealing first of all with ourselves, who, as we must agree, are particular people in a particular place.

By dealing with ourselves first I think we would be putting ourselves in a better position to deal with the writer, the reader, and society today, in as much as, having started with ourselves, we would have taken up a particular position, a particular vantage point. And from this vantage point I think we will be in a better position to assess the meaning of writing and reading as activities as having relevance to the human condition.

To recognise and accept a standpoint in this connection is of special importance. For just as the man on the peak of a mountain sees a different world from the man in the valley, just so should we, from our particular context of being, see something more and something different from anybody else.

And yet I do not propose to offer here any detailed study of society. All I will try to do is delineate the experience of the people from whom we spring. And in doing so, surely it must be unnecessary for me to trace the chronological development of life in this territory to an audience such as this.

For a long time the pattern of experience I am talking about has been clear to me, and I have written about it time and again – the institution of slavery which remains for us the unknown land, the source of our sensibility. And of course colonialism and the status colonialism connotes is an ineluctable concomitant. Thus to live here and have our being here denotes immediately a particular kind of sensibility, derived from the actuality of slavery, and a particular kind of status, derived from the actuality of colonial life. I contend too that the sensibility of the slave and the status of the colonial combine to make us what we are in the innermost meaning of the term. Thus our status as colonial will change when our sensibility is transformed, and with the transformation of our sensibility will come the birth of a people. I hesitate to use the word 'nation' for a variety of reasons, chief among which is the possibility of controversy arising as to meanings.

Professor J.H. Parry of the University College of the West Indies, in an article in one of the issues of *Caribbean Quarterly*, a publication of the U.C.W.I (University College of the West Indies), wrote as follows:

> Experience in the West Indies has shown the importance of facing squarely and objectively the history of an institution (slavery) which affected all the Americas in some degree and which in some countries left deep scars in the social memory.

I agree with Professor Parry. I know at the same time that many West Indians shift about unfortunately when slavery is brought up as an item of discussion. Nonetheless, I insist on facing 'squarely and objectively' the reality of slavery. What actually is the essential meaning of slavery in human terms? Dom Basil Matthews, the Trinidadian sociologist, in his book *Crisis of the West Indian Family* has put it this way:

> In the earth shaking upheaval, the strange new world surroundings, the new economic occupations, the African, bereft of his social controls, was lost not only to his kin but to himself.

I wish to stress here the last phrase of this quotation:

> lost not only to his kin but to himself.

Basil Matthews continues:

> The backbone of social control in West African society, namely the tribal religion, was badly broken. No alternative religion or moral system was as yet effectively introduced. The social function filled by the old tribal religion remained vacant. The results on society and the individual were disastrous. Turn to any sphere of slave activity, conduct, work, crime, folk literature, folk music, educational outlook, the reading of the cultural barometer is the same – anarchy, with a strong suggestion of cultural frustration.

In a symposium on whether a West Indian way of life exists, published in the 1955 Mid-year issue of *Kyk-Over-Al*, I wrote that emancipation in the 1830s took the chains off the hands and the feet, but that the psychological constitution woven in the gloom of the plantation remained. And I went on to say that, to me, the essential meaning of slavery is the loss of self, the loss of identity and its inevitable consequence, the most shattering self concept. What I mean by the loss of self and the loss of identity is the loss of those relationships which allow choices, the loss of those equivalences between inward necessity and external situations. And I mean too the disruption in which integration and action remains action, remote from any possibility of being transformed into destiny. That I contend is what slavery means in human terms.

After the abolition of slavery the social process took a certain direction. This direction and the results of this process are summed up very well by Dr Raymond Smith who in his book *The Negro Family in British Guiana* writes:

> Since the white group is the apex of the social pyramid and extremely close to the cluster of positively evaluated elements it forms the most isolated and solitary sub-group. Numerically small and culturally homogenous (at least within the colony) its members participated solely at the executive, managerial and administrative levels of the occupational structure...it preserves its social distinctions vis a vis the rest of the population by means of an intricate and usually covert mythology of racial purity and superiority. But it is equally true that the black group retains a good deal of social solidarity, not so much as a large cohesive group extending all over the colony as in small territorial clusters such as villages. Once again this solidarity is maintained by an elaborate mythology, this time of inferiority... Portuguese, Chinese and East Indians all came to British Guiana after the foundations of the colour class system had been laid and all are in a sense marginal to it.

The quotation I have used from Dr Smith refers to the 'colour class system', but I wish to confine them to the slave actuality, in which the social pattern is bounded at one limit by the 'nigger yard' and at the other limit, by the 'Big House', to use Gilberto Freyre's terminology. And if we examine our experience in this context many things seem to emerge.

What stands out most forcibly during slavery and at the abolition of slavery? The flight of the slave from the plantation. Who has not read of slaves escaping from estates and attempting to set up homesteads in the jungle? Who has not heard of the desperate flight of the slaves from the plantation and the hunting down of these slaves by Amerindians hired for the purpose by the slave owners? And after abolition too we see porknockers leaving the estates in haste and going to the jungle in search of precious minerals. Some may say this is something natural and to be expected. I suggest that this general flight from the plantation is not only a simple flight but also a profound search. It is, I contend, not only a search for identity as such, but indeed a search for the self lost in the circumstances of slavery. I go further and say for example, that the emigration of West Indians to Britain is not purely and simply an economic affair. I suggest that here too at a certain level, a search is implied, although of course by now this search has lost the marks of its origin and assumed new masks and disguises, even as the slave who was taught carpentry by his owner makes out in due process of time that it was always his ambition to become a carpenter. Purely for illustration and with no claim to argument I refer to the Freudian concept of childhood conditioning and its relation to individual motivation.

'The Flight of the Slave and the Search' is the essential meaning of West Indian life, I believe. I invite your attention to the music and the poetry we call West Indian. What actually is the secret of the music, the native music? All I can find is the rhythm. But even this rhythm is not our own, in the sense of having been created by us. For are these rhythms not actually the germ motifs of African music? We certainly didn't create these rhythms. Far from it. All we have done, so far as I can see is to batten or hem and repeat them over and over again without developing them; without allowing them to challenge us to creation. I am not, of course, by any means, trying to argue away their value or any such thing. All I am trying to do is to put them in perspective. Again, look at the poetry we call West Indian. What has the larger part been, other than a series of poor imitations of English models? If, for instance, at a given period Tennyson is the leading English Poet, then the poems written are poor copies of Tennyson. If Swinburne is the leading English Poet, then the poems written are poor copies of Swinburne. It is, of course, true that all artists go through a pastiche period, and further that the world of the arts must have its great family spirit and resemblances: Dylan Thomas for example and Gerard Manley Hopkins are remarkable poets in their own right, though the influence and background of Hopkins and Thomas is plain. It is well known that the French Symbolists were heavily influenced by the literary theories of Edgar Allan Poe, the American poet. But this certainly is a family spirit – a kinship – not a relationship between master and slave.

The vantage-point spoken of therefore at the beginning of this introduction is the standpoint of the slave which we must learn to accept as a reality. Acceptance of this reality will be the first step to self identity, the first step on the journey in search of ourselves. But this is no easy task. It will call for the emergence of men of genius, men who by a gift of nature are able to assimilate the experience of their heritage and transform it into meaningful symbols and images, so that all of us, on looking at those symbols and images, will be looking into a mirror and seeing ourselves for the first time.

In this connection we can prepare ourselves by considering the words of Salzberger, who in an essay on Hölderlin, the German poet, wrote:

> Genius, the agent of the dialectical process of history, has to transgress against the laws of moderation which govern the lives of ordinary men, in order to bring to a crisis the conflicts of his age and restore a healthy equilibrium.

Unfortunately, however, the circumstances obtaining here and now do not give rise to feelings of optimism in this respect. For the slave is still in headlong flight and the flight has not yet consciously become the search. And that is one aspect of the human condition in the world today.

[1958]

A Letter

In discussing our contemporary shambles, almost every visitor to this country ultimately comes round to asking about local publications of the nature of this one. And when the answer is given that there is none, the visitor's shoulders slump and he quickly changes the subject, afraid, perhaps, of saying something uncharitable.

Life in a country as materialistic and philistine as B.G. soon blunts the edge of the mind. The almost fanatical preoccupation with hollow issues, the gossip-mongering which passes for conversation, and the inevitable political hysteria, leave little time for the serious examination of ideas. I know that the psychological squalor of everyday life is exhausting. I know that the urgent practical problem of making a living comes first. What I do not know is why only so few revolt, either by word or by deed against such acute spiritual discomfort.

These are the conditions which make me welcome the appearance of this publication. The editor and the contributors, I know, are well aware of the high death rate of magazines. But at least they can console themselves with the thought that in order for something to die, it first had to be alive. And there is so much material in this country awaiting critical examination that I cannot see why shortage of copy should ever prove a difficulty. On the other hand, of course, there is indifference, frightening indifference.

I have been told that this magazine will contain independent analysis, comment and opinion, and that those who make contributions will try to be as objective as possible. In our present condition few things can be as important as objectivity. I feel that much of the good which will come out of this publication will come from the ability of the contributors to maintain their objectivity in the face of fixed allegiance and uncritical response.

[1964]

A Question of Self-Contempt

Continuously subjecting nightmare to daytime censorship I know that nightmare – that most original form of self-criticism – participates in the operation of valid judgements, and censorship, of the truth of a special condition. Being not either historian, sociologist, anthropologist or psychologist, I depend only on the tool of imagination to examine and probe a condition which, since I remember myself, has oppressed me and led me into action not immediately perceivable either as reasonable, in the social sense, or as useful, in the sense of expected function. Concerned with certain forms of self-denial and the demanding presence of crowding faces scarred by what living time has prescribed as real, and has authorised as the actual minimum for survival, I have not always understood the nature of the sacrifice heart must make to ensure continuity. For, given remains the world. Place to enter and have place within. Brutalities of non-response. Assaults on sensibility. Wayward indiscipline. Contingencies which contain the least meaning in a world of fantasy dominated by new intentions, badly expressed in repeated proposals for any kind of revolution.

In this condition of unawareness, I came into a contact of different character with the spiritual facts of the life I have lived. Encountering them, I recognised their phenomenal relevance and symbolic challenge. Self was here in visible location, aware of the datum and exigence of land and community. But, who was my? who self? On black knees before the great white names of civilisation and human power, I claimed my own humanity in terms of flesh and blood; in the endurance and the suffering, the defeat and achievement I discovered written inside the abstractions of European philosophy and experience. I made inevitable identifications. Homeland is everywhere. All skies are blue. The green, and world of the freedom of feeling is, by definition, accessible. And whenever, as so regularly, real shadows loom too close, the wild whore-houses of irresponsibility are available, where it is possible always to effect self-change in the very midst of all-reducing squalor, and, like a gifted lizard, make skin turn cloak like a smile.

Out of these swirling confusions I stepped into a world of action. I became a member of an organisation formed by Cheddi Jagan, friend of great days. And every Sunday night a meeting in an unpainted hutch with grey dust like history's night-soil between the creases in the floor. Sometimes no more than five of us. Five bewildered creatures on a Sunday night repeating ourselves like desperate obeahmen. Outside the world. Dog dung in the street. A black man in South Africa. Love beneath the gay stars. Firelight in cane-pieces. Degradation, absolute vomit. Same tomorrow. Tomorrow again. Tomorrow always.

Among those who came on the Sunday nights of our desperation, was a talkative middle-aged black gentleman I knew as Bovell. Stoop of a tired tree. Face of a face. One of the best of us all. So strange and disheartening therefore to discover that he came no longer to meet with us on Sunday. I could not understand. Ill? I would search him out and find him.

Until one afternoon, walking along Vlissengen Road, I saw him cutting grass for his donkey, arcing scythe flashing like dark silver beside the grey and asphalt carriageway.

And I went up to him.

'Bovell.'

I saw the scythe sweep and tender blades of grass collapsed.

'Bovell.'

The scythe jerked in his hand, and a certain green leaf lived a little longer.

'I haven't seen you for a long time,' I said, exaggerating.

'Why don't you come anymore?'

Turned his old head slowly. Recognised me. Smiled his recognition. And leaned on the smooth and brown handle of his scythe.

Then took a bundle of dirty cloth from his trouser back pocket and wiped his sweat face very carefully. That way I wipe my eyes.

'Boy,' and I heard something I do not want to hear again.

'Week after week I come to you meeting. I hear you talk about exploitation. I hear talk about how poor people must rise up. About socialism. About revolution.'

I stared at his hopeless hands as he spoke. Eyes and hands.

He leaned forward. A new intensity informed his very eye.

'Tell me,' he said suddenly, and I responded to the fury in his voice and heart.

'Just tell me something,' and I knew I had no answer. 'You and your friends really believe you can fight white people? Rass!'

Spat, shook his head, turned his back to me, and the impartial grass was again victim.

By the side of the road his donkey stood yoked. The iron tyres of the two-wheeled cart were shining in spots. No rust anywhere. And I looked at Bovell's skull and saw a bump.

I wondered whether an owner had turned homuncule and taken up residence. My own head I rubbed. He was wondering why.

Incapable of explanation, I remained silent.

Not long after the rubbing of my head Cheddi Jagan and Forbes Burnham brought the People's Progressive Party into existence. I became a member of its executive committee. Same weekly procedure. Political economy, dialectical and historical materialism straight from Engels, from slim pamplets, British-provided fuel for the engines of our embarrassing enthusiasm. And some of us who could not even spell 'economics' nonetheless argued passionately about surplus value, the defects of the capitalist system and the glories of the classless society to come. One night I talked about Karl Marx, his carbuncles, and Jenny von Westphalen, and my challenge in calling their names was defeated by the subservience of those who listened to me. Not one question.

One Sunday night after one such meeting was over I was accosted by an East Indian gentleman known to me as Mr Singh.

He asked me to spare him a moment.

'Comrade,' he said sententiously, shaking hands, shrewd eyes sharp behind gleaming gold rimmed spectacles. I knew him to be a dispenser and I smelt cough medicine.

'I knew your father very well,' he continued, 'we used to work in the Civil Service together.'

'Thank you,' I replied, not knowing what else to say, 'Are you working Comrade?' he asked, cocking his head like a hawk, shrewd eyes suddenly suspicious behind gold rimmed spectacles.

'I am a Civil Servant,' I told him shortly. I was getting bored.

'A Civil Servant!' he exclaimed, shocked.

His lip seemed to tremble.

'What are you doing in this thing?' he demanded.

The lenses of his spectacles seemed to contract.

'What thing?' I asked, wondering what his questions could possibly mean.

'Dis ting,' he ejaculated, pointing with a crooked thumb over his shoulder.

'Don't you know the white people watching everybody what belong to this party?'

I waited. He measured me coolly. Theodolite spectacles. A whole face frowning.

'Don't you have any ambition?' he finally exploded.

I do not remember how I responded to his shattering logic. But as I walked through the choking night of the city I remembered the story I had heard of a man, who, applying for the post of hangman, had written the Superintendent of Prisons to say that since he was a little boy it had been his ambition to become a hangman one day. I even wanted to turn back and tell Mr Singh of it. But I was apprehensive of his possible comment.

In the early days of the People's Progressive Party funds were always scarce. In order to collect as much as we could, we developed the practice of placing an old tin, with a slot in the cover, on a table in full view of the members, so that anyone who attended could make a contribution.

If, for instance, one member could afford only a penny, then that member could slip the penny into the tin without anyone knowing how much he or she had contributed. This way there would be no embarassment. The system worked well.

One evening, however, after a meeting was over, I saw a middle-aged woman of African descent approach the table. I knew her. Often had I seen her pushing her handcart selling starch in the streets of the city, in broken shoes, on hard feet, through a long walk.

She approached the table confidently. Then she reached into a pocket of her worn dress, took out a sixpence and dropped it into the tin. She did it ostentatiously and that was why it was possible for me to see the size and silver glint of the coin.

As she turned away I went up to her.

'Many thanks, comrade,' I said. She nodded.

'Don't misunderstand me,' I continued, 'but I saw you put a sixpence in the tin just now. We need it. But I know how hard things are for everybody nowadays. You must not strain yourself.'

She understood immediately.

'Comrade,' she said, looking straight into my face, 'I know you see me put twelve cents in the tin, and you wondering if I can afford it.'

I nodded, glad to see that she had understood so easily what I had been trying to convey.

'Comrade,' she continued, 'you think if was like you so, or Dr Jagan so, I would put a whole twelve cents in that tin?'

'Never,' she said, emphatically.

'But you want to know why I put so much?'

She was smiling.

'I put all that twelve cents because of Mrs Jagan.'

I was puzzled.

'That big, nice, great white lady come all the way from America to help we, comrade. That nice white lady. That's why.'

She spoke triumphantly, and I knew she felt that all who belonged to the organisation thought and behaved in the self same way.

She had enunciated the theorem of situational equality.

She had, in her own terrible words, told me part of the story of her way of life and of mine too – ugly history of the movement from slavery to parasitism. Not indeed the obvious slavery of some wretched African tribesman captured in a jungle and transported to a Guyanese plantation. Not the obvious parasitism of the urban middle class which consists of being always on the right side of power, imperial or native. Not even the parasitism of the so-called intellectual elite, whose representatives hide in offices, enjoy the benefit of non-commitment, and claim specific rights.

What the seller of starch had implied for me was more than all of this. She had indicated the existence of spiritual parasitism, the dynamic principle at work in the very groin of the land.

That night I went for a long walk, and when I reached home at last, I looked at the books which had helped to keep me alive. I examined the shape and structure of the house in which I had lived since I knew myself, noting the disposition of kitchen and bedroom, back step and living space.

I thought of my father's face and tried to guess the face of the original slave ancestor, as it lived and died. Useless. No matter how I surrendered mind to association and symbol, the imaginary plantation I summoned yielded not one of the secrets I knew existed. Between me and them was silence, broken by the sound of voices I invented out of desperation, and continuing converse with those I kept hearing in nightmare.

[1966]

A Free Community of Valid Persons

In the year 1865, in the Jardin des Plantes, in Paris an event of more than ordinary biological, for biologists, but for us, symbolic significance occurred. Certain creatures known by their Aztec name of AXOLOTL, long held to be sexually mature adults, metamorphosed and took on what in the common process of growth would have been their expected physiological configuration.

Symbolically significant for us here is that these creatures, in their native habitats in certain lakes in Mexico, attain sexual maturity in larval form, which is aquatic, and apparently in that habitat never metamorphosed beyond that form.

According to investigators of this phenomenon, the permanent aquatic larval form of the creature – it is terrestrial when completely metamorphosed – is brought about by a suppression of the thyroid gland, the secretion of which is responsible for metamorphosis in AMPHIBIA; and that treatment of AXOLOTLS with thyroid secretion, at any stage of that halted growth, would bring about metamorphosis; would bring about, that is to say, transformation from the aquatic larval form to the terrestrial adult form, as is the normal case with creatures we are all familiar with – the frog or the crapaud.

What in this phenomenon fascinates me and makes me pause relates to the whole concept of transformation and the startling possibility that, in some ways, I believe we are somewhat like AXO-LOTLS, which is to say that, for some reason or other, something seems to have gone awry with that process of metamorphosis, which, if we are to accept what our leaders tell us, should work to trans-form us from what we function as – an aggregation of begging, tricking, bluffing, cheating subsistence seekers and assorted hustlers – into a free community of valid persons; each of whom has existed in a way we have come to conceptualise as, at least one, among other, higher modes of being, where the essence of staying alive means fulfilment of self and self-realisation: which when achieved ceases to remain merely the accomplishment of a competence but goes onward to the acquisition of the status of a function of the personality; a function which consummates itself in the enrichment of every self that participates with it in the creation of a free com-munity of valid persons.

You may well want to ask – Is not every person a valid person? And I say: Yes. I say yes only if that person's person outweighs his babble in the war against the reduction of himself, because every word or deed a person utters or commits which fails to recognise or increase the value of another ends up by effecting a reduction of the provenance of the intention.

So that is why when we look at the contemporary condition, nationally and internationally, we want to mutter 'All gone', acutely aware of our victim role in a ruthless world; profoundly critical of what to only too many of us seems to be serious malfunctioning on the part of those who decide how we should live; self-righteously indignant at what is considered the demoralisation and apathy of the so-called masses and that outlook which exposes itself as one that sees as irrelevant anything which does not serve its own and immediate crassest self-interest; and these all combine to make our contemporary and civic behaviour an ungodly scramble, where each one of us is prepared to exploit the other. It may be, I would like to suggest, the perception of this, accidentally or unconsciously, which causes ministers and official spokesmen, whenever they say anything, to find it necessary to resort to caustic admonition, and also to seek, at almost every opportunity, to describe some one or other individual or section of the community as anti-Guyanese, as though indeed there is some holy text somewhere which spells out what being pro-Guyanese is.

But the truth is that every society is made of conflicting interests: the interests of the rulers and the interests of the ruled; competition within the ranks of the rulers and competition within the ranks of the ruled; and it is from the creative encounter of these interests, from the clash of all these forces that a valid hierarchy of values emerges to challenge the very premises that sponsored them.

Nor can this encounter be abolished. It may be obscured and take perverse forms of expression, in which eventually the individual personality suffers erosion and ceases to function in a creative way, until, inevitably, general paralysis of the spirit overcomes.

This is the war we have to fight, the war against paralysis of the spirit, for I am tempted to think in a metaphorical way, that just as the suppression of the thyroid gland in the AXOLOTL could have halted that creature's metamorphosis, just so this paralysis of spirit if not itself overcome, can delay, if not corrupt, our transformation into a free community of valid persons.

Greater and greater daily seems to grow this paralysis as the individual person is confronted with the sometimes inscrutable workings of political and bureaucratic power; when faced with the crises which present themselves in the form of seemingly unresolvable problems of conscience, dilemmas created by a lack of courage or conviction or situations in general about which he feels he can do nothing – a condition of being which hobbles the mind, induces varying degrees of hysteria and provokes adventurism, especially among the young.

In the Caribbean and Guyana we have a sufficiency of historians, political scientists, sociologists, economists and politicians who, from time to time, depending upon the occasion, or conditioned by the audience, go to great trouble to speak learnedly or rhetorically about the historical, social, economic and political backgrounds of these territories and who also, sometimes tentatively, sometimes dogmatically, seek to lay down guidelines for the Caribbean Naissance.

In nearly all of the prescriptions, in addition to the often mechanical recital of moral imperatives, there is to be found a preoccupation with the concept of systems and institutions – a preoccupation which communicates that there is, in the minds of these savants, a conviction that the solution of most of our troubles lies in the construction of adequate systems and institutions.

And no one would dare to question the legitimacy of this pre-occupation if in what is proposed as its consequence, the adjective, 'adequate', necessarily connoted the inclusion of informal social and psychological elements, elements that defy codification, like commitment to the name but not the substance of some one or other political ideology; or the prejudices associated with skin-colour; or the failure of communication that accompanies racial cleavage; or, most important of all, the exercise of state power which brooks little interference and distorts men and laws in the overt and covert processes of its consolidation and hegemony.

It is the action of these informal elements in their many combi-nations, which can and does bring about the perversion of creative strategies and exacerbates those very ills these strategies were orig-inally planned to control.

In all of what I have been saying I have attempted to bring to your attention some considerations, which in a world shaken by economic and attendant crises, people like housewives and politicians may want to deem less urgent than their own immediate concern with pragmatic issues.

But I am afraid in certain circumstances such concern can be manipulated and used, if not to justify, then at least to conceal transgression. On the other hand, it is precisely in times of crisis that we must re-examine our lives and bring to that re-examination contempt for the trivial, and respect of the riskers who go forward boldly to participate in the building of a free community of valid persons.

[1974]

Open Letter to the People of Guyana

Like other régimes of similar character, the PNC's main preoccu-pation is self-perpetuation. In principle the pre-occupation with self-perpetuation is understandable, since it accords with the fun-damental idea of self-preservation.

But while a truly democratic régime would try to ensure self-perpetuation by acting in a way such as would make it acceptable and needed by the people, what does the PNC, which poses as socialist, actually do?

The PNC's method of ensuring self-perpetuation consists of

indulging in a deliberate policy of degrading people. And the reasoning behind this is that degraded people are incapable of effective resistance.

Hamilton Green's statement, published in the *Chronicle* of August 4, to the effect that a certain unnamed Roman Catholic priest was responsible for the death of Father Darke, is the latest flagrant example of this deliberate policy of degradation. It is so because it expresses contempt for the intelligence and humanity of people.

Green's statement is in character with the PNC's deliberate policy of degrading the people.

Of this policy, the following examples should be kept in mind:

Item: In the rigging of elections in which many ordinary and by no means vicious people were cajoled into doing indecent things, and were thereby compromised.

Item: In corruption as a way of life, in which people were made to accept that stealing, cheating, lying, bearing false witness, informing on each other was a positive sign of loyalty to the régime; was what was expected of them, and were thereby further compromised.

Item: In the budget of information presented to the people by the régime's rigidly controlled mass media, in which the very language used is perversion, facts falsified; threats against individuals and groups openly advertised; internal events of significance ignored; local events of significance suppressed; all contributing to the whole process of moral and intellectual honesty, one end of which is to make mental independence a crime, and mental subservience to the régime the highest qualification in the land. And the greatest damage done in this area is to young people who are led to believe that they can do anything, no matter how selfish, how intolerant, how mindless, how coarse, since they identify this attitude with the attitude the régime underwrites. The result is the warp of personality, the degradation of the spirit that is so much abroad in the society.

Item: In the militarisation of the people in which poorly fed children are made to march in the sun like soldiers, playing militia at the expense of their lessons; in which paramilitary forces enjoy a spurious social prestige at the expense of the rights of their fellow citizens, thereby putting a premium on authoritarian bullying in clear mirror image of the behaviour of the leaders of the régime, all serving to bring about in the consciousness of people and their children that parading is more important than learning, and uniforms more important than respect for law.

These are but a few examples, but for the people they have come to constitute to some extent what socialism, as the PNC endorses it, signifies to them.

Socialism is a system based on lofty ideals and its end is the liberation of man: the enloft of being.

What the PNC régime has brought the people to experience as socialism is a system based on degradation, the end of which is the régime's self-perpetuation.

The ideology of the PNC is not based on a philosophy of man. It is based on disrespect for people. The only way to deal effectively with this process of degradation is by example. The example required is the example of resistance, the very things the degradation is designed to prevent and to destroy.

Resistance has to be on two fronts. Resistance to the brute fact of degradation itself. Resistance to the exploitation of this degradation by the régime.

The first front is the refusal to be further degraded, as individual and as group. One goes with the other. Thus individual repudiation and civil disobedience.

The second front is exposure of the PNC's ideology of self-perpetuation, as this ideology can be perceived to have its base on the degradation of the people. Thus the waging of the psychological offensive, the continuous "war of nerves".

Who do we think we are?

I sign my name,
Martin Carter

[1979]

218

Out, Out the Fire

Outside, in the city the sun burns madly upstairs in the sky. The streets blaze white near green grass, and galvanised iron roofs shimmer like vapour. When the sun is high the city lies rigid, tense and trembling in the stark light. And the sky is far away like a foreign country, and the clouds are like new sails on old ships sailing forever.

Every street is straight and white like a chalk line. On either side houses stand up on stilts like angular insects, reaching for something to eat. The fronts of the houses are separated from the green parapets by fences made of wallaba paling-staves. But some are broken and jagged like splintered teeth, dirty and discoloured. The fronts of the houses are like open mouths and the stumps of the paling-staves are like the strained stumps of broken teeth. And just as down a human mouth, the food of life goes everyday, just so into the broken mouth of the houselot, life goes everyday, passing forward and backwards as if some giant face were eating with a morbid relish, spitting out the more tasteless morsels and swallowing all the rest.

The street is wide and full of dust. In the white sunlight it lies down passively. From the wide world come motor cars, lorries and vans, making a lot of noise, shaking up the white dust and leaving the air full of the smell of fume. Wooden donkey carts, creaking and shaking, rattle over the pieces of white marl lying all about. Dogs fight in the grass, snarling and snapping angry white teeth until they lock into each other, twisting violent muscles. And little naked black children, with rags for shirts, run about with discarded bicycle tyres, jumping over the furious dogs, the grass and the stones. Sometimes, but sometimes only, the whole street goes suddenly quiet, as though everything has stopped for a moment to listen to itself. But then it begins all over again, iron wheels turning, sun wheels turning, sky wheels turning, hub and rim, centre and circumference, point and limit, core and boundary.

And when the sun goes down the whole yard becomes a slab of darkness, like a block of black ice. In the night-wrapped city, where the streets intersect, the light from lantern posts falls into yellow pools on dust and pebbles. Trees grow tall above the roof tops and some of them look as if they were trying to go to sleep.

Crapauds in the damp grass begin to rattle and whistle like birds who can fly. And even the dogs bark with a different meaning. The night is like a door that closes in the afternoon locking everything into a black room. And as it comes down, the sky seems to rise high up into space, only to come down again. Below, in the streets, boys and girls on bicycles ride past men and women walking. And a donkey cart would appear around the corner moving slowly. The cartman droops over the donkey's rump, half-asleep. In his fist he clutches a bottle from the narrow spout of which protrudes a tongue of yellow fire. And as the donkey walks, the cartman rolls forwards and backwards in rhythm with the hooves. And in the yards, the women sit on their doorsteps looking out at the street, spitting at the night, gossiping with their neighbours and laughing at themselves, in strange and secret amusement.

Miss Agnes always sat out on her front steps watching the street after dusk. She would sit down and look at the people passing for an hour or two before going to prepare for sleep. But as somebody from the yard would come to look out too, she invariably had a companion to talk to.

That night she was sitting on her front step in the dark as usual when suddenly she heard a voice from the shadows behind her.

'Like you looking out,' the voice said.

'Eh heh,' Miss Agnes replied, turning her head to see who it was. Recognised Old Katie's voice and repeated, 'Eh heh, ah looking out lil.'

Old Katie came up and stood beside Miss Agnes.

'But wait! Was to ask you. Is wha' kind of shrimp shells you throw away in the alley dis morning.'

Miss Agnes started. The sudden question surprised her. She did not reply at once but wondered why Old Katie had asked the question at all. Before she could say anything else Old Katie continued:

'If you only smell the place now. It smell like some dead ram-goat bury with rotten eggs. I never smell nothing so bad in all my life.' As she spoke she grimaced as though something was stuck up in her nose. In the dark her flabby face twisted around her nose like a mask of soft rubber.

'But is wha' you mean at all,' Miss Agnes asked her after a moment. 'Is only today I throw way' dem shrimp shells in de alley. You never smell shells before?' She demanded, turning fiercely on Old Katie.

Old Katie sighed. She was not a quarrelsome old woman so she said quietly, 'I custom to smelling shrimp shells yes, but I ain't custom to smelling shrimp shells like dem at all. I telling you Miss Agnes, dem shrimp shells really smell bad. But you must come with me and tek a smell for yourself.'

Miss Agnes did not reply. She was wondering how the few shrimp shells she had thrown away that morning could ever smell as bad as Old Katie was making out.

'You sure is shrimp shells you smelling in de alley,' she asked quietly, looking at Old Katie.

'Is wha' den',' the old women replied. 'Is only you use shrimps today and throw way de shells in de alley. It didn't smell so last night, so it could only be you shrimp shell that got de place smelling so nasty.'

'Well,' said Miss Agnes. 'Well ah really don't feel like smelling no nasty thing tonight. But if you sure is me shrimp shells smelling so high in de alley, I going to come down in de morning and tek a smell foh myself.'

Old Katie turned away grumbling to herself. 'Just fancy, she don't feel like smelling no nasty thing tonight! But I who living in de backhouse got to sleep with it, and bathe with it, cook with it, eh! eh?'

As she walked back through the yard to her house at the back she continued grumbling in her mouth.

'But look at me trial,' she grumbled. 'Dey come and dey throw away dey nasty things all about the place and when you talk to dem about it dey bex. People like them should live in de pasture where dey could do what dey like.'

She walked up her steps and entered her shaky house. Across the alleyway she could see the lights in the other houses giving off a sickly yellow glow as though the lights was weak and anaemic with living in all the darkness.

And when midnight comes and every light is out except the street lights, all is quiet as a grave yard. In the silence the beat of the wind on the sea comes gently, floating over the sleeping roofs. In the grass near the land crickets and candle flies exchange places on hidden leaves. Dogs snarl and bark out suddenly. And somewhere in the world of night, man lies on top of woman closing his eyes and emptying himself into the invisible depths of her body. And then when he is quite empty, he becomes light like a feather and floats through the black silk cotton of sleep like a seed on wings. And far away to the north of the city the sea surrounds the world, dark under the keen stars. Up and down, forever and forever, the broken waves run from shore to shore, from night to night and from man to man.

In the morning, bright and early, Miss Agnes went down to the alleyway. The sun was lifting itself over the city and the sharp light made clear shadows on the earth. The wind was fresh and moist and the sky sparkling like wet grass.

'Ah come foh smell de thing you was telling me about last night,' she called out as she came up to Old Katie's house.

Old Katie looked through the window.

'Wha' happen,' she asked, 'you mean to say you ain't start smelling yet?' She looked at Miss Agnes suspiciously.

Miss Agnes took a noisy sniff, holding her nose to the air.

'You ain't got to do all dat,' Old Katie cried out, 'just come round by the back step and you gin know.'

Miss Agnes walked around and took another loud sniff.

'Oh Jesus Christ!' she exclaimed suddenly, 'Oh Jesus Christ, but is true. But is wha got dis place smelling so bad!'

As she stood up there she could see the shrimp shells she had thrown away lying on the ground. Surely those few shrimp shells could not be giving off that smell. And yet, she reasoned, it had to be the shrimp shells. There was nothing else lying about that could possibly give off such a cloud of stink.

Miss Agnes stood up looking about her. She couldn't say anything to defend herself. And all she did was to cry out again and again about the smell.

Behind her at the window Old Katie was waiting to hear what she would say.

'You believe now?' Old Katie asked, 'you believe now about what I was telling you last night. And you only smelling it now you deh here standing up. But if you was like me living in dis house you would dead long ago. Last night smell was so bad that I dreamed I was living in the latrine, not no clean big shot latrine, but them brum down nasty latrine some people got in the yard where dey say dey living. And dis morning ah wake up and smell the smell, ah know de dream was not no dream at all. Because up to know ah got one splitting headache.'

Miss Agnes turned around sympathetically.

'Ah know how you must be feeling wid dis nastiness so near you.' She walked away slowly wondering what she should do. As she turned around she noticed a piece of cloth sticking out from under a pile of old boards lying half in the yard and half in the alleyway. She walked over and looked at it curiously. As she bent down to inspect it, the smell rose in her face like a dense spray of water.

She put her hand over her mouth and bent lower.

'But is wha dis?' Miss Agnes asked again. She looked around on the ground and picked up a short piece of stick and started to probe at the half-hidden cloth.

As she probed at it a piece of pinkish fabric broke away.

'Eh Eh,' she remarked aloud. 'But this look like blood.' The smell was stronger than ever and Miss Agnes kept her mouth tightly closed so as to prevent any of the bad smell going down her throat.

Suddenly she jumped back as though something had leaped from the ground straight into her eyes.

'Oh Gawd,' she screamed, 'Oh Gawd.' She spun around to face Old Katie. 'Is a dead baby, is a dead baby.' She bawled, 'come quick.'

'An was dat got the place smelling so bad an' got me blaming Miss Agnes shrimp shells,' Old Katie told Policeman who was writing in his notebook standing near the spot where the bundle showed under the wood. Around his black uniform the women from the adjoining houses were discussing the pitiful discovery. They had all come running when Miss Agnes gave the alarm, leaving their pots cooking on the fires in their kitchens.

'But why you all people don't go home and cook you husband food?' Policeman asked them nudging one of the women with his elbow.

They were all grouped around him listening as he spoke with Old Katie, and from time to time they interrupted him.

The woman he nudged sucked her teeth loudly.

'But like you is a anti-man nuh?' she asked, cutting her eyes at Policeman. All the women laughed out boisterously, and Policeman looked back into his book writing industriously so as to appear as busy and official as possible. He knew he dared not attempt to exchange remarks with the women and so he tried to ignore them.

The policeman was a young man with a dark brown skin and a very serious expression on his face. The women knew that he was very young in the force and that he felt he had one of the most important jobs in the world and that he meant to live up to the dignity of it. He had been sent out from the Station when old Katie went and gave a report. And now he was taking a statement from Miss Agnes, who all the time had remained on the spot watching the bloody bundle that showed under the wood.

'Is somebody living around here throw away dat thing,' one of the women said.

'But ah wonder is who,' another asked, leaning forward as if to inspect anew and discover some clue as to its origin.

'Is somebody living around here,' the woman who had spoken

first repeated again, emphatically.

'Like you know is who,' Policeman said suddenly, turning to look directly at the woman.

'Oh me Jesus,' the woman cried out in alarm, 'What I know about anything like dat. And to besides leh me go and see what happening to me pot before it boil over.'

She bustled away hurriedly, leaving Policeman looking behind her inquisitively.

He turned back to face the women.

'Now listen,' he said 'if anybody here got any information about who throw away that ting in dis alley, dey bettah come forward right away. Because if you know and you don't tell is an offence.'

He spoke proudly, aware of his authority. But nobody answered.

'All right, all right,' he warned. 'You all people know to lie down wid man when the night come and enjoy yourself. But when you get ketch you don't want to mind pickney. You don't think about the consquences. All you want is the sweetness. Ah know, ah know, but we going to see what is going to happen. Somebody looking for trouble and is one of you.'

As he spoke he frowned. The women, who a few minutes before were laughing at him, now watched at him with troubled eyes.

'And this is a serious offence,' he continued. He saw that he had them frightened and he was happy.

'Last year in the country,' he said, 'a woman get baby and when the baby dead she wrap it up in an old newspaper and throw it away in the alley. And you know what happened? Was only because the Magistrate sorry foh her that she didn't get jail.'

'Is true,' one of the women said. Every eye fixed on Policeman. Standing in his black uniform stiff and erect, he seemed to tower over them. Suddenly Miss Agnes took a step forward.

'But boy,' she said, without warning 'But boy, is wha you name?' She had been listening to Policeman while he was speaking and her sudden irrelevant question fell like a bucket of cold water over him.

'Constable Cecil Joe No. 4914,' Policeman almost shouted, almost saluting. But quickly he caught himself and relaxed.

He glanced at Miss Agnes.

'Like you is a botheration woman,' he said softly with cold anger in his eyes. The question had really caught him and his immediate parrot-like recitation of rank, name and number made him feel ashamed. He realised how stupid he looked and he knew that the women who only a few moments ago were looking at him with awe, were now more or less normal again and ready to laugh at him.

Just then another policeman came up to the crowd with an old toffee tin in his hand.

'You tek down the statement and everything?' he asked constable Joe.

'Yes a got it.'

'Well all right then, leh we pick up dis thing and carry um down to the police station one time.'

The second policeman picked up the bundle and put it in the toffee tin. 'I am going to have to ask some more questions,' Constable Joe told Miss Agnes as he started to leave. 'This investigation only now start.'

Miss Agnes stared at him for a moment, then she laughed out, with a forced bitterness.

'But hear he!' she shouted at his back. 'But hear he! You could start anything like investigation!'

She turned to the women. But they had all begun to walk away and so Miss Agnes went back alone through the yard to her room. And on the grey ground beneath her feet as she walked, the hard little brown ants journey through the dust leaving no trail. In the yard the lean chickens scratch with impatient feet at mounds of dirt, searching for a worm, a shrimp shell, a grain of rice. Green blades of grass choking beneath weeds, lean back their clean points to the land in a mute repudiation of light and sun. Only the winged marabuntas and the slender-tailed pond flies dance through the air, flitting from earth-floor to roof-top and darting from cool shade like memories seeking a place to rest. And high above, beyond the tall interruption of coconut palm heads, the unsympathetic sun burns out its white insistence, contemptuous of ant or chicken, grass or weed, roof top or dust, memory or wing.

[1958]

A Note on Vic Reid's *New Day*

When Vic Reid's book *New Day* first appeared it was warmly greeted by some and rudely challenged by others, in both cases for extra-literary reasons. Those who greeted warmest were those who felt that Reid had created or at least led the way to the creating of a 'West Indian literary style', whatever that may mean. As Arthur Seymour expressed it: 'Reid's adaptation of Jamaican dialect points the way for a distinctive West Indian style'.

Now it seems to me that the idea contained in the term 'West Indian style', derives from a preoccupation with something other than literature. For the term 'West Indian' presupposes of course 'West Indies' and the term 'West Indies' presupposes a community. Thus 'West Indian style' must mean a style informed by the communal life of those who live in the West Indies. While this is so anthropologically speaking, I do not know if it is in terms of literature. So far as I know, a book, a piece of literary art, is produced by an individual, who no matter how much influenced by the life around him, is still an individual, before, during, and after working on a book. The life that exists around him is material to be taken and transformed into art. It is his raw material. It cannot dictate what he must do. It yields to him even as he yields himself to it. Thus what he created is the particular irreducible un-analysable consequence of a process in which what is external and what is internal combine to make something new. And what matters most in the process is the artistic power of the writer, the individual at work. If in the process of working the writer stops to worry about whether he is creating a West Indian style or anything like that, it seems to me that he will be interfering in the very nature of the process, which has nothing to do with what people want but rather with what people are going to get. But perhaps what is meant by the word 'style' in this context is really language, literary language, and what Reid's admirers seek is a West Indian literary language.

If this is so it is perhaps time to take a look at a sample from the book. I quote, quoting a sample used by Arthur Seymour in one of his essays.

> All of us are waiting to see Father strike Aaron Dacre. You can see shoulder muscles a-talk to my father's arm underneath his coat; worry rides Mother and Manuel; Naomi's mouth opens wide, a meccaback fish being shored in net. For a long time my father's hand stayed on the Bible he was carrying. Then his head shook a little, the shoulder muscles stopped talking. All this time Father's and Aaron Dacre's eyes were making four with each other...

Good. As Arthur pointed out, it is an 'adaptation of Jamaican dialect'. So now we must look forward to adaptations of Barbadian, Trinidadian, St Lucian, Grenadian, Guianese, Berbician, Buxtonian dialects, and when all the adapting and writing is done we will have our body of 'distinctive West Indian styled literature' (which even those who speak the dialect from which it is contrived will not be able to read, if that is the hope and intention). Then the main problem will be to decide which is the most West Indian of all, which is the most distinctively West Indian.

Quite obviously this hankering after a 'distinct West Indian style' is a throw-off from nationalism, West Indian nationalism. The idea is well-known and popular – a nation must have national things. But many people seem to forget that even poverty can have an adjective before it, for example. That doesn't make it different though, qualitatively, from poverty in general, as a condition.

So what is Reid's contribution? It is his style created for a special purpose, for the purpose of making his book as he wanted it to be made. It may have significance outside of literature, no one denies that. But to deal with that significance is to deal with something else, something extra-literary. The problem is to avoid importing extra-literary considerations into these things.

[1958]

Sambo at Large

London: rain wet streets and enduring stone walls, begrimed with the smoke of memory.

London: and thousands upon thousands of hard hurrying feet and set faces; and the black and not so black voluntary exiles, imitating the natives' way of walking and strangling, in a cold and alien wind; their hot sun vitality under long drab coated and masked brows. And in Leicester Square, in a night street of gleaming motor vehicles and separate chattering mouths, a tall gaunt and overcoated European, with a blue stubble of beard and wild-rimmed eyes stoops like a sudden hawk and picks up a dead cigarette-end from the meaningless pavement, while all around the many worlds of London spin on in a remorseless and unlaughing merry-go-round.

Easily the most depressing sight in London is the immigrant from the West Indies, pallid, down-at-heel, shuffling along and looking thoroughly unhappy. I remember looking at one of them in a pub just off Victoria Station. Actually I am not certain whether he was West Indian or African, student or immigrant. But there he was – isolated and silent, sitting like a statue, like a fugitive from the historical department of the British Museum. I keep imagining him – sitting bolt upright at the counter, with a glass of beer before him – tense and wary – like a perai near a dentist.

I left London for the Poetry Conference at Cardiff on Sunday, September 19. The day before, Gavor Ullah, a 23-year-old Pakistani had been shot in the back as he stood in a store in Edgware Road in the middle of the afternoon. As I read the report of the incident in a London newspaper, while waiting for the train, I could imagine myself bleeding in the midst of the impersonal pigeons which foul up the fountains in Trafalgar Square. There was a black porter standing near one of the entrances to the train station and I went up to him and asked what gate the train for Cardiff was leaving from, although I knew well enough it was gate 2. But I had to have an excuse for addressing him, since it is unusual for a stranger to say anything to anyone, black or white, in London, unless it is functional. When he replied to my enquiry I detected from his accent that he was a Jamaican. But on his face was the same gloom.

The train left Paddington on time and I found myself in a coach with an American, his female partner, and an Australian. The American gentleman – small, unpleasant, bespectacled, moustached with a face which could have been the original of a Rudyard Kipling photograph – was, as I learnt subsequently a "beat" poet, a "hipster" and he too was on his way to Cardiff. Also on his way was the Australian – a nervous, fingernail-biting soft-faced young man with the eyes of an ashamed policeman.

As the train sped westwards I could see the changing countryside – now green level fields, now clustered concrete blocks of houses with limp and dreary lines of washing swinging like executed men in the foreign air. My coach-mate, the American "beat", the "hipster", after getting up and looking through the window a few times, began fretting because there was no dining-car on the train. His silent partner – a pale thin girl, wearing a jacket and a pair of black trousers and looking like a bewildered school girl, answered his regular snarls with predictable low-toned groans and a theatrical closing of the eyes. My other coach-mate, the Australian, after stealing a few glances at the American, settled himself in his seat and gave me his back. And I, to him another sambo at large, picked up the paperback I had bought at a stall, and tried to read. The train sped on.

As the train moved through the countryside, I reflected on the relationships which exist between people in general since I was bound for a poet's conference in a part of Europe, between European intellectuals and what, for the sake of convenience, I will call their counterparts in the Caribbean, Africa and Asia. From previous experience, of course, I knew that the European intellectual in general manages to retain a special form of contempt for the colonial who, instead of concentrating on knowing his place, forgets himself so far as to want to become – not a doctor or a lawyer: this is acceptable – but a man using his mind. And this I knew was partly a consequence of the European's historical position and partly a consequence of the subservient attitudes so readily adopted by the colonial. Overwhelmed by the home-ground of the master, the colonial who aspires to use his mind, quickly becomes anxious to be accepted; to be considered sophisticated; and just as anxious, too, to be separated from his less enlightened fellow colonials. His essential preoccupation is to ingratiate himself and win a tap on the shoulder. In his essay 'Black Orpheus' which deals with the poets of French Africa, Jean-Paul Sartre has written that, by and large, the usual European's attitude to the work produced by such as these is one of 'interested contempt'. It seems difficult to put it more accurately.

About two and a half hours after leaving London we arrived in Cardiff and made our way to the Park Hotel where accommodation had been arranged for us. At a first glance I could see that although the hotel staff had been warned, the sight of all together – Africans, Ceylonese, a Malayan, an Indian, long-haired British "hipsters", the Australian and my American coach-mate was rather too much. I could see in the eyes of the receptionists something closely resembling terror. And in spite of myself I sympathised, as I inspected the long-haired "geniuses" come to Cardiff to perform.

[*c.* 1965]

Apart from Both

The central issue of poetry as of politics is the destiny of the human personality. What I say is what I believe you can hear. But if we are without a common cause, then what I say is unhearable. But I am afraid that our spiritual history has caused us to see each other in terms of contempt which we borrow from ourselves. Frankly, even our self-contempt is not original. In another context and speaking hyperbolically, much of what history has done for us is to change a vowel: the vowel 'i' to the vowel 'a' in the verb deprived.

To want to be a poet and try to be one; and to participate in politics which is what all of us do whether we realise it or not, is, when we think about it, to try to have more life; to deepen the relations we have with each other; to explore one's own and each other's own capacity to respond to those challenges of being and mind and spirit we issue as we exist. It is decidedly not to reduce the human person into an object of use, a convenient thing. In this 20th century we have seen how various systems of government, founded upon conflicting political philosophies have, perhaps by different methods but similar aims, provoked anarchy and despair among the young and relegated the so-called mature to a treadmill of malicious boredom. And for all of this we have none to blame but ourselves. We become what we are.

And one cannot speak about poetry and politics without speaking about poet and politician. In this period of serious pre-occupation about sheer physical survival – in the crudest economic terms – it may seem to some a fiddling thing to speak of what may appear to be abstract concepts and intellectual refinements. But I want to insist, now as much as any other time, that the values of personality determine the values of life, and that the achievement of a good life can only be measured in terms of the victory of the personality.

A real poet is a person who, whether he knows it or not, participates in a moral and spiritual tradition which has its foundations in that dimension of thought and feeling out of which language came. The German scholar and thinker Ernst Cassirer in one of his works – *Language and Myth* – has said that 'language moves in the middle kingdom between the "indefinite" and the "infinite"; it transforms the indeterminate into the determinate idea, and then holds it within the sphere of finite determinations'. Cassirer proceeded thereafter to speak of the 'ineffables', one of which represents the lower limit of verbal expression, and the other, the upper limit; and also about the opposition between chaos and creation.

'What poetry expresses,' said Cassirer, 'is neither the mythic word-picture of gods and demons, nor the logical truth of abstract relations. The world of poetry stands apart from both, as a world of illusion and fantasy – but it is just in this mode of illusion that the realm of pure feeling can find utterance and can therewith attain its full and concrete actualisation...and recognise them for what they really are – forms of self-revelation'.

The poet Frederick Hölderlin, born in 1770, in some of his poems exemplified these concepts brilliantly. This passage comes from his poem – *The Poet's Vocation*:

> Too long now things divine have been cheaply used
> And all the powers of heaven, the kindly, spent
> In trifling waste by cold and cunning
> Men without thanks, who when he, the Highest,

In person tills their field for them, think they know
The daylight and the Thunderer, and indeed
Their telescope may find them all, may
Count and may name every star in heaven.

Yet will the Father cover with holy night,
That we may last on earth, our too knowing eyes.
He loves no Titan! Never will our
Free-ranging power coerce his heaven.

Nor is it good to be all too wise. Our thanks
Know God. Yet never gladly the poet keeps
His lore unshared, but like to join with
Others who help him to understand it.

But, if he must, undaunted the man remains
Alone with God – ingenuousness keeps him safe –
And needs no weapon and no wile till
God's being missed, in the end, will help him.

Or again as Hölderlin says: 'Man is a god when he dreams, a beggar when he reflects.' The translator of the poem quoted, commenting on Hölderlin's profound perception, has written that when Hölderlin speaks of dreaming he means the state of mind that permits communion with Nature while reflection is the self-consciousness that cuts off the individual from the rest of creation. 'It is the alternation of these states of mind', Hamburger the translator argues, 'with characteristic variation of modulations, and a gradual progression towards synthesis or reconciliation'. Hölderlin himself chose an astronomical term 'the eccentric orbit' to describe his mode of progression.

The individual perception is nothing unless there is community reception of the terms in which this perception is conceived and expressed. To speak Latin to a person you know is illiterate is not to speak, since the speaker in speaking Latin has made it clear that he had no intention of speaking at all. But then you may ask of this hypothetical situation: What did the speaker speak? I suggest that all then the speaker would be doing was to make sounds that established his presence; and that in so doing he would be establishing, in acceptable human form, that he too is a human being. For invertedly, in spite of himself, he would be seeking to signal his membership of the human community.

Three thousand, five hundred years before the birth of Christ, Aknaten, the Egyptian, prayed that he might write, and wrote:

'Behold, I am a scribe, and I have copied each day, the words of beautiful Osiris even as Thoth hath done...'

Aknaten, because he advocated monotheism was branded by the tongues of polytheists, a criminal. But who remembers the names of those who brand?

This is from *The Book of the Dead*:

> He holdeth fast to the Memory of his Identity
> In the Great House, and in the House of Fire,
> On the dark night of counting all the years,
> On the dark night when months and years are numbered, –
> O let my name be given back to me!
> When the Divine One on the Eastern Stairs
> Shall cause me to sit down with him in peace
> And every god proclaims his name before me, –
> Let me remember then the name I bore!

[1974]

The Location of the Artist

The situation in which the productive person (in particular, the artist) finds himself in contemporary Guyana is not at all unique. It is rather one manifestation of a condition which has existed in other places and at other times. Travellers and sojourners among so-called primitive peoples, for example, have noted that exhibitions of outstanding skill or conspicuously successful behaviour are usually attributed to witchcraft; and that frequently, individual exhibitors of such skills or patterns of behaviour usually ended up as victims of group hostility. Winwood Reade, the 19th-century traveller in West Africa, in his *Martyrdom of Man* tells how among certain tribes he came in contact with, 'if he (a tribesman) builds a better house than his neighbours they pull it down'. And Hannah Arendt in her *The Human Condition* exposes another aspect of this situation when she writes of 'the prohibition of excellence' and notes that within the Benedictine order 'if one monk becomes proud of his work he has to give it up'.

It seems clear that the crux of the matter here is power, productive power. And the attribution of unusual productive power to witchcraft by so-called primitive peoples implies a concept of personality consistent with a particular kind of solidarity. Anything that serves to disrupt this solidarity is harmful and must be controlled. If this argument is valid, then the situation in which the productive person (in particular, the artist) finds himself, has to be interpreted in terms of the solidarity which obtains within the Guyanese community.

What is this solidarity? A few comments on the education which the Guyanese community has had should help to answer this question. From one point of view this education has been part of a process of our being taught the correct way of learning how to read incorrectly. What has been incorrect is that we have learnt to apply literally to ourselves what others in teaching us only apply symbolically to themselves. One result of this is that we do a lot of trying to fit ourselves into positions for which the symbols we employ do have application, but which indeed are not of our fitting positions. Thus, we are continuously displacing ourselves. This displacing, which leads not only to the confusion of priorities, but also to a failure to conceive of the very nature of priority, is among the chiefest of the factors bringing about our productive inferiority in general. This productive inferiority is reflexive, and in turn, produces creatures inferior to it, to wit, the producers, our community. And so, the exertions of these producers, in a situation such as the one described constitute a negative process. Negative productivity therefore, is the solidarity which obtains in the Guyanese community.

It is in the light of these considerations that the location of the artist, a particular type of productive person in the Guyanese community, has to be understood. Because the important and interesting point to be noted here is that precisely because the community sponsors a process of negative productivity, the artist is the chief target. Because in fact art is negative productivity, and presupposes a process of positive productivity as its proper environment. To bring about a reversal of this state of affairs seems to be the objective of much of what passes among us as 'cultural imperatives', among which are proposals for the organisation of art to serve ideological purposes, and the induction of the artist into groups with vested interests.

But a word or two about what is meant by negative productivity is indicated here. The first consideration to be dealt with concerning art and the artist has to do with satisfaction and fulfilment. This satisfaction and fulfilment has to do with the development of self-consciousness. Self-consciousness itself is an issue, itself subsumed by the issue that subsumes all issues: human fate. The artist cannot change the nature of this fate: all he can do is endure it. At the same time it is his society which has to provide the conditions that make this fate endurable. It is in these senses that art is described as negative productivity and positive productivity suggested as the required environment of the artist. Where there should be interaction of negative and positive productivity we find instead only the contiguity of two negative productivities, one seeking to retain its integrity through independence and autonomy, the other attempting to assimilate this independence and autonomy into a system which, since it does not have the requirements of positive productivity, is not in a position to offer co-existential status.

The provenance of the productive power of the artist resides to a very great extent in his independence and autonomy. In this context these two terms connote interdependence, which contiguity certainly is not. Not being able to enjoy interdependence and autonomy the artist is a displaced person, and therefore not in a situation really different from other members of his community. But while displacement is consistent in a situation which is negative when it should be positive, it is not so in a situation where, through sheer environmental inadequacy it is not negative as it should be, but rather is made into something different from what it should be, that is to say, into something dependent, having a position rather than a location.

[1979]

NOTES

The following notes provide bibliographical details and commentaries relating to specific phrases in the poetry and prose. Collations of lexical differences are given when there are multiple versions of a poem. A list of abbreviations for people and works consulted follows these notes.

COLLECTED POEMS

TO A DEAD SLAVE (1951) *(59-65)*
No manuscript exists, but a published copy bearing Carter's ink corrections is housed in the A.J. Seymour Collection in the National Library, Georgetown, Guyana. The poem has not been republished since Carter first financed its publication in 1951. It is the only poem for which he provides a preface. The poem was printed by the Magnet Printery on Holme Street, Georgetown and Carter distributed it free of charge. It is unknown how many copies were produced.

1-2. *To you dead slave:* Although the slave trade was abolished by Britain in 1807, Carter's 'Guiana' comprised the Dutch colonies, Demerara, Essequibo and Berbice until 1816, when they were taken into British possession. In 1831 the colonies were united as British Guiana. Slavery was abolished in the British West Indies in 1838, after a four year "apprenticeship" (for emancipation) had been served by enslaved peoples.

38. *Pomeroon:* river that runs from the interior to Charity.

39. *Demerara:* river that runs from Makari Mountains to Georgetown.

40. *Essequibo:* river that runs from Acarai Mountains to Parika.

52. *Caribs:* Amerindian people who colonised the north-east coast of South America.

53. *Wichabai:* town in the south of the country in the Upper Takutu-Upper Essequibo Region.

53. *Kanaku:* mountain range in the Rupununi.

54. *Ganges:* sacred river in the Indian subcontinent.

55. *Quamina:* An African (possibly Coromantee) man enslaved on Plantation Success in Demerara, Quamina was the head carpenter and 'first deacon' at Bethel Chapel, the missionary Church for slaves, led by John Smith during the time of the rebellion. Emilia da Costa speculates on whether Quamina's role within a Christian church mirrored a prior African traditional role of 'conjurer' or 'fetishman' (EdC, 194). In 1823, believing rumours that freedom was to be granted to slaves, Quamina and his son, Jack Gladstone, emerged as leaders of a large group of insurgents, organising what is now known as the Demerara Slave Rebellion. After early successes in capturing plantations and imprisoning the planters, the rebellion was quashed. Quamina became a fugitive in the interior of Guyana and is said to have claimed that no white man would capture him alive. In September 1823, Quamina was spotted. He refused to give himself up to the search party and was shot and killed by an Amerindian. His body was hung in chains in a gibbet outside his former plantation (EdC, 229).

60. *how human is a rock:* Human-carved rock patterns, known as timehri, can be found in much of Guyana's interior. Animism of Amerindian religious belief suggests that gods inhabit and take the form of inanimate things.

63-65. *or ship that moves...names the slaves inherited:* Carter conflates here two practices during slavery: the slaveship logbook, which contained the numbers of the unnamed slave cargo, and the plantation account book, which contained the new names imposed upon slaves in the Americas.

95. *some pelt ripe padi seeds into the soil:* In the 20th century, in addition to producing sugar, Guyana became a large rice producer.

149. *corial:* a Guyanese term for a dugout canoe with pointed ends, possibly derived via the Spanish from the Arawak, *koriara* (DCEU). The OED dates the word as late 18th-century.

150. *kitchen midden:* refuse heap left by prehistoric settlements, common in Guyanese interior.

151-52. *Europe keels / which sailed:* Christopher Columbus first landed in the Caribbean, thinking that he had discovered a new route to the East Indies.

153. *brown:* In the 1950s it would have been standard to describe people of mixed white (European) and black (African) ancestry, like Carter himself, as either 'brown', 'Creole' or 'coloured'.

154-61. Carter's description here of a specific form of English (one that is distinctly Caribbean in rhythm, tone and meaning, and therefore capable of articulating the Caribbean's cultural history) is an early articulation of the growing linguistic and literary interest in Caribbean English.

167. *six hands:* One of the mottos of Guyana is 'Land of Six Peoples': Amerindian, African, Indian, Chinese, British and Portuguese.

167. *citadel:* As a description of Georgetown, 'citadel', plays on the fortress role of settlements in the years of European colonisation in the Americas.

180. *benab:* A Guyanese term for a shelter made of a framework of poles, covered with leaves and branches. The OED states that the word is derived from the Arawak, *bannabuhu.*

209-13. *I / must bend down...:* Compare 'Listening to the Land'.

223. *Hebo:* variant of Igbo, an ethnic group from the north-east of present Nigeria.

224. *Mosambos:* Probable reference to ethnic group from the Congo, but it could also refer to Guyanese people of Angolan or Mozambiquan descent. I would like to thank Adeola James for this information.

224. *Ochus:* Probable variant spelling of 'Oku', a title used in Guyana to describe people of Yoruba descent. It is derived from a variation of the phrase used to begin most Yoruba greetings: *'o ku...'* [familiar, singular], *'e ku...'* [plural, polite]. The common use of this phrase led to its adoption as a descriptive noun. I would like to thank Adeola James, Molara Ogundipe and Karin Barber for this information. Karin Barber notes that people of Yoruba descent who were resettled in Sierra Leone in the early 19th century came to be known as 'Aku'.

223-24. *dances pound... beat their goat skin drums:* Goat skin is widely used as a drum membrane. Carter's lines suggest the cultural survivals and syncretisms of African ethnic groups in the Americas.

225: *kurtaed:* A kurta (derived from the Urdu, *kurtah* [OED]) is a loose shirt or tunic worn especially by Hindu men and women.

225: *magi:* member of ancient Persian priestly caste.

227. *pandit:* a Hindu learned in Sanskrit and in Indian philosophy, religion and laws.

247-52. History, as taught in Britain and its colonies, dissembled the British role in world slavery, concentrating on the abolitionists of the late 18th- and early 19th-centuries, rather than the three prior centuries of slave-trading in the Americas.

261-62. *fire stick:* torch.
275. *Guiana:* notably not 'British Guiana'.
276. *Carib sea:* This is not a typographical error. Guyana is not geographically part of the Caribbean Sea, but Carter can rightly claim his country's place in the waters sailed by Caribs.

THE HILL OF FIRE GLOWS RED (1951) *(66-73)*

Carter's first collection of poetry, *The Hill of Fire Glows Red*, was published in a series edited by A.J. Seymour, called the Miniature Poets Series. It appeared in October, a few months after Wilson Harris's pamphlet of poems, *Fetish*. The print run was one hundred copies. Poets paid five dollars for twenty copies and 'the remaining eighty would be sold to friends, teachers, Ministers of religion, civil servants, fellow poets for one shilling per copy' (AJSP, 33). Seymour writes in his unpublished notes that *The Hill of Fire Glows Red* was the only collection in the Miniature Poets Series to have had a second edition. Janet Jagan, as secretary of the PPP and editor of *Thunder*, paid Seymour to reproduce a hundred more copies to go on sale at the PPP bookshop. In the title of the first edition, 'glows' was not capitalised.

'Not I with This Torn Shirt' *(66)*

No manuscript exists. First published in *Hill of Fire Glows Red* (Georgetown: author, 1951), p.3. Not included in *Poems of Succession*.

Magnificent Province: In Shakespeare's *The Merry Wives of Windsor* Falstaff discusses Mistresses Ford and Page in terms of the promised treasures of the 'New World': 'She [Ford] is a region in Guiana, all gold and bounty. I will be cheaters to them both, and they shall be exchequers to me. They shall be my East and West Indies, and I will trade to them both' (1.3. 63-66).

mud...flood...feudal coast: Reference to the character of Guyana's plantation geography, which consists of land reclaimed from the coastal plain by Dutch planters in the 17th century. Although colonial Guyana never supported a feudal system, the plantation economy could justifiably allow Carter to compare slaves to serfs.

white mansions: The colonial geography of Guyana was typified by wooden buildings painted white.

trench: Guyanese term for a ditch or canal built to irrigate cane fields and to control water levels throughout the coastal belt.

El Dorado: Walter Ralegh's *The Discoverie of the Large, Rich, and Bewtiful Empyre of Guiana with a relation of the great and Golden Citie of Manoa which the Spanyards call El Dorado* (1596) located the Guianas as the place to cement Elizabeth I's New World empire.

white dust: White marl was used to cover the roads of Georgetown. Compare 'freedom is a white road with green grass like love' ('The Knife of Dawn').

How are the mighty slain: A reworking of David's biblical lament: 'The Beauty of Israel is slain upon thy high places: how are the Mighty fallen' (Samuel 21.19).

this new science of men alive: See Karl Marx and Friedrich Engels, *The German Ideology*: 'We do not set out from what men say, imagine, conceive, nor from men as narrated, thought of, imagined, conceived, in order to arrive at men in the flesh. We set out from real, active men, and on the basis of their real life-process we demonstrate the development of the ideological reflexes and echoes of this life-process' (KMFE, 47).

COLLATION

14. and a battering] and battering [SP1989, SP1997]

'Do Not Stare at Me' *(67)*

No manuscript exists, but Carter's fair copy typescript is extant in the *Poems of Succession* manuscript. First published in *Hill of Fire Glows Red* (Georgetown: author, 1951), p.4.

Do not stare at me from your window, lady: Carter's experience of taking part in PPP political marches in Georgetown could have occasioned this poem. I would like to thank Eusi Kwayana for this suggestion. Phyllis Carter remembers that Carter refused to learn to drive, preferring to walk around Georgetown; this decision could sometimes arouse suspicion from people in the large urban houses.

the slums in the south of the city: Carter is likely to be thinking of Albuoystown and Tiger Bay.

rear: (1) rise in anger or fear (2) bring up children.

COLLATION

15. waggon] wagon [PS, SP1989, SP1997]

'Old Higue' *(67)*

No manuscript exists. First published in *Hill of Fire Glows Red* (Georgetown: author, 1951), p.5. Not included in *Poems of Succession*. Carter's mother knew many stories from Caribbean folklore and would certainly have told him about old higue. I would like to thank Phyllis Carter for this information.

higue: A female vampire in Caribbean folklore, also known as succubus, soucriant, soucouyant. It takes the form of an old woman and when it sheds its skin at night it reveals a ball of fire. It is said to fly through the night feeding off sleeping children. 'Higue' is a Caribbean variant form of the SE word 'hag'.

peel...took...pound: The phrasing reflects Creole usage, by alternating present-tense and past-tense verbs, and by using present-tense verbs to describe past events.

mammy: mother or kin term used to mark respect for elders and strangers.

pepper: hot chilli pepper is a traditional weapon for killing the higue.

Cool um water cool um: Creole phrasing 'cool it water cool it'. 'Um' is the third person singular pronoun.

meringue: Variant spelling of merengue. A dance of Dominican and Haitian origin, usually in duple and triple time. DCEU states that the phrase 'dance merengue' in Guyana means 'to writhe in pain'.

COLLATION

12, 14, 18. meringue] merengue [SP1989, SP1997]

'Like the Blood of Quamina' *(68)*

No manuscript exists. First published in *Hill of Fire Glows Red* (Georgetown: author, 1951), p.6. Not included in *Poems of Succession*.

the river: the Demerara river.

whenever cane is ripe: Before sugarcane is cut, the fields are set on fire in order to burn away the excess leaves, exposing the bare canes.

this city: Georgetown.

O Jesus Christ man!: exclamation that works as both Standard English and Creole.

tiger: Guyanese term for jaguar. William Blake's 'tiger' provides the obvious comparison here for a symbolic animal (in Carter's poem it represents 'the soul of slavery') that seems to offer both a threat and a promise to the world (WB, 214-15).

Quamina: See note to *To a Dead Slave, l.* 55.

forest: tropical interior of Guyana.

'Shines the Beauty of My Darling' *(69)*

No manuscript exists. First published in *Hill of Fire Glows Red* (Georgetown: author, 1951), p.7. Also published in four sequences under the heading 'Poems of Resistance': PR, PRMagnet, PRMasses and PRWIIP. See introductory note to *Poems of Resistance from British Guiana*. Not included in *Poems of Succession*.

Malaya: Between 1948 and 1960, Malaya (a British colony until 1957) was governed under a state of emergency. During this time the 'Malayan Races Liberation Army' – Communist forces opposed to British control – fought a long, but eventually unsuccessful campaign.

Vietnam: In May 1941 the Central Committee of the Indochinese Communist Party formed the 'Revolutionary League for the Independence of Vietnam' (the Viet Minh). In 1946 a war of independence began, with France and Communist anti-colonial guerrillas fighting to control an area known then as French Indo-China.

revolt of India: India, as the first British colony to gain independence and as the ancestral home of many Guyanese people, was a touchstone for the anti-colonial movement in Guyana and much of the British Empire.

Africa like guardian: Africa, as the ancestral home of many Guyanese people, was an important focus in colonial Guyana and the Caribbean. The Martinican poet and politician, Aimé Césaire, and the Senegalese poet and politician, Léopold Sédar Senghor, had already named the political and cultural renascence of Africa and its diaspora as *negritude*. The left-wing anti-colonial movements in Africa, particularly that headed by Kwame Nkrumah in the Gold Coast (now Ghana) were also a source of inspiration to members of the PPP in Guyana, and were extensively reported in the PPP journal, *Thunder*.

my darling: Carter and Phyllis Howard were dating at the time.

COLLATION

2. night] might [PRMagnet]

6. down the light] dawn light [PRMasses, PRWIIP, SP1989, SP1997], down light [PR, PRMagnet]

9. brain] brains [PR]

10. new are] now ere [PR]

23. shines] shine [PRWIIP]

'Three Years After This' *(69)*

No manuscript exists. First published in *Hill of Fire Glows Red* (Georgetown: author, 1951), p.8. The poem was reprinted in *Thunder* to mark the anniversary of the deaths. Not included in *Poems of Succession*.

Enmore: Plantation on the East of the Guyana coast.

down the long red road: The road leading from Georgetown along East Coast Demerara towards Enmore was made of burnt red clay. I would like to thank Dudley Kissoore for this information.

five men bleeding: Five male sugar workers, known as Harry Jug, Lalla Bagi,

Pooran, Rambarran and Dookhie, were shot and killed by Colonial Police on 16 June 1948 during a strike. They were part of a crowd fired on while protesting against a field system that would have resulted in the loss of wages (CJ, 90). The five killed workers became known as the Enmore Martyrs, and a statue was eventually erected in their honour.

I walked behind: A march from Enmore to Georgetown took place every year to commemorate the Enmore Martyrs.

my city had no shame: Nobody was prosecuted for these deaths.

'Looking at Your Hands' *(70)*

No manuscript exists, but Carter's fair copy typescript is extant in the *Poems of Succession* manuscript. First published in *Hill of Fire Glows Red* (Georgetown: author, 1951), p.9. Republished, along with a new poem – 'Death of a Slave' – in *Kyk-Over-Al Anthology of West Indian Poetry*, 14 (1952), 52. Also published in three sequences under the heading 'Poems of Resistance': PRMagnet, PRMasses and PRWIIP. See introductory note to *Poems of Resistance from British Guiana*.

No: a possible response to the ellipsis that ends 'Three Years after this'.

fire: Multiple implications of this word include anti-colonial revolution, slave rebellion and Phoenix-like metamorphosis. Compare the discussion of fire in 'Time of Crisis'.

who could not die...who did not sleep to dream, but dream to change the world: Carter had obviously been reading Shakespeare, but he finds a way to keep the Shakespearean influence and topicalise the subject of sleep, death and dreaming with his revolutionary aspirations. See *The Tempest*, IV.1.156-58: 'We are such stuff / As dreams are made on; and our little life / Is rounded with a sleep'; and *Hamlet* III.1.65-68. 'To sleep, perchance to dream. Ay, there's the rub; / For in that sleep of death what dreams may come, / When we have shuffled off this mortal coil, / Must give us pause'.

looking at your hands: Compare 'not hands like mine / these Carib altars knew' ('Not Hands Like Mine').

COLLATION

Looking at Your Hands] I Will Not Still My Voice [PRMagnet, PRMasses, PRWIIP]

6. looking at books] deleted [PRMagnet]

7-8. or coming to your house / or walking in the sun] Walking in the sun / Or coming to your house [PRMagnet]

13. without a light] without light [PRMagnet]

20. ranks] vaults [PRMagnet]

'Tomorrow and the World' *(71)*

No manuscript exists. First published in *Hill of Fire Glows Red* (Georgetown: author, 1951), p.10. Also published in four sequences under the heading 'Poems of Resistance': PR, PRMagnet, PRMasses and PRWIIP. See introductory note to *Poems of Resistance from British Guiana*. Not included in *Poems of Succession*.

I walk...the seller of sweets...the shoemaker: Carter is significantly positioned on the street – the locus of revolution.

'Friend': common greeting, if old-fashioned, in Caribbean.

the songs of life: Compare Walt Whitman, 'So Long!': 'I have sung the body and the soul, war and peace have I sung, and the songs of life and death' (WW, 433).

awake: Compare Carter's interest in awakening in 'Run Shouting Through the Town' and 'Let Freedom Wake Him'.

COLLATION

5. happy is it] happy it is [PR, PRMasses, PRWIIP]

8. flame] flames [SP1989, SP1997]

11. everywhere the light of the day] deleted [PRMagnet]

12. songs of life] songs of light [PRMagnet]

13. like new ships] like might ships [PRMagnet]; life new ships [PRWIIP]

'It Is for This That I Am Furious' *(71)*

No manuscript exists. First published in *Hill of Fire Glows Red* (Georgetown: author, 1951), p.11. Not included in *Poems of Succession*, nor *Selected Poems*.
coughing infant...bawdy house: Compare William Blake, 'London': 'How the youthful harlot's curse / Blasts the new born infant's tear' (WB, 213-14).
byre: cow shed.

'Run Shouting Through the Town' *(72)*

No manuscript exists. First published in *Hill of Fire Glows Red* (Georgetown: author, 1951), p.12. Not included in *Poems of Succession*.
Oh! wake: Compare William Blake, 'Jerusalem': 'Awake! awake, Jerusalem! O lovely Emanation of Albion, / Awake and overspread all nations as in ancient time – / For lo! the night of death is past and the eternal day / Appears upon our hills!' (WB, 844).
I would rip off my clothes / run shouting through the town: Carter's carnivalesque draws on Caribbean practices, most notably the midnight Canboulay (literally *cannes brullées*, 'burning cane') processions of Trinidad, illuminated by torches carried by revellers (EH, 24).
naked: This can refer to both the poverty of the child and to the bacchanalian frenzy promoted in the poem.

'Listening to the Land' *(72)*

No manuscript exists, but Carter's fair copy typescript is extant in the *Poems of Succession* manuscript. First published in *Hill of Fire Glows Red* (Georgetown: author, 1951), p.13.
That night when I left you: Possibly addressed to Sydney King (now Eusi Kwayana), referring to a visit they made together to Buxton.
the old brick chimney: There is an old chimney, a well-known landmark, along the East Coast at Mon Repos. I would like to thank Phyllis Carter for this information.
as if some buried slave wanted to speak again: Compare Carter in his essay 'A Question of Self-Contempt': 'the imaginary plantation I summoned yielded not one of the secrets I knew existed. Between me and them was silence, broken by the sound of voices I invented out of desperation, and continuing converse with those I kept hearing in nightmare'.

COLLATION

12-16. but all I heard...listening to the land] deleted [PS, SP1989, SP1997]

'A Banner for the Revolution' *(73)*

No manuscript exists. First published in *Hill of Fire Glows Red* (Georgetown: author, 1951), p.14. Not included in *Poems of Succession*, but added to the

1964 edition of *Poems of Resistance*.

Banner for the Revolution: Compare Soviet National Anthem: 'In the victory of Communism's deathless ideal, / We see the future of our dear land. / And to her fluttering scarlet banner, / Selflessly true we always shall stand'.

that night there will be thousands of torches: Indirect reference to the burning of the cane, either for harvesting or as part of slave and colonial rebellion.

eager to be men: Compare 'a city of clerks became a city of men' ('Black Friday 1962').

THE KIND EAGLE (POEMS OF PRISON) (1952) *(74-78)*

This was the first of two collections that Carter self-published in Georgetown in 1952 when he was working as Secretary to the Superintendent of Prisons (see my Introduction, pp.26-27). The collection was published in June. There are no records of the print run, but given what is known about the Miniature Poets Series, we could estimate one hundred copies maximum, sold at a price of at least one shilling. Copies of this pamphlet are extremely rare, and are held in the A.J. Seymour Collection in the National Library, Georgetown, Guyana. All the poems were published in italics. At the end of 1952 the seven poems from *The Kind Eagle* were reprinted in *Kyk-Over-Al* under the title 'Poems of Prison', with an additional poem, 'Discovery of Companion'. This poem is included as the final poem of *The Kind Eagle* in the present edition. The third poem, 'You Are Involved', and fifth poem, 'The Kind Eagle' (retitled 'The Knife of Dawn') were also published as part of *Poems of Resistance from British Guiana*. In the present edition I have placed these two poems in this subsequent location, in order to preserve the integrity of this major collection. See 'Note on the Text'.

'Bare Night Without Comfort' *(74)*

No manuscript exists. First published in *The Kind Eagle* [n.p., p.2]. Also published in 'Poems of Prison', *Kyk-Over-Al*, 15 (1952), p.27. Not included in *Poems of Succession*.

a bare night without comfort: Compare King Lear on the heath, speaking of 'unaccommodated man' as a 'poor, bare forked animal' (III.4.109). In the first publication, 'without' is given as 'with out'.

drum: Compare 'O Where to Hide' and *To a Dead Slave*: 'like drum beats throbbing with a jungle noise'.

Like dark ball: The lack of definite article suggests a Creole grammatical pattern.

hurling curse at me: The absence of plural-marking suggests Creole phrasing.

'Who Walks a Pavement' *(74)*

No manuscript exists, but Carter's fair copy typescript is extant in the *Poems of Succession* manuscript. First published in *The Kind Eagle* [n.p., p.3]. Also published in 'Poems of Prison', *Kyk-Over-Al*, 15 (1952), p.28.

Iron gate: The omission of the indefinite article draws on Creole grammatical patterns (compare 'slant roof', 'tight cell', 'lash', 'shell' and 'heart').

prison: Eusi Kwayana (then known as Sydney King) remembers Carter's political campaigning: 'He would say something like this to a meeting, large or small: "Now I am sure you all agree with me that this colony called British Guiana is a jail. Now why is it a jail? It is not because you and I are in some cell with an iron bar and a big key. No, it is not that kind of jail. Why is it a jail then?"' (EK, 160).

go back: If read as standard English the phrase can be interpreted as an imperative. If read as Creole, the phrase operates multiply – as an imperative (perhaps inverting and strengthening the Creole imperative, 'galang' or 'go along'), as a new composite noun (prison is 'a go-back'), and as part of an abbreviated sentence (meaning 'a prison forces a person to go backwards').

lash of two things: 'Lash' is the felt experience of the slave, prompted by 'back'. Kamau Brathwaite opens his 'New World Trilogy', *The Arrivants*, with words that confronted slavery in the Caribbean and its African cultural inheritance: 'Drum skin whip / lash, master sun's / cutting edge of / heat' (EB, 4).

shell which is the heart / and heart which is the shell – the hollow tear: Possibly brought together because of their comparable shapes. Compare 'drain out my heart and husk it into shell' ('Sunday Night').

The man of time whose look can stain a sky / who walks a pavement, walks and disappears: It is possible to link this poem to Carter's rare discussions of his role as a poet. When asked how he became a poet Carter replied: 'In jail it is hard to walk forward, so you walk back, and you walk through to yourself; in the process of walking back you walk through to yourself.' I would like to thank Moses Nagamootoo for asking Carter this question and sharing his answer.

'O Where to Hide' *(75)*

No manuscript exists, but Carter's fair copy typescript is extant in the *Poems of Succession* manuscript. First published in *The Kind Eagle* [n.p., p.5]. Also published in 'Poems of Prison', *Kyk-Over-Al*, 15 (1952), p.28.

time's black candle: Within the practice of obeah, black candles can be used to symbolise one's enemy, or people to be avoided. Burning the candle is meant to bring harm to one's enemy. Carter was interested in obeah practices but did not consult them personally.

drum beat: Compare Carter's claim in 'Immortal Like the Earth' that a poet 'is the drum beating their doom like music'.

stamp foot: Compare 'Kick off yuh shoe and stamp down the spot' ('Number Two', *Three Poems of Shape and Motion*).

'All of a Man' *(75)*

No manuscript exists. First published in *The Kind Eagle* [n.p., p.7]. Also published in 'Poems of Prison', *Kyk-Over-Al*, 15 (1952), p.29. Not included in *Poems of Succession*.

strike kind eagle: The eagle is favoured in many cultures. In Amerindian folklore the eagle represents the North of America (compared to the Condor of the South). The eagle is the sacred animal of the god Jupitus, protector of the city, state and empire of Rome, and symbol of the United States of America. Carter's explicitly kind eagle could be seen as a corrective to the aggressive imperial ambitions with which the eagle had been associated.

'O Human Guide' *(76)*

No manuscript exists, but Carter's fair copy typescript is extant in the *Poems of Succession* manuscript. First published in *The Kind Eagle* [n.p., p.8]. Also published in 'Poems of Prison', *Kyk-Over-Al*, 15 (1952), p.30.

burnt earth: possible reference to the burning of cane before harvesting, or to the burning of clay to make road surfaces. Also note the implication of religious sacrifice and revenge. See Aeschylus's *The Eumenides:* 'I loose my poison over

245

the soil, aieee! – / poison to match my grief comes pouring out my heart, cursing the land to burn it sterile' *(ll. 795-97).*

I dip my hand... I splash the pool: An act of baptism. See Jacques Roumain, *Les Gouverneurs de la rosée* (1944): 'Plunging her hand into the dust Délira Déliverance said, "we are going to die"' (JR, 23). Although he died in 1944, as the founder of the Haitian Communist Party in 1934, Roumain could have been known to Carter.

furies of this world: Aeschylus's Eumenides are the avengers of the gods.

the rampart spiked with pain: During plantation slavery the heads of executed rebel slaves would be displayed on spikes (EdC, 243).

guilty heaven: Compare 'the guilty cage of heaven' ('All of a Man').

O human guide: Commonly angel or priest in Christianity, *murshid al-kamil* (perfect spiritual guide) in Islam, *guru* (teacher) in Hinduism and Buddhism.

a wild black horse of terror: The black horse of the Apocalypse is commonly understood to represent commerce. 'And when he had opened the third seal, I heard the third beast say, Come and see. And I beheld, and lo a black horse; and he that sat on him had a pair of balances in his hand. And I heard a voice in the midst of the four beasts say, A measure of wheat for a penny, and three measures of barley for a penny; and see thou hurt not the oil and the wine' (Revelation 6. 5-6). Note also that in Haitian voudoun and Cuban Santería during spirit possession, the lwa or god is considered to 'ride' those who he/she possesses as a 'horse' (JD, 74).

COLLATION

'O Human Guide'] 'Human Guide' [PS]

4-5. I splash the pool that feeds my painful flowers / I find the lake whose source leaks from a river] I find the lake whose source leaks from a river / I splash the pool that feeds my painful flowers [PS, SP1989, SP1997]

9. The guilty heaven promising a star] deleted [PS, SP1989, SP1997]

15. but every night] and every night [PS, SP1989, SP1997]

'The Discovery of Companion' *(77)*

No manuscript exists, but Carter's fair copy typescript is extant in the *Poems of Succession* manuscript. This poem was not published in *The Kind Eagle (Poems of Prison)*. First published in *Kyk-Over-Al*, 15 (1952), pp.30-31, as part of the sequence, 'Poems of Prison'. This poem is published in *Selected Poems* as the final poem of the collection, *The Kind Eagle*, and represents Carter's final intentions concerning the ordering and naming of the 'kind eagle' poems; there it is not divided into numbered sections.

the return of arrival is merciless: a possible gesture to Aimé Césaire's major Caribbean poem, *Cahier d'un retour au pays natal* [*Notebook of a Return to My Native Land*] (1956).

pillar of endurance: Compare 'so river flood, drown not my pillar feet' ('The Knife of Dawn').

THE HIDDEN MAN (OTHER POEMS OF PRISON) (1952) *(79-81)*

The Hidden Man (Other Poems of Prison) was the second collection of poetry to be self-published in Georgetown in 1952 when Carter was working as Secretary to the Superintendent of Prisons (see Introduction, pp.26-27). The collection was published in December. As with *The Kind Eagle* there are no records of the print run. Matching estimates about the Miniature Poets Series, a reasonable guess would suggest a maximum of one hundred copies, sold for at least one shilling. Copies of this pamphlet are extremely rare, and one is held in the A.J. Seymour Collection in the National Library, Georgetown, Guyana. All the poems were published in italics. *The Hidden Man* was not republished in Carter's *Poems of Succession*, and in *Selected Poems* it was mistakenly placed before *The Kind Eagle*. Of the seven poems originally published in the 1952 collection ('I Stretch My Hand', 'Cartman of Dayclean', 'Sunday Night', 'Looking Again', 'I Walk and Walk', 'Till I Collect', 'No Madness Like This Sanity'), 'Cartman Of Dayclean' and 'Till I Collect' are published as part of *Poems of Resistance from British Guiana* in this edition. See 'Note on the Text'.

'I Stretch My Hand' *(79)*

No manuscript exists. First published in *The Hidden Man* [n.p., p.1].

I stretch my hand: Compare Abraham 2.7: 'I stretch my hand over the sea, and it obeys my voice; I cause the wind and the fire to be my chariot; I say to the mountains "Depart hence" and behold, they are taken away by a whirlwind, in an instant, suddenly.'

tap root: a long, prominent root in a plant.

rest is death: A challenge to Pascal in *Pensées*: 'Movement is the essence of our nature; complete repose is death to us' (BP, 149).

my dark: Possible Creole phrasing, abbreviating 'darkness'. DCEU states that 'dark' can be used adjectivally to refer to weak sight, making Carter's stretched hand a response to blindness.

'Sunday Night' *(79)*

No manuscript exists. First published in *The Hidden Man* [n.p., p.2].

the wall of life: Carter's interest in the metaphor of the wall may be prompted by the fact that Guyana's coastal plain is protected by a sea wall. Carter, like many Georgetown people, would commonly walk on the sea wall on Sunday evenings.

yonder: DCEU states that it is used in informal Caribbean English, and that it need not be understood as a literary or archaic term.

The congregation only hears the priest / but more I hear: Carter did not attend church regularly, but in 1952 he would sometimes attend Brickdam Catholic Cathedral, if he knew that Phyllis Howard and her friends and cousins would be there. I would like to thank Phyllis Carter for this information.

drain out my heart and husk it into shell: Compare 'shell which is the heart / and heart which is the shell – the hollow tear' ('Who Walks a Pavement').

'Looking Again' *(80)*

No manuscript exists. First published in *The Hidden Man* [n.p., pp.2-3].

old mad house: The Fort Canje hospital (now the National Psychiatric Hospital) was known as 'the mental hospital' or 'mad house'. I would like to thank Phyllis Carter for this information.

yard: can refer to any exterior domestic enclosed area, although the Guyanese term, 'nigger-yard', is used to refer to a yard in a slum area or plantation. Compare 'I Come from the Nigger Yard'.

'I Walk and Walk' *(81)*

No manuscript exists. First published in *The Hidden Man* [n.p., p.3].

I taste the bitter world: See Revelation 8. 11: 'And the name of the star is called Wormwood: and the third part of the waters became wormwood; and many men died of the waters, because they were made bitter'. Also compare Carter's 'Bitter Wood'.

is blood! is black! is coal!: See Revelation 8. 7: 'The first angel sounded, and there followed hail and fire mingled with blood, and they were cast upon the earth: and the third part of trees was burnt up, and all green grass was burnt up'.

COLLATION

5. lidded with glass] lidded in with glass [SP1989, SP1997]

'No Madness Like This Sanity' *(81)*

No manuscript exists. First published in *The Hidden Man* [n.p., p.4].

in such fashion marry to the world: Compare Giovanni Pico della Mirandola's *Conclusions*: 'to work magic is nothing other than to marry the world' (FY, 87-88).

earth no mother, sky no father: Guyanese poet, David Dabydeen, writes in his long poem, *Turner*: 'No stars, no land, no words, no community, / No mother' (DD, 40).

At a dark day's end a darker night will choke us: Night provided enslaved peoples with the opportunity to exercise a limited amount freedom, and for this reason the hours of darkness were feared by slave-owners. Compare 'Night comes from deep forest / in a boat of silence' ('Death of a Slave').

COLLATION

4. bones naked, hopes barren – beautiful world!] bones naked, – beautiful world! [SP1989, SP1997]

18. How in such fashion marry to the world?] deleted [SP1989, SP1997]

TWO FRAGMENTS OF 'RETURNING' (1953) *(82-83)*

These fragments were published in *Kyk-Over-Al* in the middle of 1953. Carter had resigned from the Civil Service and ran but failed to gain a seat in the general elections of April 1953. His return to the subject of slavery links the poem to *To a Dead Slave*. It is not clear whether these two fragments are drawn from a longer poem called 'Returning'. There is no evidence of the longer text, other than that provided by the title. *Poems of Succession* and *Selected Poems* publish them as two poems, titled 'One' and 'Two', with the abbreviated title, *Returning*.

No manuscript exists, but Carter's fair copy typescript is extant in the *Poems of Succession* manuscript. First published in *Kyk-Over-Al*, 5.16 (1953), pp.138-39.

1.

1. *heavy iron:* (1) manacles used on slave ships; (2) manacles of punishment used on the plantations.

2. *twisted leather:* whip.

3. *wet cord stung with cruelty:* Strikes of a leather whip were the most common form of whip punishment in the Caribbean. Rope whips were more common on ships during slavery, but were not unknown in the Caribbean, particularly in workhouses in the early 19th century. 'Stung' suggests whip, but it could

also suggest the tying of hands or feet. I would like to thank Diana Paton for these suggestions.

4. *hot jungle thrusting to a mountain:* Escaped slaves in the Caribbean would head for the interior mountains. In Jamaica and on the South American colonies communities of escaped slaves, known as Maroons (or in Dutch-speaking areas as Djukas), flourished in these areas.

8-9. *Tattered... trousers:* commonly represented dress of male slaves in the Caribbean.

10. *roasted green plantain:* common ground provisions on the plantation.

10. *creek:* Guyanese term for river.

17. *birds who speak like squat brown men:* Many Amerindian cultures have developed a sophisticated ability to mimic animals.

18. *the stretch of Asia over Africa:* Reference to global population movements of Africans and Indians to the Americas.

23. *the gap of footprints and the coin:* Plantation society encouraged a population of bounty hunters, employed to recapture escaped slaves. In the Guianas, Amerindians were often paid to carry out this job.

2.

In this section the poetic voice is ambiguous; it could be the modern poet contemplating (or mentally 'returning' to) the condition of the slave, or it could be the voiced consciousness of the slave, returning to the plantation, or possibly returning to a life of freedom.

36-37. *I dissolve like mist and turn myself to air / golden as liquid fire:* Compare 'Only men of fire will survive / all else will move to ashes and to air' ('The Discovery of Companion').

39. *sea waters crumble:* Compare 'the crumbled waters' [*les eaux écroulées*] in *Cahier d'un retour au pays natal* (AC, 130-31).

40. *wood around my head:* A possible reference to punitive stocks.

COLLATION

41. earth bending nearer like a tree] earth bending nearer – nearer like a tree [PS]; earth bending nearer nearer like a tree [SP1989, SP1997]

53. and behind myself and behind the light and behind the wood around my head] and behind myself and behind the light / and behind the wood around my head [PS, SP1989, SP1997]

54. and behind the crumbling sea waters behind the regions of daylight] and behind the crumbling sea waters / behind the regions of daylight [PS, SP1989, SP1997]

POEMS OF RESISTANCE FROM BRITISH GUIANA (1954) *(84-104)*

Perhaps Carter's most famous collection, *Poems of Resistance from British Guiana* was published in London by Lawrence & Wishart in 1954 (selling at 1s. 6d.). Fourteen of the 18 poems had appeared either in a different form, with a differ-ent title, or independently before the collection was published. The collection was borne out of the PPP's electoral victory, subsequent dismissal and the state of emergency called in British Guiana by the British Governor. Lawrence & Wishart also published Cheddi Jagan's *Forbidden Freedom* in the same year, 1954. The records of the publishers were destroyed by flood, making it now impossible to recover the sequence of decisions leading to publication. It is probable that Janet Jagan, as editor of *Thunder*, either encouraged Carter to send the poems to the publishers, or sent them directly herself. The Communist links of Lawrence & Wishart made them the obvious publishers of a volume lambasting colonialism in the Caribbean and linking the Guyanese political struggle to an international anti-colonial and socialist movement. Lawrence & Wishart in their catalogue write that Carter, 'the foremost poet of the Caribbean people, is a true people's leader' (L&W, 9).

Carter produced several poems under the heading 'Poems of Resistance' before the Lawrence & Wishart publication. A pamphlet (here referenced as PRMagnet) of six anonymously written poems was seized from the Magnet Printery, 29 Holme Street, Georgetown, by police on 29 October 1953, just days after Carter had been arrested (British National Archives CO1031/777). The poems were 'I Will Not Still My Voice', 'This Is the Dark Time My Love', 'Shines the Beauty of My Darling', 'Tomorrow and the World', 'Let Freedom Wake Him' and 'I Clench My Fist'. The archives show that A.J. Seymour was first thought to be the author of the poems, a concern given that Seymour was by then a senior civil servant (CO1031/1177). The US journal, *Masses & Mainstream*, printed these six poems under Carter's name, with the title, 'Six Poems of Resistance', while Carter was imprisoned. See Martin Carter, 'Six Poems of Resistance', *Masses & Mainstream*, 6.12 (December 1953), pp.20-23 (here referenced as PRMasses). In addition, the West Indian Independence Party published the same six poems under the title *I Sing My Song of Freedom: Poems of Resistance* (Port of Spain: Education Department of the West Indian Independence Party, n.d. [*c*. 1953]) (here referenced as PRWIIP). There is a further undated pamphlet (here referenced as PR), titled 'Poems of Resistance', held in the A.J. Seymour Papers in the National Library, Georgetown. A single sheet stating on its cover 'Poems of Resistance by Martin Carter' includes only three poems: 'Shines the Beauty of My Darling', 'Tomorrow and the World' and 'I Clench My Fist'.

The Lawrence & Wishart edition concludes with a letter to the reader and a biographical note written by Phyllis Carter:

Dear Reader,

The author of these poems and four other members of the People's Progressive Party in British Guiana were arrested and kept under detention for over two months without charges being instituted against them and without being brought to trial for any offence alleged to have been committed by them.

Whatever your views concerning events in British Guiana, you will agree that any one deprived of his freedom is entitled to know the reason why, and that he should be brought to trial as speedily as possible for offences committed.

The Guiana Defence Fund has been set up to assist these men, and an English Barrister has been briefed to represent them. The total costs are anticipated to be £1,000.

An appeal is therefore made to all friends in Britain and elsewhere to subscribe to this Fund to assist a cause which needs so very much assistance. Will you please help? Your donation should be sent to:

GUIANA DEFENCE FUND
16 SOHO SQUARE
LONDON, W.1

MARTIN CARTER

Martin Wylde Carter was born in New Amsterdam, British Guiana, in 1927, the son of a civil servant. He obtained his secondary education at Queen's College, Georgetown, which he attended for five years. From college he entered the civil service and worked as a clerk for four years, when he was forced to resign because of his persistent struggle for the rights of his fellow Guianese.

From an early age Martin showed a keen interest in poetry and wrote several poems which remained unpublished. In 1951, however, he published his first poem, *To a Dead Slave*, and some months later he published a collection of poems under the Miniature Poets: *The Hill of Fire Glows Red*. In 1952, he published two collections of poems in prison – *The Kind Eagle* and *The Hidden Man*. In an anthology of West Indian Poetry published this year, Mr A.J. Seymour in his biographical notes, describes him as 'direct and energetic in his poetry which concentrates on social protest'. Mr Sydney King, his contemporary and comrade, in his booklet *Friends of Youth* refers to Martin thus: 'This young poet is an artist with a mirror for spectacles, with an axe in one hand and a watercan in the other. He is an enemy of death, darkness, slavery and meekness. When spoken by him the truth makes us jump.'

This beloved people's poet was arrested along with other leaders of the People's Progressive Party, because 'his freedom constitutes a threat to public safety in his homeland'.

British Guiana, October 1953   PHYLLIS P. CARTER

Two editions of *Poems of Resistance from British Guiana* have been published since 1954. The second edition, *Poems of Resistance*, was published in 1964 by the newly founded University of Guyana, with an introduction by Neville Dawes; the poems were re-ordered, with the additional inclusion of 'A Banner for the Revolution' from *The Hill of Fire Glows Red*. Release Publication (Carter's publisher of *Poems of Affinity*) published the third edition, *Poems of Resistance from Guyana*, in 1979 with the original ordering. Here I have followed the text of the first edition with collations of emendations and textual variations from the other editions. See 'Note on the Text'.

'University of Hunger' *(84)*
No manuscript exists, but Carter's fair copy typescript is extant in the *Poems of Succession* manuscript. First published in *Kyk-Over-Al*, 17 (year end 1953), pp.208-09. Republished, with some alterations, as the first poem in *Poems of Resistance from British Guiana*, pp.1-2. Included in *Poems of Succession* (pp.34-35), but it is ordered third in the selection included from *Poems of Resistance*. In *Poems of Succession* and *Selected Poems*, the first five lines all end with full stops.
University of Hunger: Compare Maxim Gorky's *My Universities* (1923); a pioneer of Soviet socialist realism, Gorky did not attend university. Compare Aimé Césaire: 'you know that it is not from hatred for other races / that I force myself to be the digger of this unique race / that what I want / is for universal hunger / for universal thirst / to summon the race free at last...' (AC, 117-19).
1. *is the university of hunger the wide waste:* Creole phrasing. In SE this might be rendered: (1) It is the university of hunger that is the wide waste; (2) It is

251

the university of hunger, and it is the wide waste; (3) Is the university of hunger the wide waste? (Note that Carter rejected reading [3].)

2. *the long march:* Recalls the Long March of the Chinese Communist Party troops in 1934-35, during which 100,000 troops regrouped, retreating from government forces to complete a 6000-mile trek from southern to northern China.

7. *They come treading in the hoof marks of the mule:* Possible reference to the route taken by villagers coming into the city.

10. *sudden flight:* Compare *Returning* and the flight of slaves from the plantation.

11. *the terror and the time:* This phrase was adopted as the title of Rupert Roopnaraine's and Ray Kril's 1979 film about the 1953 political emergency in Guyana.

12. *distant village of the flood:* Apt description of coastal villages in Guyana.

13. *middle air to middle earth:* See Keats 'Endymion: A Poetic Romance': 'That one who through this middle earth should pass / Most like a sojourning demi-god' (JK, 151 [i *ll.* 723-24]) 'Abrupt, in middle air, his way was lost' (JK, 190 [ii *l.* 656]).

16. *twin seasons:* Drought and flood. Guyana has two rainy and two dry seasons per year.

18. *is the dark ones:* Creole phrasing. The phrase can draw on multiple meanings of 'dark': (1) of African ethnicity; (2) of Indian ethnicity; (3) of non-white skin; (4) unknown, indistinct; (5) obscured, shadowed; (6) concealed, secret; (7) ignorant; (8) non-illuminated; (9) gloomy, sombre; (10) sinister; (11) sad; (12) angry; (13) remote, uncivilised.

23. *mud floor of the year:* Carter describes Guyana as 'province of mud' ('Not I with This Torn Shirt').

24. *dark heavy water:* The Hindi phrase *kala pani* ('black water') translates as 'ocean' and has been used specifically to refer the 19th- and 20th-century crossings of the Atlantic by Indians travelling to the Caribbean as indentured labourers.

26. *O long is the march of men:* Compare William Morris's 'March of the Workers' ' "On we march then, we the workers, and the rumour that ye hear / Is the blended sound of battle and deliv'rance drawing near" ' (WM, 114-15).

28. *is air dust and the long distance of memory:* Creole phrasing. A signal to Africa as an ancestral focal point. I would like to thank Gordon Rohlehr for making this suggestion.

29. *sleepless toads are silent:* Nocturnal frogs inhabit much of Guyana and are widespread in Georgetown.

33. *the broad city:* Georgetown

49. *beating drum:* Use of drums is prevalent in Guyanese cultural expression, from drums associated with obeah practices to the Indian dholak drum and tassa drum used at weddings.

54. *shell blow:* (1) call to slaves to begin work and end work on plantations; (2) fishsellers in Georgetown would blow the conch shell as an announcement; (3) Hindus in Guyana blow the conch shell as part of religious ceremonies; (4) in the early 20th century a conch shell was blown to announce the arrival of mail in the interior.

54. *iron clang:* possible reference to shackles from slavery; or to the slamming of the jail door. Compare 'Clang the illiterate door' ('After One Year').

6. roofs] huts [*Kyk-Over-Al* 1953]

7. hoof marks] hoofmarks [PS, SP1989]; hoof-marks [SP1997]

24. water] waters [*Kyk-Over-Al* 1953, SP1989, SP1997]

28-38. is air dust... is the span.] deleted [PS]

32-33. They come in long lines / toward the broad city] They come in long lines toward the broad city [SP1989, SP1997]

35. floor] flood [*Kyk-Over-Al* 1953]

'I Am No Soldier' *(86)*

No manuscripts exists, but Carter's fair copy typescript is extant in the *Poems of Succession* manuscript. First published in 'Two Poems', *Masses & Mainstream*, 7.5 (May 1954), 49-51 (pp.49-50). Published in *Poems of Resistance from British Guiana*, pp.3-4.

1. *comrade:* A common term of address for members of the PPP, as well as in international socialism.

19. *iron bars:* Compare 'twin bars of hunger' ('University of Hunger').

21-22. *dark island in a dark river... forest of torture:* Mazaruni Prison is located on an island in the Essequibo River, in the interior of the country near Bartica. Cheddi Jagan was imprisoned in this complex in 1954.

35. *Malaya:* See note to 'Shines the Beauty of My Darling'.

37. *Kenya:* In 1954, a British colony, and ruled under a state of emergency since October 1952. The Mau Mau (or Kenya Land and Freedom Army), an anti-colonial militant guerilla movement, and Jomo Kenyatta's Kenya Africa Union, were known to the PPP and reported in *Thunder*. While imprisoned in 1953-54 Carter held a month-long hunger strike partly in protest against British bombing in Kenya.

39. *Korea:* After World War Two, Korea was divided into the Soviet-backed North Korea, under Kim Il-Sung, and the American-backed South Korea, under Syngman Rhee. The invasion of the South by the North in 1950 led to a three-year dispute involving the US, the UN, the Soviet Union, China, the UK and the Commonwealth. The war ended in stalemate; the border was reasserted and a demilitarised zone was created, perhaps occasioning Carter's 'where land is desolate'.

48. *Stalin:* Although Joseph Stalin and the Soviet Union were disgraced in many Socialists' and Communists' eyes by 1954 (and much earlier), he remained popular within the PPP. On his death in March 1953, tributes were published in *Thunder*.

48. *Mao Tse-tung:* Chairman of the Chinese Communist Party in 1935 after the Long March, and created the People's Republic of China in 1949, following the Sino-Japanese War and the Chinese Civil War. His anti-imperial and pro-agrarian stance made him popular with the PPP.

49. *Accabreh:* Also spelt Accabre. A leader of the Berbice Slave Rebellion of 1763, which began on 23 February 1763 at Plantation Magdalenenburg during Dutch rule of the colony and almost simultaneously on the Berbice river. Accabreh worked at Plantation Stevensburg on the Canje river and was probably of Kongo origin. At first the rebellion united Akan, Kongolese and Angolans, and the rebels almost forced the Dutch out of Berbice. Accabreh became more prominent in the military decisions of the rebellion after the leader, Cuffy (also spelt Kofi), committed suicide following a leadership contest. The rebellion was quashed in 1764 after 14 months of conflict. Accabreh was captured and

sentenced to death by the Dutch authorities (see WRS). Compare 'Ancestor Accabreh'.

51. *astronomer of freedom:* Compare John Donne, 'The Good-Morrow' (JDP, 60).

59. *soldier hunting in a jungle:* possible reference to the guerilla tactics used in all the struggles referred to above.

COLLATION

1. Wherever you fall] Whenever you fall [SP1989]

2. Wherever and whenever] Whenever and whenever [SP1989]

15. and pointing at my grandfather's continent, unhappy Africa / unhappy lake] and pointing at my grandfather's continent, unhappy / Africa / unhappy lake [SP1989]

27. nightmare] night mare [PS]

35-36. flesh, like beasts / I shall arise] flesh, like / beasts / I shall arise [PS]

37-38. stain of famine / I shall arise] stain of / famine / I shall arise [PS]

42. I will come to the brave] I shall come to the brave [PR1964]

42. red and yellow flowers blooming in the tall mountains of their nobility] red and / yellow flowers blooming in the tall mountains of their / nobility [PS, SP1989]; red and / yellow flowers blooming in the tall mountains of their nobility [SP1997]

44. Led by thy] Led by my [PR1979, PS, SP1989, SP1997]

59-60. I am no soldier hunting in a jungle / I am this poem like a sacrifice.] deleted [SP1989, SP1997]

'Death of a Slave' *(88)*

No manuscript exists. First published in *Kyk-Over-Al Anthology of West Indian Poetry*, 14 (1952), p.53. Published in *Poems of Resistance from British Guiana*, pp.5-6. Not included in *Poems of Succession.*

green cane arrow: feathery green sprouting on the top of sugar cane.

river... forest... field: These are the dominant topographical features of Guyana: arterial rivers running throughout the country, interior rainforest, and coastal agricultural fields.

Aie!: Compare 'A-a-a-h!' ('O Where to Hide') for apparently non-verbal utterances, often related to the contemplation of slavery or colonialism. Under 'Ai!2' DCEU states possible West African Twi origins for the exclamation: 'ai, aai, aii "ah me!, alas!, woe!"'.

looks / over the world: An aerial perspective that, according to Afro-Caribbean folklore, could be gained as a dead slave flew back to Africa.

This is another world: This line marks a possible shift from the voice of the dying slave to the contemporary voice of the poet; or a temporal shift from the period of slavery to the period of emancipation.

sun falls down like an old man: Quetzalcoatl, associated with the Morning Star, was a serpent-bird god worshipped by the Toltec Mexicans as the bringer of light and fertility. He appeared arched across the sky, and also adopted human form – either a young man in a feathered cloak, or an old man with a broken walking stick and a white beard.

white birds: On the trees along the riverbanks of Guyana white herons can be seen roosting at dusk. In Christianity the white dove is a sign of peace and, when settled on dry land, the dove is associated with the renewed Covenant of the Old Testament. Quetzalcoatl was also represented as a god who would reintroduce a period of peace for the Aztecs.

10. red is heart!] red is the heart! [SP1989, SP1997]
29. biting the neck of a slave] biting the neck of slave [*Kyk-Over-Al* 1952]
30. But sun falls down like an old man] but sun falls down like old man [*Kyk-Over-Al* 1952]
35-51. Night comes from down river...time plants the seeds of anger] [absent in *Kyk-Over-Al* 1952]

'Death of a Comrade' *(90)*

Carter wrote the poem in memory of Ivan Edwards, a trade unionist and fellow Guyanese member of the PPP who drowned while swimming off the coast of Barbados. First published in *Thunder*, 3.5 (May 1952), p.7, on a two-page spread under the headline 'Workers Lose Great Leader', along with a tribute by L.F.S. Burnham ('A Great Man Dies'). Carter's poem appears without note or introduction. However, Janet Jagan, editor of *Thunder* at that time, retained the fair copy manuscript of the poem. At the bottom of the undated, handwritten copy of the poem, a note reads, 'Janet, If you can find space for this you are free to use it. Martin.' Published in *Poems of Resistance from British Guiana*, pp.6-7. Carter's fair copy typescript is extant in the *Poems of Succession* manuscript. The poem was read at Carter's funeral in 1997.

Death must not find us thinking that we die: Compare Milton's assertion in 'Lycidas' (1637), a poem that deals with the death by drowning of a friend: 'Lycidas, your sorrow, is not dead, / Sunk though he be beneath the wat'ry floor' (*ll.* 166-67).

banner... scarlet fold: See note to 'A Banner for the Revolution' on Soviet National Anthem.

Death of a Comrade] For a dead comrade [Jagan manuscript]; For a Dead Comrade [*Thunder* 1952]
1. Death must not find us thinking that we die] Death will not find us thinking that we die [Jagan manuscript]; Death will not find us / thinking that we die [*Thunder* 1952]
12. down and beyond this dark dark lane of rags] down and beyond this / dark dark lane of rags [*Thunder* 1952]
20. for even now the greener leaf explodes] for even now / the greener leaf explodes [*Thunder* 1952]
23. Now from the mourning vanguard moving on] Now, from the mourning / vanguard moving on [Jagan manuscript, *Thunder* 1952]
24. dear Comrade I salute you and I say] Dear Comrade I salute you / and I say [*Thunder* 1952]
25. Death will not find us thinking that we die] Death must not find us thinking that we die [Jagan manuscript]; Death must not find us / thinking that we die [*Thunder* 1952]

'Not Hands Like Mine' *(91)*

No manuscript exists of this poem, but Carter's fair copy typescript is extant in the *Poems of Succession* manuscript. First published as '"New Day"' in *Kyk-Over-Al*, 12 (mid year 1951), p.114. Republished in *Kyk-Over-Al Anthology of Guianese Poetry*, 19 (year end 1954), pp.64-65. Published in *Poems of Resistance from British Guiana*, pp.7-8, where the punctuation, layout and capitalisations were revised. This new poem was titled, 'Not Hands Like Mine'. These revisions were retained in the 1964 and 1979 editions. Several more changes in punctuation and layout were made when 'Not Hands Like Mine' was published as the opening poem to the selection from *Poems of Resistance* in *Poems of Succession*. The *Selected Poems* versions of 'Not Hands Like Mine' are different in layout from earlier versions. '"New Day"' was the first poem by Carter to be published in its entirety in *Kyk-Over-Al*.

Carib altars: Walter Roth claims that Carib islanders 'dedicated no temples or altars to their divinities' (WR, 161). Carter may be referring to the 'consulting room' of Carib *piais* (medicine men), constructed from 'kokerite leaves set up on end' (WR, 334). J. Walter Fewkes offers another reading: 'Locally [in the Lesser Antilles] the boulders on which these pictographs occur are called "jumbles" or "altar" stones, the latter term implying a belief in their former use in sacrifices. The West Indian pictographs resemble those of Porto Rico on the one hand, and of British Guiana, on the other, and generally occur near the shore or on the banks of streams, convenient to landing places' (JWF).

forgotten are the gods: Colonialism in the Americas saw the increasing marginalisation of Amerindians, and their belief systems.

silent people: George Simon suggests 'it is necessary to be silent so that one hears the voices of the spirits. To this day no one really knows why the Amerindian speaks in whispering tones. The forest, savannahs, mountains and rivers demand that they be approached in quietude and reverence. It is a code of conduct to walk in the forest silently' (private correspondence, 24 November 2005).

spend: The present tense forces us to consider the contemporary rights and visibility of Amerindians in colonial Guyana.

not like more human years: Lines 7 to 10 make grammatical sense if this line is read as a parenthetical statement, describing the present's difference from 'more human', perhaps humane, times.

aged and brown their rivers flow away: The leaf- and bark-stained brown rivers of Guyana are mostly named in Amerindian vocabulary.

ocean's flood: reference to Guyana's position below sea-level.

muttering sea: Compare D.H. Lawrence's *Sons and Lovers*: 'Again he saw her, the merest white speck moving against the white, muttering sea-edge' (DHL, 402). See also Vastey's response to Henri Christophe's plan to build his new kingdom, in Derek Walcott's play *Henri Christophe: A Chronicle* (1950): 'That one [hill], where the gulls achieve halfway, / Then slide back screaming to a muttering sea?' (DWHC, 40). It is unknown whether Carter had read *Henri Christophe* or seen it performed, but both he and Walcott would probably have read *Sons and Lovers*, and the notion of a 'muttering sea' – with its implication of drowned people and aggrieved voices – could have had increased relevance for writers attuned to the history of slavery and the middle passage in the Caribbean.

right at my feet / my strangled city lies: Compare the Priest of Zeus in Sophocles' *Oedipus the King:* 'lift this state so that it falls no more!' (*l.* 50).

a slave: Carter's poetic voice is tied to the genealogy of slavery in the Caribbean. The reference to slavery can refer to Amerindian as well as African enslavement. Compare *To a Dead Slave*, 'Listening to the Land', 'Death of a Slave'.

new day: Redolent phrase in the British West Indies. V.S. Reid's novel, *New Day* (1949) is a fictionalised account of the 1865 Morant Bay Rebellion in Jamaica, representing the awakening of Jamaican national consciousness and resistance to British imperialism (VR).

killing my rice: The flooded rice padi. The cultivation of rice is mostly asso-
ciated with Indian and Chinese labourers in the Caribbean.
COLLATION
Not Hands Like Mine] "New Day" [*Kyk-Over-Al* 1951]
11-12. Yes / pressing on my land] yes, pressing on my land [*Kyk-Over-Al*
1951, PS, SP1989, SP1997]
25. Now still are the fields] Now still / are the fields [PS, SP1989, SP1997]
26. the flood] the floods [PS, SP1989, SP1997]

'Letter 1' *(92)*

No manuscript exists, but Carter's fair copy typescript is extant in the *Poems of
Succession* manuscript. First published as 'Letter from Prison' in 'Two Poems',
Masses & Mainstream, 7.5 (May 1954), 49-51 (pp.50-51). Published in *Poems
of Resistance from British Guiana*, pp.8-9. Most probably composed during
Carter's imprisonment at Atkinson Field. Phyllis Carter believes that this
could have been one of the poems that she smuggled out for her husband.
Each prisoner was only allowed one visitor at Atkinson Field and written
permission was needed from the authorities. Mrs Carter, a nurse at Georgetown
Hospital, had been caring for David Rose (a prominent Guyanese-born govern-
ment official) who was recovering from typhoid. Mrs Carter asked if he could
help, and he arranged for her to get permission to visit her husband. Mrs
Carter was never searched when she visited Atkinson Field.
they: the British authorities
in prison: Carter was imprisoned at Atkinson Field US air base along with
Sydney King (now Eusi Kwayana), Rory Westmaas, Bally Latchmansingh and
Adjodha Singh.
nor kill my thoughts, nor murder what I write: Carter's work was not officially
banned in Guyana, but personal and PPP papers were confiscated from his
home, and an early version of *Poems of Resistance* was destroyed at the Magnet
Printery in 1953. See introductory note to *Poems of Resistance from British Guiana.*
Proud as the tree the axeman cannot tumble: Inversion of well-known Caribbean
proverb 'little axe cut down big tree'.
In Kenya today they drink the blood of black women: Carter inverts stereotypical
images of the guerilla Mau Mau (or Kenya Land and Freedom Army) and the
British forces as reported in the British press. Mau Mau initiation ceremonies
involved blood sacrifice, leading to accusations of barbarism (WOM, 73).
In Malaya the hero is hunted and shot like a dog: Readers of the Socialist press
would have seen critical coverage of British forces during the Malayan Emergency.
My son: Carter's first son, Keith, was born in May 1953 before Carter was
imprisoned.

'Letter 2' *(93)*

No manuscript exists, but Carter's fair copy typescript is extant in the *Poems of
Succession* manuscript. If we accept the documentary status of the reference to
'twenty days', we can date the composition of this poem as between 14 and 15
November 1953. First published in *Poems of Resistance from British Guiana*,
pp.9-10.
twenty days and twenty nights in prison: Carter was arrested on 25 October 1953 at
Plantation Blairmont. After a night in the plantation prison, Carter and his four
PPP comrades were transferred the next day by armed guard to Atkinson Field.

14-15. *my darling... my dear wife:* Phyllis Carter *née* Howard. It took two days to discover the location of Carter. Although the road from Georgetown was unmetalled, Phyllis Carter regularly visited her husband.

16. *creeping:* Guyanese Creole, referring (especially to children) to crawling on all fours.

23. *I cannot come to the city:* Atkinson Field was 25 miles from Georgetown, on the eastern bank of the Demerara River.

25. *sharp vines of barbed wire:* As a US air base, we can presume the perimeter of Atkinson Field was bounded with barbed wire.

32. *let our red banner fly in the city:* Banned activity in the colony during the Emergency.

COLLATION
25. sharp vines] sharp lines [PR1964]

'Letter 3' *(94)*

No manuscript exists, but Carter's fair copy typescript is extant in the *Poems of Succession* manuscript. First published in *Poems of Resistance from British Guiana*, pp.10-11.

A soldier marching: Soldiers were positioned at Atkinson Field during the Emergency.

'Let Freedom Wake Him' *(94)*

No manuscript exists, but Carter's fair copy typescript is extant in the *Poems of Succession* manuscript. First intended for publication in PRMagnet. First published in 'Six Poems of Resistance', *Masses & Mainstream*, 6.12 (December 1953), 20-23 (pp.22-23), and also included in PRWIIP. Published in *Poems of Resistance from British Guiana*, p.11. The discussion of 'a soldier searching for me' probably dates the composition as between 8 and 25 October 1953, the period between the arrival of British soldiers and Carter's arrest.

little one: Keith Carter.

my little child lies sleeping / Let freedom wake him – not a bayonet point: Carter's house was searched while he was imprisoned. Some papers and poems were hidden under the sheets of Keith Carter's cot as he slept. I would like to thank Phyllis Carter for this information.

songs of freedom: Compare 'I Clench My Fist'; Carter may also have known Paul Robeson's film *Song of Freedom* (1936), as Robeson contributed to *Thunder*.

COLLATION
4. heart in heart] heart in hand [PRWIIP]
10. morn green] morn the green [PRMagnet]
11. Here] Hear [PRWIIP]

'Till I Collect' *(95)*

No manuscript exists, but Carter's fair copy typescript is extant in the *Poems of Succession* manuscript. First published in *The Hidden Man* (Georgetown: Author, 1952), pp.3-4. Published in *Poems of Resistance from British Guiana*, pp.11-12. Included in *Selected Poems* under *The Hidden Man*.

moon is blood: See Peter in Acts 2. 20: 'The sun shall be turned into darkness, and the moon into blood, before that great and notable day of the Lord come.' A common description of a lunar eclipse (where sunlight is refracted though the earth's atmosphere creating a red glow on the moon).

fence of lights: During Divali (the Hindu festival of lights that is celebrated in Guyana during the October/November new moon), lamps (called 'diyas') line and illuminate fences, driveways, windows, to symbolise the triumph of light over darkness.

The fisherman: Compare Jesus's command to Peter, the fisherman: 'Put out into the deep water and let down your nets for a catch' (Luke 5. 4).

the islands of the stars: a mirror of the Caribbean archipelago.

my scattered skeleton: Alludes to (1) the Caribbean archipelago; (2) fragmented historical identity; (3) fragmented slave ancestry; (4) Armageddon.

'Cartman of Dayclean' *(96)*

No manuscript exists, but Carter's fair copy typescript is extant in the *Poems of Succession* manuscript. First published in *The Hidden Man*, pp.1-2. Published in *Poems of Resistance from British Guiana*, p.12. Published as part of *Poems of Resistance* in *Poems of Succession* and as part of *The Hidden Man* in *Selected Poems.* Carter provided the voice for a reading of the poem in Rupert Roopnaraine and Ray Kril's Guyanese film, *The Terror and the Time*. It was accompanied by 1970s footage of a man driving his horse and cart to Georgetown.

iron cartwheel: In the 1950s it was common (as today) for horse-pulled dray carts to be used to bring goods into Georgetown.

hidden man consistent in the dark: In the Bible Peter uses the phrase 'hidden man' to mean 'soul' or 'conscience'. 'Whose adorning let it not be that outward adorning of plaiting the hair, and of wearing of gold, or of putting on of apparel; But let it be the hidden man of the heart, in that which is not corruptible' (I Peter 3. 3-4).

day clean: Creole term used throughout the Caribbean, meaning daybreak or dawn.

appellant man: legal term, referring to the maker of appeals.

cupric: of the quality of copper.

till journey done: Creole phrasing. The contrast with SE is in the omission of the copula verb 'is'.

COLLATION

5. day clean] dayclean [PS, SP1989, SP1997]
14. iron wheel will spark] iron wheels will spark [HM, SP1989, SP1997]

'Weroon Weroon' *(97)*

No manuscript exists, but Carter's fair copy typescript is extant in the *Poems of Succession* manuscript. First published in *Poems of Resistance from British Guiana*, p.13.

Weroon Weroon: My God, My God. I would like to thank George Simon for this translation.

benab: See note to *l.* 180 in *To a Dead Slave.*

hammock: traditional Amerindian bed.

calabash: A gourd indigenous to Guyana, often used for carrying liquid.

Land of the waters: 'Guiana/Guyana' in Arawak means 'land of many waters'.

corial: See note to *l.* 149 in *To a Dead Slave.*

'The Knife of Dawn' *(98)*

Undated fair copy manuscript held in the Box File 'Non-AJS Poems' in the A.J. Seymour Room, University of Guyana. Carter's fair copy typescript is extant in the *Poems of Succession* manuscript. First published as 'The Kind Eagle' in *The Kind Eagle*, p.5.

the kind eagle: See note to 'All of a Man' in *The Kind Eagle*.

endure the spike: See note on the ramparts in 'O Human Guide' in *The Kind Eagle*.

pillar feet: the poet becomes here the finished monument, carved out of 'a jagged block of convict years'.

COLLATION

The Knife of Dawn] The Kind Eagle [KE, PS, SP1989, SP1997]

2. wall of prison] wall of a prison [KE, PS, SP1989, SP1997]

10. block of convict] block convict [PR1954]

19. drench] drown [KE, PS, SP1989, SP1997]

'This Is the Dark Time My Love' *(99)*

No manuscript exists, but Carter's fair copy typescript is extant in the *Poems of Succession* manuscript. Phyllis Carter believes that this could have been one of the poems that she smuggled out of Atkinson Field during Carter's imprisonment. First intended for publication in PRMagnet. First published in 'Six Poems of Resistance', *Masses & Mainstream*, 6.12 (December 1953), 20-23 (pp.20-21), and also included in PRWIIP. Published in *Poems of Resistance from British Guiana*, p.14.

dark time: Compare Bertolt Brecht, 'Motto to the Svendborg Poems': 'In the dark times / Will there also be singing? / Yes, there will be singing / About the dark times' (BB, 320).

carnival: Like most of the southern Americas, Guyana holds a carnival (now known as Mashramani), and is similar to Mardi Gras and Trinidad's Carnival.

COLLATION

2. all round] all around [PR1964]

11. strange invader] stranger invader [PR1964]

'I Clench My Fist' *(100)*

No manuscript exists, but Carter's fair copy typescript is extant in the *Poems of Succession* manuscript. Phyllis Carter believes that this poem could have been smuggled out while Carter was imprisoned. First intended for publication in PRMagnet. First published in 'Six Poems of Resistance', *Masses & Mainstream*, 6.12 (December 1953), 20-23 (p.23), and also included in PRWIIP. Included under the title 'I Clinch My Fist' in the undated 'Poems of Resistance' pamphlet, PR. Published in *Poems of Resistance from British Guiana*, pp.14-15.

warships: British troops were brought to Guyana by boat. A warship is featured on the front cover of the first edition of *Poems of Resistance from British Guiana*.

Korean blood: See note on Korea in 'I am No Soldier'.

finger trembles on a trigger: After his arrest in 1953, Carter was transferred under armed guard from Plantation Blairmont to Atkinson Field.

curse: Although the phrase 'to put a curse on' is obviously implied here, the dominant meaning in the Caribbean would be 'to abuse loudly and angrily' (DCEU).

Accabreh: See note to Accabreh in 'I Am No Soldier'. Compare 'Ancestor Accabreh'.

come in thousands: 500 British soldiers landed in British Guiana on 8 October 1953 (CO1031/1166).

point your gun straight at my heart: See note above, to *finger trembles on a trigger*.

I Clench My Fist] I Clinch My Fist [PR]

7. Accabreh] Accabre [PR, PRMagnet, PRWIIP]

9. night] nights [PRMagnet]

10. eyes] eye [PR, PRMagnet, PRMasses, PRWIIP]

13. come] came [PRMagnet]

15. although you point] although point [PRMagnet]

16. clench] clinch [PR]

16. song of FREEDOM] song of freedom [PR, PRMagnet, PRMasses, PRWIIP, SP1989, SP1997]

'I Come from the Nigger Yard' *(101)*

Undated fair copy manuscript held in Box File 'Non-AJS Poems', A.J. Seymour Room, University of Guyana. Carter's fair copy typescript is extant in the *Poems of Succession* manuscript. This poem was not published in *Kyk-Over-Al*, but the poem had evidently been to sent to Seymour. There is no accompanying letter so we can only speculate about the circumstances of its composition. First published in *Poems of Resistance from British Guiana*, pp.15-17. The poem features in the film, *The Terror and the Time* (1979). I have corrected four apparent errors in PR1954, following the fair copy manuscript. See collation, lines 2, 11, 53 and 55.

1. *nigger yard:* Yard is the name given to dwellings in the Caribbean and implies either a shared dwelling, or an individual one carved out of a larger one (e.g. a room in a house or a shack built in the yard of a house). Here it can refer to the simple, often shared and overcrowded, dwellings of slaves, indentured workers and paid workers who worked on the plantations in Guyana. It also refers to an enclosed exterior area in slum districts.

3. *scorn of myself:* Compare Carter's essay, 'A Question of Self-Contempt'.

8. *who cannot see will hear:* A possible rephrasing of Creole grammar (e.g. who kyan see, mus 'ear). I would like to thank Peter Patrick for this suggestion.

15. *searching the dust:* The floors of the plantation dwellings were commonly made of packed earth.

18. *meeting strange faces:* Compare W.B. Yeats's 'Easter, 1916': 'I have met them at close of day / Coming with vivid faces' (WBY, 181).

24-25. *sad music... / like a bugle and a drum:* instruments commonly played at military funerals.

47. *a coffin space for home:* Compare Emily Dickinson's 'A Coffin – is a small Domain' (ED, poem no. 943).

60-61. *hammers...anvils:* Combines the two prominent emblems of the Communist Party and the Spanish Socialist Workers Party.

64. *whores:* Compare 'all origins of creation, whores and virgins' ('Black Friday, 1962').

2. oppressor's] oppressors [PR1954, PS]; oppressors' [PR1979, SP1989, SP1997]

11. rocking] racking [PR1954]

47. and a coffin] and coffin [PS, SP1989, SP1997]

53. angry] anger [PR1954, PR1979]

55. bleeding her life in clots] bleeding her of her blood life clots [PR1954]

'On the Fourth Night of Hunger Strike' *(103)*

No manuscript exists, but Carter's fair copy typescript is extant in the *Poems of Succession* manuscript. If we are to accept the timing of four days within the poem, we can date the composition of this poem to approximately 27 November 1953. This contradicts Carter's discussion of 'December' in the poem. First published in *Poems of Resistance from British Guiana*, p.18.

I have not eaten for four days: Hunger strike began on 23 November 1953 to complain about the diet in the internment camp; the fact of martial law in British Guiana; the injustice of indefinite detention; and the use of heavy bombers in the British government's fight against the Mau Mau in Kenya. See note to Kenya in 'I Am No Soldier'.

my comrade lies in his bed: Sydney King, Rory Westmaas, Ajodha Singh and Bally Latchmansingh were imprisoned with Carter, although Latchmansingh was released early due to ill-health.

Christmas: Carter and his comrades were told that they might be released before Christmas.

my wife brought me a letter: Phyllis Carter believes it would have been a letter from Janet Jagan.

'You Are Involved' *(104)*

First published in *The Kind Eagle* [n.p., p.4]. Published in *Poems of Resistance from British Guiana*, p.18. Not included in *Poems of Succession*.

jig: (1) a structure to hold and guide tools for the manufacture of goods; (2) a dance.

web: Anancy, the Yoruba and now Afro-Caribbean spider god, is known as a trickster. He is hero and villain or anti-hero of many folktales.

COLLATION

4-5. hero or monster / you are consumed!] hero or monster / You are involved! / You are consumed! [KE]

THREE POEMS OF SHAPE AND MOTION – A SEQUENCE (1955) *(105-08)*

First published in *Kyk-Over-Al*, these poems cemented Carter's relationship with the journal. It was now the forum to which Carter most often turned to release his work. His relationship with the editor, A.J. Seymour, was friendly, and Seymour seems to have published almost all the poems that Carter submitted without editorial intervention. There are no records of the publication of these poems, nor manuscripts, but it should be noted that the poems were published while Carter was deemed a rebellious member of the PPP. His profile as a Communist-supporting activist meant that Seymour's decision to publish Carter's work was a brave editorial act.

'Number One' *(105)*

No manuscript exists but Carter's fair copy typescript is extant in the *Poems of Succession* manuscript. First published in *Three Poems of Shape and Motion – A Sequence*, *Kyk-Over-Al*, 20 (year-end 1955), 141-43 (p.141). A revised version of this poem was published in *Poems of Succession* (London and Port of Spain: New Beacon, 1977) under the title 'Shape and Motion One' in a section titled *Poems of Shape and Motion*.

space in my soul / be filled by the shape I become: Compare Aimé Césaire in 'Poetry and Knowledge': 'The poet approaches the poem not just with his whole soul but with his whole being' (MRKF, 138).

6. I was wondering if I could stand as tall] I was wondering if I could as tall [*Kyk-Over-Al* 1955]
10. door of morning] door of the morning [PS, SP1989, SP1997]

'Number Two' *(106)*

No manuscript exists. First published in *Three Poems of Shape and Motion – A Sequence*, *Kyk-Over-Al*, 20 (year-end 1955), 141-43 (pp.141-42). This poem was excluded from the selection in *Poems of Succession*, but reinstated in *Selected Poems*.

Pull off yuh shirt: Compare 'Run Shouting Through the Town' for the carnivalesque impulses in Carter's poetry.

yuh… 'way: Along with 'Old Higue', these are the only poems in which Carter uses obvious Creole orthography.

left foot, right foot: Possible reference to the road marching of Carnival.

boy: Form of address that in the Caribbean is historically associated with servitude, but is here exclamatory.

Far   far: The layout is deliberate and is reproduced in *Selected Poems*.

COLLATION
4. you] yuh [SP1989, SP1997]
8-9. Run down the road / Run up the sky] Run up the sky / Run down the road [SP1989, SP1997]

'Number Three' *(107)*

No manuscript exists but Carter's fair copy typescript is extant in the *Poems of Succession* manuscript. First published in *Three Poems of Shape and Motion – A Sequence*, *Kyk-Over-Al*, 20 (year-end 1955), 141-43 (pp.142-43). Published in *Poems of Succession* and *Selected Poems*, but without the section headings.

walk slowly: contrasting with the contemplative first poem, and riotous second poem.

I walk because I cannot crawl or fly: Carter draws on the distinction between living things but does not repeat the hierarchy of mankind in Genesis 1:26: 'let them have dominion over the fish of the sea, and over the fowl of the air, and over the cattle, and over all the earth, and over every creeping thing that creepeth upon the earth'.

COLLATION
15. that walk and deeds] that walk / and deeds [SP1989, SP1997]
29-32. I walk slowly…all the life of man] deleted [PS, SP1989, SP1997]

CONVERSATIONS (1961) *(109-12)*

A gap of six years separated the collection from Carter's last sequence of poems. He had published individual poems in the intervening years, but this was the first sequence. Published in *Kyk-Over-Al*, the poems were laid out in a two-page spread, in italics, without titles, and each poem was separated by the icon of a star. Following Carter's conventional approach, they appeared without comment. A bound copy of *Conversations* is held in the National Library, Georgetown, suggesting that the sequence was also distributed as off-prints.

[They say I am a poet write for them] *(109)*
Fair copy manuscript held by Ian McDonald in his Martin Carter File for *Kyk-Over-Al*, and Carter's fair copy typescript is extant in the *Poems of Succession* manuscript. First published in Conversations, *Kyk-Over-Al*, 28 (1961), 154-55 (p.154). The first in the sequence and titled as 'They Say I Am' in *Poems of Succession* (p.61) and *Selected Poems* (p.73).
write for them: Homophone of 'right'. Phyllis Carter remembers her husband saying 'Look at these people asking me to write for them'.
the dying…the unborn: Carter's readers mark the temporal boundaries of society.
born again: See John's acceptance in the Bible that the seed needs to die before it can be reborn as wheat: 'Verily, verily, I say unto you, Except a corn of wheat fall into the ground and die, it abideth alone: but if it die, it bringeth forth much fruit' (John 12.24).
COLLATION
8. Or for the unborn] or the unborn [PS, SP1989, SP1997]

[I dare not keep too silent, face averted] *(109)*
Fair copy manuscript held by Ian McDonald in his Martin Carter File for *Kyk-Over-Al*. First published in Conversations, *Kyk-Over-Al*, 28 (1961), 154-55 (p.154). This poem is not included in *Poems of Succession* or *Selected Poems*.
I dare not keep too silent, face averted / That tells too much, it gives the heart away: A vow of silence is often associated with spiritual devotion. *Qalb* (heart) and *hahut* (silence) are key words in Sufism (a religion that interested Carter), and central to gaining *hikmat* (religious wisdom).
smiling lips: Derogatory, as in 'skin-teeth'. Compare Guyanese proverb: 'every skin-teet[h] ain['t] a laugh' (DCEU, 512).
silence of the heart: Compare Albert Camus on suicide in *The Myth of Sisyphus*: 'An act like this is prepared within the silence of the heart, as is a great work of art' (ACMS, 12).
laugh and talk and drink: at this time informal drinking sessions took place on a Sunday at the Anira Street house in Georgetown, Carter's former family home, where his brother Keith and his mother, Violet, lived. There was a theatricality to these meetings where the participants honed a peculiar brand of Guyanese absurdism. David de Caires remembers: 'We would all be drinking rum […] and then poetry would be recited, often the same stuff week after week. […] One I think I mentioned to you was that passage near the end of "Easter 1916". Keith [Carter] would sometimes recite Pericles' "Funeral Oration", and Rory [Westmaas] would sing a song from the Spanish Civil War. […] And then Martin would jump up, and the first time this happened I was deeply shocked because I thought something would happen. He would say "I can't stand these people any longer" at the top of his voice "this place is unbearable. I don't know how I can live in it. These are not people, these are swine".'

[The wild men in prisons, they who rot like rust!] *(110)*
Fair copy manuscript held by Ian McDonald in his Martin Carter File for *Kyk-Over-Al*, and Carter's fair copy typescript is extant in the *Poems of Succession* manuscript. First published in Conversations, *Kyk-Over-Al*, 28 (1961), 154-55 (p.154). Third in the sequence and titled as 'Who Can Share?' in *Poems of Succession* (p.63) and *Selected Poems* (p.75).

The loud men who cry freedom and are so full of lies: the Constitutional Conference of 1960 and the elections of August 1961 had provided many opportunities for the discussion of British Guiana's political independence. Carter had resigned himself from formal politics *circa* 1956, and this poem could be seen as a condemnation of the ambitions of the political parties in British Guiana. Compare 'shining governments of the damned' ('After One Year') and 'Where Are Free Men'.

prisoners, politicians and drunk men: Three prominent social roles that Carter played throughout his life.

What only souls that blaze and burn can win: A common image in Christianity, Islam, Buddhism and Hinduism for religious wisdom.

COLLATION

3. the street!] the street [C]
7. To prisoners] With prisoners [PS, SP1989, SP1997]

[Trying with words to purify disgust] *(110)*

Fair copy manuscript held by Ian McDonald in his Martin Carter File for *Kyk-Over-Al*, and Carter's fair copy typescript is extant in the *Poems of Succession* manuscript. First published in Conversations, *Kyk-Over-Al*, 28 (1961), 154-55 (pp.154-55). It appears fourth in sequence in *Poems of Succession* and *Selected Poems* and is titled 'To Substitute a Temple' (p.64 and p.76).

Trying with words to purify disgust: Carter appeared on BBC Radio with Fred D'Aguiar and Grace Nichols in 1992, talking about the purpose of poetry. Discussing Nichols's 'Blackout', D'Aguiar said, 'If it wasn't for the articulacy of the writing, it would be a picture that is utterly depressing'. Carter replied, 'Of course. It has to liberate her from precisely what she's saying, so that she knows it better for having written it and therefore she has acquired some psychological distance from the raw, empirical fact. In doing so, of course, there are two gains, I think. One is for Grace as a person, and also for people who will read it and who would come to realise that it is possible to know it and not to be defeated by it. So there is a possibility of triumph through a work of art; that art should not only be communication – the word that everybody talks about – but also a triumph of the spirit' (SB, 329).

To substitute a temple for a shop: See John 2.15-16, in which Jesus clears the temple of market-traders: 'he drove them all out of the temple, and the sheep, and the oxen; and poured out the changers' money, and overthrew the tables; And said unto them that sold doves, Take these things hence; make not my Father's house an house of merchandise.'

[Now there was one whom I knew long ago] *(111)*

Fair copy manuscript held by Ian McDonald in his Martin Carter File for *Kyk-Over-Al*. First published in *Conversations, Kyk-Over-Al*, 28 (1961), 154-55 (p.155). Not included in *Poems of Succession*. Sixth and last in the sequence that appears in *Selected Poems*, titled 'Now There Was One' (p.78).

But all is gone: Compare W.B. Yeats's 'September 1913': 'Romantic Ireland's dead and gone' (WBY, 108).

They did not mean to kill only to burn: presentiment of the violence that would characterise Guyana in the early 1960s.

[Groaning in this wilderness of silence] *(111)*
Fair copy manuscript held by Ian McDonald in his Martin Carter File for *Kyk-Over-Al*, and Carter's fair copy typescript is extant in the *Poems of Succession* manuscript. First published in *Conversations, Kyk-Over-Al*, 28 (1961), 154-55 (p.155). Second in the sequence and titled as 'Groaning in this Wilderness' in *Poems of Succession* (p.62) and *Selected Poems* (p.74).

wilderness of silence...voices hardly human shout at me: See Matthew 4:1: 'Then was Jesus led up of the Spirit into the wilderness to be tempted of the devil'.
pavement in the city: The wilderness is topicalised as Georgetown.
Seeing a human turn into a dog...when I tried to utter words – I barked: Compare 'Every few weeks or so, some official or expert or advisor arrives in British Guiana, and, after spending a few days in the company of assorted reactionaries, completes the visit by making oracular disquisitions either about the Soviet Union or "the communist conspiracy to rule the world", or some such thing, all very much in the manner of the character Shakespeare parodied by crediting with the lines: "I am Sir Oracle, when I open my mouth let no dogs bark".' Martin Carter, 'An American Oracle', *Kyk-Over-Al: A Martin Carter Prose Sampler*, 44 (May 1993), 45-47 (p.45). [First published in *Thunder*, 24 August 1954.] Also compare Shakespeare, *The Merchant of Venice*: 'There are a sort of men whose visages / Do cream and mantle like a standing pond, / And do a wilful stillness entertain / With purpose to be dressed in an opinion / Of wisdom, gravity, profound conceit, / As who should say, "I am Sir Oracle, / And when I do ope my lips, let no dog bark"' (I. 1. 88-94). The barking voice of the poet thus holds a number of implications: the poet can be protesting, that is his bark can be read as a paradoxically articulate response to the Sir Oracles surrounding him. However, the poet can also be a Sir Oracle – a false prophet – barking, but saying nothing.
COLLATION
11. nodded] noddled [C]

[In a great silence I hear approaching rain] *(112)*
Fair copy manuscript held by Ian McDonald in his Martin Carter File for *Kyk-Over-Al*, and Carter's fair copy typescript is extant in the *Poems of Succession* manuscript. First published in *Conversations, Kyk-Over-Al*, 28 (1961), 154-55 (p.155). Fifth in the sequence and titled 'So That We Build' in *Poems of Succession* (p.62) and *Selected Poems* (p.74).
a sound of conflict in the sky: Carter's words are prophetic of the following years' violence.
What we have lost in floods of misery: The reference to the Biblical flood is also a reminder that Guyana's coastal belt suffers from periodic flooding.

JAIL ME QUICKLY (1964) *(113-16)*
At the end of 1964 Carter offered *Jail Me Quickly* to David de Caires to publish in *New World Fortnightly*, a new Guyanese magazine that de Caires edited with another lawyer, Miles Fitzpatrick. The goal of the magazine was to offer a forum for political and cultural debate that was non-partisan, but which interrogated the post-colonial future of Guyana and the Caribbean. When de Caires received the poems he was not able to pay Carter, nor did Carter ask for payment: 'This fabulous series of poems were given to us. We were a

struggling little magazine publishing four, five, six hundred copies at best and this recognised poet gave us these poems.' The editors of *New World Fortnightly* republished the five poems in 1966 with an introduction by Ian McDonald. McDonald notes that the poems 'created a considerable impression' when they were first published (IM, 19). Note that in the *Poems of Succession* manuscript, Carter dated *Jail Me Quickly* as 1963.

'Black Friday 1962' *(113)*

No manuscript exists, but Carter's fair copy typescript is extant in the *Poems of Succession* manuscript. First published in *New World Fortnightly*, 2 (13 November 1964), pp.5-6, with the following note: 'Mr Carter has given us several poems under the general title "Jail Me Quickly". In this issue we publish the first two' (p.5). This poem was not published until two years after the event it describes. In the time between the event and publication, violence in Guyana had escalated and new elections had been set for December 1964. Republished as a continuous sequence, with an introduction by Ian McDonald in *New World Fortnightly*, 34 (18 February 1966), 19-25 (p.21).

Black Friday 1962: On 16 February 1962, riots broke out in Georgetown. Cheddi Jagan's PPP was in power and was attempting to implement the Kaldor budget (named after Nicholas Kaldor, an economist from Cambridge University brought in by the PPP via the United Nations to offer tax recommendations). At the time, *The Catholic Standard* reported that thousands of people were protesting against the budget (AM, 13). One sign erected outside Government House read: 'Slavery begins if Jagan wins Independence now' (AM, 14). The general strike was motivated by political competition, racial division, historical differences, imperial and Cold War concerns. Guyana was politically divided between the predominantly Indian-Guyanese PPP and the predominantly African-Guyanese PNC (led by Forbes Burnham). The sign outside Government House articulated the fear that Jagan, and therefore the Indians and the Communists whom he represented, would inherit the colony. Slavery became a metaphor for new deprivations that would face African-Guyanese people in Jagan's independent Guyana, as well as for the economic loss of freedom that all Guyanese people would suffer if the Communist PPP kept power. *The Catholic Standard* blamed Jagan for his combative approach to demonstrations and the general strike; Jagan argued that the strike was manipulated by US and British imperial interests to remove him from power. Demonstrations were banned, the centre of Georgetown was burned down, tear gas was used on the protesters, large-scale looting took place and Jagan called in British troops to regain order on the streets. Carter and his brother, Keith, were both on the streets and injured during the riots on Black Friday. Carter's daughter, Sonia Dolphin, recalls that they went out to see what demonstrations were taking place. Eusi Kwayana (formerly Sydney King) suggests that they played a more active role in the protests. Confidential reports to the Colonial Office also reported the brothers' active role (CO1031/4029-30). Dolphin remembers that Keith was shot in the hip and that Carter was wounded in the arm and that her mother had to dress their wounds (SD; EKI).

were some: Draws on Creole phrasing in omitting the pronoun [in SE: There were some...].

city of clerks...city of men: Compare W.B. Yeats's 'Easter, 1916': 'I have met them at close of day / Coming with vivid faces / From counter or desk among grey / Eighteenth-century houses' (WBY, 180).

whole of a morning sky: Phrase used as the title of Grace Nichols's first novel, *Whole of a Morning Sky* (London: Virago, 1986).

hair was a mass of fire: In ancient mythology Phaeton, son of Phoebus/Helios/ Apollo, over-ambitiously asked to ride the chariot of the sun for a day. His father reluctantly agreed, fearing that his mortal son would not be able to carry out this divine action. Phoebus failed, setting the world on fire. He fell to earth, his body and hair in flames, becoming a shooting star.

hand upon a groin: Common mode of swearing an oath in the ancient world. See Genesis 24.2, 'Put, I pray thee, thy hand under my thigh'.

For is only one way, one path, one road: Creole phrasing omits the pronoun 'there' or 'it'.

dead who shoot: Rioters were fired on by the police during the disturbances of 16 February 1962.

creatures rise from holes: Phrase suggests a brief victory against a repressive tide, but note that the image of 'crabs in a barrel', scrambling ahead of one another, is a common Guyanese proverbial reference to competitive human nature.

claw a triumph like a citizen: In ancient Rome a victorious General could be allowed to make a processional entry (a triumph) into the city.

vultures practising to wait: Vultures, or carrion crows as they are known in Guyana, are a common sight.

True, was with them all: Creole phrasing omits the pronoun. In SE it could be understood as 'Truly, I was with them all'. 'I' is plausible but it is not the only possibility.

now I repeat it here: Compare Yeats's, 'Easter, 1916': 'I write it out in a verse' (WBY, 182).

COLLATION

23. leaves to sunlight] leaves sunlight [SP1989, SP1997]

'After One Year' *(114)*

No manuscript exists, but Carter's fair copy typescript is extant in the *Poems of Succession* manuscript. First published with 'Black Friday 1962' in *New World Fortnightly*, 2 (13 November 1964), p.7. Although this poem seems to refer to the events described in 'Black Friday 1962', it was not published until over a year after the 'one year' it describes. In the time between the events and publication, there were increasingly violent clashes between Indian- and African-Guyanese. Republished as a continuous sequence, with an introduction by Ian McDonald in *New World Fortnightly*, 34 (18 February 1966), 19-25 (p.22).

Old hanging ground is still green playing field: Independence Park (previously known as Carmichael Square and used as the parade ground for the colony's militia and troops) had been used for hangings during earlier colonial periods. In 1851 it became an open promenade area and was known as the Parade Ground until 1966. This area was used for the public executions of slaves involved in the Demerara Slave Rebellion of 1823.

mocking great dreams: Possible reference to Carter's earlier lines: 'I do not sleep to dream, but dream to change the world' ('Looking at Your Hands').

Rude citizen: Compare Brutus's speech in Shakespeare's *Julius Caesar*: 'Who is here so rude that would not be a Roman? If any, speak; for him have I offended. Who is here so vile that will not love his country? If any, speak; for him have

I offended. I pause for a reply' (III. 2. 26-29).

as men must murder men: Compare Brutus's logic: 'As Caesar loved me, I weep for him; as he was fortunate, I rejoice at it; as he was valiant, I honour him: but, as he was ambitious, I slew him' (III. 2. 21-23).

'What Can a Man Do More' *(115)*

No manuscript exists, but Carter's fair copy typescript is extant in the *Poems of Succession* manuscript. First published in *New World Fortnightly*, 3 (30 November 1964), p.7, as part of the *Jail Me Quickly* series. Republished as a continuous sequence, with an introduction by Ian McDonald in *New World Fortnightly*, 34 (18 February 1966), 19-25 (p.23).

rain and fire: Guyana's tropical climate ensures high rainfall, and the tradition of wooden buildings creates a constant threat of fire. In 1945 much of Georgetown was accidentally burnt down, and it was again razed in 1962. Rainfall and the burning of canefields were vital to the sugar industry, but the 1950s and 1960s saw the return of disruptive cane-burning as part of the political and racial violence running throughout the country.

pick the blossoms: Compare Jamaican folk song 'Longtime Gal': 'Peel head John Crow [vulture] sit upon the tree top / Pick out the blossom.' Also compare William Blake's 'The School Boy', which Carter's lines invert: 'Oh, father and mother, if buds are nipped, / And blossoms blown away, [...] / How shall the summer arise in joy' (WB, 63).

village of the angry streets...gateways of the bleeding houses: Against the background of a general strike and violence carried out by both Indian- and African-Guyanese, the predominantly Indian-Guyanese areas of Mackenzie (now Linden), Wismar and Christianburg were sites of extreme violence: between 24 and 26 May 1964, houses belonging to Indian-Guyanese people were bombed, burnt down and looted, Indian-Guyanese people were murdered and raped, and the Indian-Guyanese populations had to be evacuated from these areas to Georgetown. On 6 July 1964 an explosion on a launch named *Sun Chapman*, travelling from Georgetown to Wismar, killed approximately 38 people, the majority of them African-Guyanese. In response five Indian-Guyanese people were killed at Mackenzie and seven seriously injured (CO1031/4758-9).

COLLATION
6. and hours spent measuring footsteps to the grave] and hours spent digging hopes out of a grave [PS, SP1989, SP1997]
17. I live] I stay [PS, SP1989, SP1997]

'Where Are Free Men' *(116)*

No manuscript exists, but Carter's fair copy typescript is extant in the *Poems of Succession* manuscript. First published in *New World Fortnightly*, 4 (15 December 1964), p.34, as part of the *Jail Me Quickly* series. Republished as a continuous sequence, with an introduction by Ian McDonald in *New World Fortnightly*, 34 (18 February 1966), 19-25 (p.24).

prison of air is worse than one of iron: suggestive of Ariel – a spirit of the air – in Shakespeare's *The Tempest*, who is first imprisoned in the forest by Sycorax, only to be released but enslaved by Prospero to do his bidding.

COLLATION
Where Are Free Men] Where Are Free Men? [PS, SP1989, SP1997]
12. wings have had no rest] wings have no rest [JQ1966]

'Childhood of a Voice' *(116)*

No manuscript exists, but Carter's fair copy typescript is extant in the *Poems of Succession* manuscript. First published in *New World Fortnightly*, 4 (15 December 1964), p.35, as part of the *Jail Me Quickly* series. Republished as a continuous sequence, with an introduction by Ian McDonald in *New World Fortnightly*, 34 (18 February 1966), 19-25 (p.25).

voice of childhood telling me my name: Compare Wordsworth in 'My heart leaps up when I behold': 'The Child is father of the man' (WWP, 62).

familiar white street...running east: Anira Street, where Carter was raised, and Lamaha Street, to which he had recently moved, both ran west to east.

COLLATION

3-4. Imagine it, the childhood of a voice / and voice of childhood telling me my name] Imagine it, the childhood telling me my name [JQ1964, JQ1966]

THE WHEN TIME (1977) *(117-44)*

In the period between *Jail Me Quickly* and *The When Time* Guyana had declared its political independence, and Carter had been appointed and resigned as Minister of Information and Culture in the PNC government. While a minister Carter had invited John La Rose (a Trinidadian writer and the founder of New Beacon publishers, based in London) to the 1969 Caribbean Writers' and Artists' Convention in Georgetown. In November 1970 La Rose agreed to publish a retrospective selection of poetry with the provisional title, *Poems 1970-1950* or *Deeds 1970-1950*. Delivered by hand to La Rose by the Guyanese painter, Aubrey Williams, the manuscript included Carter's request that the following 'Prefatory Note' be included in the text: 'Some of these are individuals and some are groups of individuals. They are arranged as such. And the order in which they are set out is not the chronological order in which they were made. Just the opposite. Thus, in going from the beginning to the end the reader will proceed from the more recent to the less recent' (included in letter to Aubrey Williams, 30 September 1970). This title and the ordering did not last. Over the next four years the collection stalled. Michael Wishart, based in Canada, planned to publish an edition of Carter's poems in 1971, and had asked Wilson Harris to write the introduction (Michael Wishart to Wilson Harris, 6 January 1972). This did not materialise, and letters from John La Rose show that there was a breakdown in communication concerning the New Beacon edition. In 1972 and 1974 La Rose wrote to Phyllis Carter, informing her that he had not received any news from Carter agreeing to New Beacon's offer. He returned the manuscript to Carter, but noted that New Beacon was still willing to begin again (John La Rose to Phyllis Carter, 30 July 1974). This manuscript no longer exists. Following the Carters' visit to England in 1975, the edition was brought back on track. By December 1975 a new manuscript had been delivered to New Beacon and the title had been agreed as *Poems of Succession*. However, Carter was still deliberating: in his Brown Notebook on the year planner for 1976, next to the address of New Beacon Books, he wrote: 'POEMS OF REVISION'. Aubrey Williams was originally in place to design the front cover, but Carter outlined his preference for a plain rust-red cover (Carter to La Rose, 1 December 1975). Between 1970 and 1975 the retrospective collection of poems had expanded into the edition we know now as *Poems of Succession*. Some of the poems to be gathered as *The When Time* –

the name given to the newly published work – appeared in journals and the Guyanese press: notably, *GISRA*, *Savacou*, *Kaie* and *The Sunday Chronicle*. The collection proved Carter's poetic activity: *The When Time* takes up a third of the book. The 1975 manuscript, Carter's corrected galley proofs and associated correspondence are held in the New Beacon Archive at the George Padmore Institute, London.

'Proem' *(117)*

Typescript with hand-written alterations, 1975. First published with the title 'Ever With Me' in *GISRA*, 5.4 (1974), p.64. Republished in *Poems of Succession* as a proem to the whole collection (p.9). Republished in *Selected Poems* as a proem to the whole collection (p.1). In the second edition of *Selected Poems* it is the final poem in *The When Time* (p.170). It is included as the first poem here to mark its introductory status and its pivotal relationship to the poems from *The When Time*.

Proem: a preface or introduction to a literary work.

you: Possible identities include (1) a lover, (2) the poem, (3) Guyana, (4) humanity.

Inexhaustibly: In a 12-item set of notes titled, 'Dimensions of the Riddle', Carter quotes a line from the poem, 'Before the Question', as Item 11: ' "THE ANSWER COMES BEFORE THE QUESTION": Those answers which constitute the perceived would imply the questions that have eventuated in the answers. In this sense RIDDLES are those questions which those answers have made necessary to be asked, inexhaustibly.' See Carter's Brown Notebook [1976 Diary], in an undated entry (probably written between 24 and 25 October 1979), held by Phyllis Carter in Martin Carter's private collection.

'Fragment of Memory' *(118)*

Typescript with handwritten additions, 1975. Undated fair copy manuscript held in Box File 'Non-AJS Poems – submitted for "Kyk"', A.J. Seymour Room, University of Guyana. First published in *Kyk-Over-Al*, 19 (year-end 1954), p.66. Republished in *The When Time* in *Poems of Succession* (p.77) with a stated composition date of 1956. I have kept the parenthetical dates added to all the poems in *The When Time*.

On the bed of the ocean bones alone remain: Compare Carter's 'muttering sea' in 'Not Hands Like Mine' and Derek Walcott, 'The Sea is History' (DWCP, 364-67).

'Voices' *(119)*

Typescript, 1975. First published in *Kyk-Over-Al*, 22 (1957), p.12. Republished in *The When Time* in *Poems of Succession* (p.78).

flower of fire: Hypezokos or Flower of Fire is an angel in the Chaldean cosmological scheme.

wide vase of air: Compare Herman Melville, *Pierre; Or the Ambiguities*: 'by now burning thee, urn thee in the great vase of air!' (HMP, 276).

strange dissolution of shape into spirit / was traced from a snail: There are many versions of the Yoruba creation story; one version tells that Orisha Nla created the earth from the contents of a snail shell: loose dirt, a pigeon and a five-toed hen.

'Words' *(120)*
Typescript with handwritten additions, 1975. First published in *Kyk-Over-Al*, 22 (1957), p.13. Republished in *The When Time* in *Poems of Succession* (p.79).
unlock...locked...locked...unlock: Compare Matthew 16. 19: 'What you lock on earth will be locked in heaven. What you unlock on earth will be unlocked in heaven.'

'Under a Near Sky' *(121)*
Typescript with handwritten alterations, 1975. First titled 'Under the Near Sky'. First published in *The When Time* in *Poems of Succession* (p.80).
The beat of water...hair alive as foam: Aphrodite, Goddess of love, beauty and fertility, is commonly described as having been born of or formed from sea foam (aphros).

'What We Call Wings' *(122)*
Typescript, 1975. First published in *The When Time* in *Poems of Succession* (p.81).
riddles: Responding to a review by A.J. Seymour of *Poems of Succession* (*Sunday Chronicle*, 26 June 1977, p.14), Carter wrote to Seymour: 'Your recognition of the significance of riddle in the poems fills me with joy. The association you made with me-riddle me-riddle marie, and my own with the riddle mechanisms of the oracles of Dodona and Delphi, to say nothing of the Sphinx, are most exciting; starting from the socio-linguistical implications and including the symbolic clustering', Martin Carter, letter to A.J. Seymour, 27 June 1977, A.J. Seymour Collection, A.J. Seymour Room, University of Guyana [Carter's underlining].
To heaven is their flight, on earth our sin: Compare Claudius's association of heaven with flight and earth with sin: 'My words fly up, my thoughts remain below: / Words without thoughts never to heaven go' (*Hamlet*, III. 3. 100-03).

'All to Endure' *(123)*
Typescript with handwritten alterations, 1975. First titled 'Poem'. First published as 'Poem', *New World Fortnightly*, 19 (23 July 1965), p.2. Republished in *The When Time* in *Poems of Succession* (p.82).
love's furious argument: (1) disagreement, (2) reasoning.
words out of a mouth: Compare Carter's discussion of words and silence in the five poems in *Conversations*.
conundrums: The idea of the riddle is central to *The When Time*. See note to 'Proem' and 'What We Call Wings'.

'Rain Falls Upward' *(123)*
Typescript with handwritten alterations, 1975. First published as 'Poem', *New World Fortnightly*, 39 (29 April 1966), p.2. Republished in *The When Time* in *Poems of Succession* (p.83).
human talk will tell me what: Compare 'one cry, one however begun / human cry, contains all' ('Rain forest').
A carrion time: Time of death and putrefaction. Compare the phrase, 'the when time'.
No serious hand is steady ever: (1) No serious hand is steady all the time; (2) A serious hand is never steady.

7. and heart] the heart [JQ1966]
8. and rain] The rain [JQ1966]
12. someone, somewhere] somewhere, someone [JQ1966]

'In the Asylum' *(124)*
Typescript, 1975. First published in *The When Time* in *Poems of Succession* (p.84).
abrupt runnel / mocking all the augurs / is piss not rain: A runnel can be a brook, as well as a gutter. At Dodona 'oracles seem to have been extracted in some manner from a sacred oak tree, perhaps by the rustling of its leaves (late legends say by the sound of a sacred spring or brazen gong)' (TCOCCL).
bocca della verita: a marble mask called Mouth of Truth (Bocca della Verità). According to popular belief it is said that anyone putting his or her hand in this mouth and swearing falsely, cannot withdraw it. The mask is situated in the atrium of St Mary's in Cosmedin Church in Rome, Italy.
the asylum: The Fort Canje hospital (now the National Psychiatric Hospital) was known as 'the mental hospital' or 'mad house'.

'A Mouth Is Always Muzzled' *(124)*
Typescript with handwritten alterations, 1975. First published with the title 'Occasion', *Sunday Graphic*, 15 November 1970, p.1, with the comment: 'This poem "Occasion", is the latest one to have been written by Mr Carter. Upon request he gave permission for it to be published in the *Sunday Graphic.*' The poem 'was not published at the poet's instigation at all, but by journalist Ricky Singh acting quite on his own initiative' (ACR, 234). The poem accompanied the front-page article, 'Exit Carter with a poem'. Republished as 'Occasion', *Savacou Special Issue: New Writing 1970*, 3/4 (December 1970 / March 1971), p.175. Republished as 'A Mouth Is Always Muzzled', *The When Time, Poems of Succession*, p.85. Dated 1969, we could presume that it was one of the poems that Carter had chosen for *Poems 1970-1950*.
The *Guyana Graphic* reported Carter's resignation on the front page on Saturday 14 November 1970, with the headline, 'Martin Carter quits Cabinet'. The *Graphic* reported Carter as commenting that he wanted to live 'simply as a poet, remaining with the people... I will not starve. I have friends... I have nothing more to say now. I believe in human decency. I believe in people.' The *Graphic* also wrote that Carter 'is reported to have offered his resignation to Mr Burnham since February this year, but was persuaded to stay on'.
The *Sunday Chronicle*, 15 November 1970, published a leader article titled, 'Carter goes', including the comment: 'At a time when Government is moving for some control in this area [dissemination of information] – something which Mr Carter himself believed in as a desirable part of the revolution now underway – it is all the more regrettable that his will not be the steering hand as distinct from that of another person who may confuse such control with blind and stupid dictatorship, with a purblind approach that he knows everything about matters in which from the time he starts to talk, it is apparent he needs education' (p.4). Also see 'I am my poem' and 'Nation-building and speaking again' in my Introduction.
premises: (1) house or building; (2) in logic, previous statements from which others are inferred (OED).

would shout it out differently / if it could be sounded plain: A possible comment on the sophistry demanded by his political position as Minister of Information.

'Even as the Ants Are' *(125)*

Typescript with handwritten additions, 1975. First published in *The When Time, Poems of Succession*, p.86.

In the beginning: Compare Genesis 1.1.

not of things…are seen, are known: the distinction drawn here is between what Kant describes as the noumenal (things in themselves) and the phenomenal (things as they are perceived [e.g., IK, 56]).

and ends by offering: Subject is missing, but given the doubt cast on 'the beginning' of the opening lines, the lack of an understandable grammar reinforces Carter's refusal to tell us what 'ends' and what might have begun.

mortality: According to Genesis 2.17, God tells Adam and Eve that they will die if they eat from the tree of good and evil.

our conspiracy: the Biblical Fall

how we came to possess: Article is missing, and given the Biblical context, a possible implied word is 'knowledge'.

are not allowed to speak / not even as the ants are: (1) like the ants, we are not allowed to speak; (2) the ants are allowed to speak more than us.

'For Milton Williams' *(125)*

Typescript with handwritten additions, 1975. First published in *The When Time, Poems of Succession*, p.87.

Milton Williams: a friend of Carter, Guyanese poet and author of *Pray For Rain* (1958), *Sources of Agony* (1979) and *Years of Fighting Exile* (1986). He came to know Carter in the 1950s during the height of PPP anti-colonial action, but emigrated to the UK in 1960.

The map I study has one continent: Williams responded in 'Second Poem for Martin Carter': 'In a different country, yet the same, / no matter what the map says, / I harbour your wise words' (MVW, 83).

Places I barely thought of you know well: Compare Williams's poem 'For Martin Carter': 'today I sit… and think of our negritude; / and about the history of our wounds; / our separation from our pristine hamlet / in some African village or city, / or that beside the river Ganges' (MVW, 67).

'Endless Moment World' *(126)*

Typescript with handwritten alterations, 1975. First titled 'This Endless Moment World' on typescript. First published in *The When Time, Poems of Succession*, p.88.

Would have turned to anyone: Creole phrasing that omits the first person singular pronoun.

wherefore: deliberate archaism.

just for so: Creole phrasing (in SE: 'just like that'): an adverbial phrase used to suggest something done casually, without obvious cause or particular reason (DCEU, 321).

language of the unspeakable: Compare Wittgenstein on the philosophy of language: 'of what we cannot speak we must be silent' (LW, §10, 49). 'I used to believe that language gave us a picture of the world. But it can't give us a picture of how it does that. That would be like trying to see yourself seeing something. How language does that is beyond all expression' (LW, §13, 118). *I need not tell / at all what my intention is:* Carter may have been thinking of Roland Barthes's 1968 essay 'The Death of the Author', which argued for the end of the search for authorial intentionality in readings of literature. Carter obtained a copy of *Image Music Text* in 1981 and annotated 'The Death of the Author'. He underlined the following passage thus: 'the <u>reader</u> is without history, biography, psychology; he is <u>simply that someone who holds together in a single field all the traces by which the written text is constituted</u>' (RB, 148).

rejoicing: Carter wrote in his Brown Notebook: 'The delight that attends the triumphant exertion of poetic power (the self's power over itself) is the poet's pay' (11.5.79). 'And so to a maximum extent the poet's life can be described as a pursuit of delight no matter how small the pay' (11.5.79). 'Thus the poet is a creature with an exceptional capacity for delight' (11.5.79).

if language were only sound: (1) *(n)* sound as noise detached from linguistic semantics; (2) *(adj)* sound as secure, well-founded, robust.

Nor would have made use of the breath / if the wind itself were voice: Compare the animism of Amerindian belief systems that accept the life and voices of natural phenomena.

'On a Pavement' *(127)*
Typescript with handwritten additions, 1975. First published in *The When Time, Poems of Succession*, p.89.

take / the lighted cigarette from my mouth: Carter was known for constantly smoking and sharing his cigarettes.

mind-torn lips: Compare 'mind-forged manacles' in Blake's 'London' (WB, 213-14).

swimming in some original form of obscenity: 'Classical Latin *obscenus, obscaenus* has been variously associated, by scholars ancient and modern, with *scaevus* left-sided, inauspicious and with *caenum* mud, filth' (OED).

COLLATION

8. pavements] pavement [SP1989, SP1997]

'If It Were Given' *(128)*
Typescript with handwritten additions, 1975. A.J. Seymour writes in his note-book that he had received 'Cuyuni', 'Leaves of the Canna Lily' and 'Poem (If it were)' by Carter on 13 March 1972 for Guyana Lithographic Co. Ltd. First published as 'If it were Given' in *New Writing in the Caribbean*, ed. by A.J. Seymour (Georgetown: Guyana Lithographic, 1972). Published in *The When Time, Poems of Succession*, p.90.

cupped hand of anguish / open for love...in the murdering drought: Compare Exodus 17. 3-6: 'And the people thirsted there for water; and the people murmured against Moses, and said, Wherefore is this that thou hast brought us up out of Egypt, to kill us and our children and our cattle with thirst? And Moses cried unto the Lord, saying, What shall I do unto this people? they be almost ready to stone me. And the Lord said unto Moses, Go on before the people, and take with thee of the elders of Israel; and thy rod, wherewith thou smotest the river, take in thine hand, and go. Behold, I will stand before thee there upon the rock in Horeb; and thou shalt smite the rock, and there shall come water out of it, that the people may drink. And Moses did so in the sight of the elders of Israel'.

padi: rice plant.

4-5. language / of the dead] language of the dead [SP1989, SP1997]

'For Angela Davis' *(128)*

Typescript with handwritten additions, 1975. First published in *The When Time, Poems of Succession*, p.91.

hemisphere: reminder of the continental connections between Carter's Caribbean and Davis's USA.

Angela Davis: Academic, member of the Communist Party of the United States, and civil rights activist. She was placed on the FBI's Ten Most Wanted List and arrested in 1970, after going into hiding. She was charged with murder, kidnapping and conspiracy for her alleged involvement in an attempt to free George Jackson from Soledad Prison. Davis was accused of having bought the guns for the jailbreak. Although imprisoned for 16 months awaiting trial, Davis was acquitted of all charges. Carter wrote the poem before her acquittal.

'Cuyuni' *(129)*

Typescript with handwritten additions, 1975. A.J. Seymour writes in his note-book that he had received 'Cuyuni', 'Leaves of the Canna Lily' and 'Poem (If it were)' by Carter on 13 March 1972 for Guyana Lithographic Co. Ltd. First published as 'Cuyuni' in *New Writing in the Caribbean*, ed. by A.J. Seymour (Georgetown: Guyana Lithographic, 1972). Published in *The When Time, Poems of Succession*, pp.92-93.

Cuyuni: rocky, largely unnavigable river in the interior of Guyana.

Inside my listening sleep: possible reference to trance. Also compare Wilson Harris, *Palace of the Peacock*: 'Everything Ah tell you dreaming long before the creation I know of begin' (WHPP, 87).

liberate one of its many demons: Massacruman or massacuruman – an ape-like spirit – is thought to live in the waters of the Cuyuni. *Ori-you* (mother of snakes) is believed by the Arawak to live in the large rivers of Guyana.

who could give me / weapons I shall be able to use: Amerindian myths sometimes present the relationship between humans and gods as antogonistic. According to Taino myths, the first humans often had to steal the cultural secrets from the gods. For example the attempt to steal the secrets of fire from the god Bayamanaco led to the creation of Caguama, the turtle on whose back the earth rests. Note that in the Poems of Succession Manuscript, Carter adds two lines here which were not reproduced: 'some mental arrow, magic spell or dream / to ward away the finger of its immense accusation'.

thrones of rock: some large boulders are considered sacred by Amerindians in Guyana (e.g. Shea Rock in South Central Rupunni). I would like to thank George Simon for this information.

35. much as I will have to] much as I will / have to / [SP1989]

'How Come?' *(131)*

Typescript with handwritten additions, 1975. First published in *The When Time, Poems of Succession*, p.94.

The beggar man: Compare Yeats's 'The Hour before Dawn', in which 'A cursing rogue with a merry face / A bundle of rags upon a crutch' is tempted and challenged by the underworld (WBY, 116-19).

'In a Small City at Dusk' *(132)*
Typescript with handwritten additions, 1975. First published in *The When Time*,
Poems of Succession, p.95.
a small city: Georgetown.

'And I Grope' *(132)*
Typescript with handwritten alterations, 1975. First published in *The When
Time*, *Poems of Succession*, p.96.
steeps: acceptable but rare variation of 'steepens'.
grope: In late 1979 Carter was reading Northrop Frye in order to help him
define 'riddle'. Carter quoted from Frye's broadest definition in his Brown
Notebook: 'the use of an object of sense experience to stimulate mental activity
in connection with it' (NF, 280), and underlined the phrase 'stimulate mental
activity in connection with it'. In the margin of his notebook Carter wrote,
'groping is an important element of this activity'.
god: the lower case is suggestive of the multiple gods known in Amerindian
and Indian belief systems.
ghost: in the east Caribbean, including Guyana the general term would not be
'ghost' but 'jumbie' or 'duppy'.

'My Hand in Yours' *(133)*
Typescript with handwritten additions, 1975. First published in *The When Time*,
Poems of Succession, p.97.

'The Leaves of the Canna Lily' *(134)*
Typescript with handwritten additions, 1975. A.J. Seymour writes in his note-
book that he had received 'Cuyuni', 'Leaves of the Canna Lily' and 'Poem
(If it were)' by Carter on 13 March 1972 for Guyana Lithographic Co. Ltd.
First published as 'The Leaves of the Canna Lily' in *New Writing in the
Caribbean*, ed. by A.J. Seymour (Georgetown: Guyana Lithographic, 1972).
Published in *The When Time*, *Poems of Succession*, p.98. This poem was read
at Carter's funeral by his son Keith.
canna lily: Matthew 6. 28: 'Consider the lilies of the field...Even Solomon in all
his glory was not arrayed like one of these'. Canna lilies are planted through-
out Georgetown on the road sides.
ragged like the lips: Compare 'No serious lip, uncracked, undried' ('Rain Falls
Upward').
COLLATION
12. death is a final] death is final [SP1989, SP1997]

'As When I Was' *(135)*
Typescript with handwritten alterations, 1975. First titled as 'As When I Was
a Boy'. First published in *The When Time*, *Poems of Succession*, p.99.
I tried to speak: Compare sixth poem in *Conversations*: 'when I tried to utter
words – I barked'.
fever came as sudden: Compare this entry from Carter's Diaries: 'No rainy
season has passed without bringing me fever. As soon as the months moved
into mid year, I would smell the fever in every fugitive breeze and every
arrogant gust of wind. [...] I dreaded the impotence it brought my limbs but
welcomed the privacy it afforded. That privacy which every animal needs –

fish to breathe, birds to build nests – but which all the things which add up to living seemed then and seem now to be conspiring to make impossible. Even in the galvanised latrine down in the yard, there was never privacy' (KMCT, 59-60).

'Before the Question' *(135)*

Typescript with handwritten additions, 1975. First published in *The When Time, Poems of Succession*, p.100.

Before the Question: Compare letter to A.J. Seymour, 27 June 1977: 'I was powerfully struck by your references and observations on the question of riddle in the poems. In this connection I would like to suggest that the line "and the answer comes before the question" in the poem on page 100, is of particular relevance.'

'The answer, which is an intuition, is, in effect, the riddle, & the poem the attempt at an imaginative answer to the question or questions posed by the riddle. The attempt, i.e., the poem, is then an exhibition of the structure of the virtual riddle posed by the answer that comes before the question.'

Two years later Carter added to these thoughts in his Brown Notebook (item 11 of 'Dimensions of the Riddle'): ' "THE ANSWER COMES BEFORE THE QUESTION": Those answers which constitute the perceived would imply the questions that have eventuated the answers. In this sense RIDDLES are those questions which those answers have made necessary to be asked, inexhaustibly; of course the capacity to perceive answers and to express questions presupposes that anterior questioning has predisposed perception. [...] The capacity to perceive answers is intuitive; and it is out of the experience of intuitivity that inspiration comes.'

'Intuition itself is attention of a certain quality. This is paraboloid attention when the magnitude of the curve or span of attention determines the location of the focus.'

[Held by Phyllis Carter in her private collection of Carter's papers.]
COLLATION
5. And the answer comes before the question] deleted [SP1989, SP1997]

'O My Companion' *(136)*

Typescript with handwritten alterations, 1975. First published in *The When Time, Poems of Succession*, p.101.

Where you are, I am: Compare 'If you are a beggar / so am I' ('We Walk the Streets').

O my companion: Compare 'The Discovery of Companion'.

'Only Where Our Footprints End' *(136)*

Typescript with handwritten additions, 1975. First published in *The When Time, Poems of Succession*, p.102. In *Selected Poems* the ordering of this poem and 'The Great Dark' is switched.

Colliding universes like our lips: Compare 'In the whirling cosmos of my soul there are galaxies of happiness /... O come astronomer of freedom / Come comrade stargazer' ('I Am No Soldier').

'The Great Dark' *(137)*

Typescript with handwritten additions, 1975. First published in *The When Time, Poems of Succession*, p.103. In *Selected Poems* the ordering of this poem and 'Only Where Our Footprints End' is switched. No date is given for this poem in *Selected Poems*.

ever weaving weaver: (1) Anansi, the spider (god) and trickster of Caribbean and African folklore and cosmology; (2) divine creator; (3) Penelope, the weaver in *The Odyssey*.

'What for Now?' *(137)*

Typescript with handwritten additions, 1975. First published as 'Poem' in *GISRA*, 4.3 (September 1973), p.31. Republished in *The When Time, Poems of Succession*, p.104.

What for now we want to go: Creole phrasing. In SE: 'Why do we now want to go?' (The OED quotes the example of 'What for you want to do that?')

the mountain: Possible reference to Mt Roraima (2800m), the most prominent mountain in the Guianas, bordering on Brazil and Venezuela.

went: Variant phrasing for 'recently departed'.

jaguar's roar: In pre-Columbian mythology the jaguar is associated with divinity. The Toltecs believed that the jaguar's roar was the sound of thunder and the bringer of rains.

'In the When Time' *(138)*

Typescript with handwritten alterations, 1975. Published in *The When Time, Poems of Succession*, p.105.

when time: Creole phrasing for 'when'.

the treasure of the tree's rooted / and abstract past of a dead seed: See note to *born again* in '[They say I am a poet write for them]'.

'No Consolation' *(138)*

Typescript with handwritten additions, 1975. Published in *The When Time, Poems of Succession*, p.106.

candle fly: Guyanese term for an insect with an luminous abdomen that lights up in flight. Walter Roth records a Carib story about a hunter lost in the forest at night, in which a 'Pu-yu' (candle fly) leads the man back to his companions in the forest (WR, 277). Changed from Carter's 'candlefly' in Bloodaxe edition.

a bulb of vacuum power: light bulb.

for whom is no consolation: Creole phrasing that omits the pleonastic pronoun used in SE existential constructions. In SE this would read: 'For whom there is no consolation'.

'On a Child Killed by a Motor Car' *(139)*

Typescript with handwritten additions, 1975. First published in *The When Time, Poems of Succession*, p.107. Phyllis Carter believes that no specific incident prompted this poem.

'The Child Ran into the Sea' *(139)*

Typescript with handwritten alterations, 1975. Published in *The When Time, Poems of Succession*, p.108.

The child ran into the sea: Carter, his wife and children took holidays on the coast of Guyana. Phyllis Carter remembers her husband writing poems and stuffing them in the glove compartment as she drove to and from their holidays on the coast.

4. on the horizon] at the horizon [fair copy typescript].

'On the Death by Drowning of the Poet, Eric Roach' *(140)*
Typescript with handwritten alterations, 1975. Published in *The When Time, Poems of Succession*, p.109.
Eric Roach: Trinidadian poet. In April 1974, after drinking insecticide, Roach drowned himself in Quinam Bay off the coast of Trinidad.
gunwale: upper edge of a ship's side (OED).
corial: See note to *l.* 149 in *To a Dead Slave.*
the window in the front of my house: Carter would often sit on the closed veranda at the front of his house, with the louvred 'Demerara' windows open to let in the breeze.
frangipani: tropical flowering bush or small tree, grown in Carter's garden.

'I Do Not Yet Know' *(140)*
Typescript with handwritten alterations, 19 June 1975. Published in *The When Time, Poems of Succession*, p.110.
yellow and ubiquitous butterfly: Possibly from the morpho family of tropical butterflies.

'About to Pass Me' *(141)*
Typescript with handwritten additions, 1975. Published in *The When Time, Poems of Succession*, p.111.
Behind window panes / faces that never lived stared at me: Compare 'Do Not Stare at Me'.

'Confound Deliberate Chaos' *(141)*
Typescript with handwritten alterations, 1975. First titled 'For a Nun Who Danced' (on typescript). Published in *The When Time, Poems of Succession*, p.112.
plantation earth: In an interview with Wordsworth McAndrew, Carter said that Guyana was 'not a country, but a refined plantation' (WMMC, 9).
canal beside a convent: the convent of the Corpus Christi Carmelites on Lamaha Street is next to Lamaha Canal.
Amazon: The large South American river does not run through Guyana but its estuary is north-west of the Guyanese border.

'For a Man Who Walked Sideways' *(142)*
Typescript with handwritten alterations, 1975. First published as 'To the Man Who Walked Sideways' in the *Sunday Graphic*, 11 August 1974, p.9, with a commentary by Eldon Stuart-Medas. Published in *The When Time, Poems of Succession*, p.113.
Proudful: Carter's neologism.
my shirt: Compare 'I will make my shirt / a banner' ('A Banner for the Revolution').
bruised heel: Adam in Genesis is cursed to have his heel bruised by the serpent.
Having failed to learn / how to die: Compare 'Before the Question'.
Laocoon: Carter refers to the death of the Trojan priest, Laocoön, and his two sons, who were crushed to death by two sea-serpents. See *The Aeneid* II. See

also Wilson Harris's 1954 poem 'Laocoon': 'Death is never treason / it is always rout. It is the unrealised associations / of the world the gods hide to bring out in the heart / of time's dying priest and eternity's valiant soldier, / creation's cunning hidden marriage and increase / of peril and of love' (WHES, 45-46).
COLLATION
9. Laocoon] Laocoön [SP1989, SP1997]

'We Walk the Streets' *(142)*

Typescript with handwritten additions, 1975. First published in *GISRA*, 5.4 (December 1974), p.64. Republished in *The When Time, Poems of Succession*, p.114.
We walk the streets: Compare 'To walk the street, that man whose heart is whole, / must never care' ('The Leaves of the Canna Lily').

'Whence Come They' *(143)*

Typescript with handwritten additions, 1975. Carter was Writer in Residence at the University of Essex from April to July 1975 and may have written this poem there. Phyllis Carter remembers his residency as a period of constant writing but only three poems dated from 1975 (and one of these – 'There Is No Riot' was published prior to the residency) are published in *The When Time*. Published in *The When Time, Poems of Succession*, p.115.
Whence come they: Compare William Morris, 'The March of the Workers': 'Whither go they, and whence come they? What are these of whom ye tell? / In what country are they dwelling 'twixt the gates of heaven and hell?' (WM, 114).
visitants: Compare William Wordsworth, *The Prelude* (1850): 'O there is blessing in this gentle breeze, / A visitant that while it fans my cheek / Doth seem half-conscious of the joy it brings / From the green fields, and from yon azure sky' (WWP, 495).

'There Is No Riot' *(143)*

Typescript with handwritten additions, 1975. First published in *The Sunday Chronicle*, 23 March 1975, p.14. No comment accompanies the text. Republished in *The When Time, Poems of Succession*, p.116.
Empty bottles, no longer trophies: Antique glass bottles from the colonial period are collectors' items in Guyana.
bombs are well remembered: The blowing up of the statue of Queen Victoria in Georgetown remained an iconic act of resistance during the Emergency. The riots of 1961-1964 were still in recent memory. See note to 'What Can a Man Do More'.
there is no riot: Carter's ambiguous support of rebellion is also marked in 'Black Friday 1962'.

'Two in One' *(144)*

Typescript, 1975. Carter was Writer in Residence at the University of Essex in 1975. Republished in *The When Time, Poems of Succession*, p.117.
the hsien: Immortal beings depicted in Chinese mythology as bird-like people or wise old men who could fly great distances and change their appearance.

POEMS OF AFFINITY 1978-1980 (1980) *(145-63)*
Some of the poems in this collection had been published before. Carter offered seven new poems ('Our Number', 'Rice', 'Paying Fares', 'Talking Names' [this poem was not published in *Affinity*], 'Rain Forest', 'Playing Militia' and 'Our Time') to *The Georgetown Review*, a journal newly founded and edited by Andaiye, Brian Rodway and Rupert Roopnaraine (all active members in a new anti-PNC and multi-racial political party, the Working Peoples Alliance).

The collection includes an introduction by Bill Carr and 'an appreciation' by Stanley Greaves. Greaves's appreciation consists of line drawings wrapped around 21 poems. On the contents page of the collection, the titles of the poems are presented in title case (e.g. 'I Still Stare'); however, only the first letter of the first word of each title is capitalised in the titles appearing with the poems. Even though the titles appear in title case in *Selected Poems*, and might suggest Carter's final revisions, this edition gives the titles of the poems as they appear with the text of the poems in *Poems of Affinity*. A year before publishing *Poems of Affinity*, the Georgetown-based Release publishers had reissued *Poems of Resistance from British Guiana*, retitled *Poems of Resistance from Guyana*. Carter was now employed at the University of Guyana and was working closely with Rayman Mandal, who owned and ran Release. Carter contributed to the publisher's journal, also called *Release*, introducing readers to the work of new Guyanese writers. An interview between Carter and Carr ran in the first issue of the journal. It is thanks to the foresight of Mandal that the *Poems of Affinity* manuscripts are the most comprehensive extant collection of Carter drafts. All manuscripts referred to below are held in Poems of Affinity Manuscript Book, Private Collection of Mrs Phyllis Carter.

Heidegger on Holderlin: This prefatory quotation is from Martin Heidegger, 'Hölderlin and the Essence of Poetry' (1936) (MH, 54).

'Our time' *(145)*
Fair copy manuscript. First published in 'New Poems', *The Georgetown Review*, 1.1 (August 1978), 127-34 (p.134). See above note on *Poems of Affinity*. Republished in *Poems of Affinity*, pp.14-15 (p.15), with an illustration by Stanley Greaves.
trenches: See note to *trench* in 'Not I with This Torn Shirt'.
fury should be fire: Compare 'Immortal Like This Earth', 'Let Freedom Wake Him', 'The Knife of Dawn', 'I Come from the Nigger Yard', 'It Is for This That I Am Furious' and 'I Am No Soldier'.
one dream / is enough: Compare 'dream to change the world' ('Looking at Your Hands').

'Playing Militia' *(146)*
Three manuscripts (one a fair copy). The fair copy and one draft are undated. A third, written in Carter's Brown Notebook II, is dated 17 August 1977 and titled 'Bearing Arms'. First published in 'New Poems', *The Georgetown Review*, 1.1 (August 1978), 127-34 (p.133). Republished in *Poems of Affinity*, pp.16-17 (p.17).
crow...carrion: vulture.
Girls, unbreasted: Possible reference to the reported practice of mythological female Amazon warriors to cut off one breast in order to use their bows more easily.

guns: During Burnham's era in government, Guyana became increasingly militarised. In Carter's 'Open Letter' he complained against 'the militarisation of the people in which poorly fed children are made to march in the sun like soldiers, playing militia at the expense of their lessons'.

Boys, ungamed: In the second manuscript Carter writes and deletes: 'Boys ungamed, / hold them like slingshots. What here / is their target?'.

spree: In the third manuscript Carter experiments with Creole phrasing, writing and deleting 'Time for spree' and 'Time fo' spree' to conclude the line beginning 'grip them like tickets.'

'I still stare' *(147)*

Two undated manuscripts (one a fair copy). First published in *Poems of Affinity*, pp.18-19 (p.19), with an illustration by Stanley Greaves. Titled 'STARE OF THE SLOPE' on the contents page of the manuscript book.

slats: Demerara windows are made from wooden slats; Carter's closed veranda and study had these windows.

I still stare: Compare 'Do Not Stare at Me'.

Time's fabulous fall down is / the slope of a strange mountain, / a shelf of books: (1) time falls fabulously (i.e. like a story or fabula) rather than chronologically; (2) our downfall (the phrasal verb turned noun, 'fall down', could be a Creole inversion of the standard English word, or new single noun, 'fall-down') is written in books. In the earliest manuscript Carter writes: 'I retain my stare, the slope / of my birth's day particular / mountain. My own time's fabulous / and kneeling down climb. Of many / human hands this is a legacy, like / a library which having been written / cannot write otherwise'.

Title: (1) name; (2) claim; (3) physical book.

'In a world' *(147)*

Two undated draft manuscripts, titled 'In a purple world'. First published in *Poems of Affinity*, pp.20-21 (p.21), with an illustration by Stanley Greaves.

purple: Can denote (1) purpleheart – wood from the heart of an indigenous Guyanese tree; (2) imperial, royal rank; (3) regal or ecclesiastical mourning; (4) venous blood; (5) the brilliant, gaudy; (6) the feverish.

sky's miserable convocation: A rewriting of the Biblical covenant of the rainbow shown to Noah after the flood.

'As new and as old I' *(148)*

Undated fair copy manuscript. First published in *Poems of Affinity*, pp.22-23 (p.23), with an illustration by Stanley Greaves.

new day: Compare 'new day must clean' ('Not Hands Like Mine').

Alphabet / of hope: Compare 'if freedom writes no happier alphabet' ('After One Year').

Crawl / of the beast in a season of days: Compare Yeats's 'The Second Coming': 'And what rough beast, its hour come round at last, / Slouches towards Bethlehem to be born?' (WBY, 187).

betrayed / old gods: Compare 'nameless and quite forgotten are the gods' of Amerindians ('Not Hands Like Mine').

'As new and as old II' *(148)*

Untitled fair copy manuscript, dated 26 July 1979. First published in *Poems*

of Affinity, pp.24-25 (p.25).
a kind of music: Compare the music of the spheres in Ancient cosmology.
A green leaf: Compare 'the greener leaf explodes' ('Death of a Comrade').
We / are its measure: Compare 'The more the men of our time we are / the more our time is' ('Our time').

'In a certain time' *(149)*
Undated draft manuscript, titled 'Defiance of Dark'. First published in *Poems of Affinity*, pp.26-27 (p.27), with an illustration by Stanley Greaves.
an owl hoots: Also known as 'jumbie-bird' in Guyana and believed to be a messenger of death.
vile eye of a toad: DCEU notes that in Caribbean English 'toad' is almost never used, 'crapaud' being the favoured term to describe both frogs and toads. The animal is associated with obeah practices.
destiny: Compare 'like a spark seed in the destiny of gloom' ('I Come from the Nigger Yard'). Compare 'The Location of the Artist': 'The artist cannot change the nature of this fate: all he can do is endure it.'

'Our number' *(149)*
Undated draft manuscript. First published in 'New Poems', *The Georgetown Review*, 1.1 (August 1978), 127-34 (p.128). See above note on *Poems of Affinity*. Republished in *Poems of Affinity*, pp.28-29 (p.29), with an illustration by Stanley Greaves.
The pins of the slack pin seine: A fishing net, thrown out by hand, used in the Caribbean.
the tide / has gone them bare: Possible Creole phrasing (SE: 'the tide has laid them bare').
denizen: inhabitant(s) (of a foreign land) admitted some rights (OED).
Is so / we stay: Creole phrasing (In SE: 'That's (just) how we are').
Is a way of counting born we: Creole phrasing (In SE: 'We are born to this way of counting').

'With that loan' *(150)*
Untitled fair copy manuscript, dated 10 March 1979. Published in *Poems of Affinity*, pp.30-31 (p.31), with an illustration by Stanley Greaves.
every answer / creature of a question: Compare 'the answer comes before the question' ('Before the Question') and 'But life is the question asking / what is the way to die' ('A Mouth Is Always Muzzled').
language of our negative yes: Kamau Brathwaite argues that this phrase summarises the poetry of antithesis and synthesis found in *Poems of Affinity* (SB, 207).

'Paying fares' *(150)*
Undated draft manuscript. First published in 'New Poems', *The Georgetown Review*, 1.1 (August 1978), 127-134 (p.130). Republished in *Poems of Affinity*, pp.32-33 (p.33).
the powerful crab: Possible reference to the Prime Minister and subesquent President of Guyana, Linden Forbes Burnham, and 'crab politics'. See note to *creatures rise from holes* in 'Black Friday 1962'.
What, they wonder / does he eat: A possible reference to food shortages that dominated Guyana during the late 1970s.
who his obeahman: A possible reference to Burnham's unrealised plans to legalise

obeah in the 1970s.

flags: A possible reference to the nationalism that Burnham sought to foster since Independence. See 'Open Letter' for Carter's reckoning of the PNC's nationalism.

'Rain forest' *(151)*

Undated fair copy manuscript. First published in 'New Poems', *The Georgetown Review*, 1.1 (August 1978), 127-34 (p.132). Republished in *Poems of Affinity*, pp.34-35 (p.35), with an illustration by Stanley Greaves.

raindrop: changed from Carter's 'rain drop' in Bloodaxe edition.

green towers: Compare phrase to W.H. Hudson, *Green Mansions: A Romance of the Tropical Forest* (1904), a novel set in the south-west interior of Venezuela.

white sand...bright gold: The interior of Guyana is rich in minerals such as gold, found by dredging the white sands of the interior rivers.

and still: (1) reference to calm waters; (2) synonymous phrase for 'and yet'.

'Rice' *(151)*

Undated fair copy manuscript. First published in 'New Poems', *The Georgetown Review*, 1.1 (August 1978), 127-34 (p.129). Republished in *Poems of Affinity*, pp.36-37 (p.37), with an illustration by Stanley Greaves.

quick wind padi: Possible reference to winnowing rice by tossing it into the air to let the wind blow off the chaff.

full moon: Phagwah (also Phagwa) is the Indo-Caribbean celebration of the Hindu festival known as Holi in India. It is the festival of spring, held during the full moon, to celebrate the victory of good over evil, and the renewal of the agricultural seasons.

cheated: In his 'Open Letter' Carter stated that the PNC régime had created a society in which people 'were made to accept that stealing, cheating, lying, bearing false witness, informing on each other was a positive sign of loyalty to the régime'.

'Beans of God' *(152)*

Two draft manuscripts, one undated and untitled, and one titled '~~The~~ Beans of God', dated 11 November 1979. This latter manuscript contains the note 'written in and with Rayman in Rayman's car at [illegible word] at about 7.00 pm on 10 January 1979'. First published in *Poems of Affinity*, pp.38-39 (p.39).

disunderstand: Carter's neologism

anaeming: Carter's neologism. In the untitled manuscript he writes 'anaemia'.

beans of God: Black Henbane, a wild flower, known in Ancient Greece as *dioskyamos* (literally meaning 'bean of the gods'). It was used in medicine and religious rites because of its poisonous quality, causing sedation, delirium or death.

'Bent' *(152)*

Manuscript draft, dated 11 January 1975. First published in *Poems of Affinity*, pp.40-41 (p.41), with an illustration by Stanley Greaves. Written in 1975, Carter could have published this poem in *Poems of Succession* as part of *The When Time*. There would have been other opportunities for Carter to publish the poem, particularly in the 'New Poems' published in *The Georgetown Review*. It is possible that Carter forgot about 'Bent', or that it was mislaid, but that seems unlikely with such a striking poem.

bent back: Recalls Atlas supporting the heavens. Compare Wilson Harris's *The Secret Ladder*: 'the old man straightened his bent back (upon which the sky revolved). He lifted a load of firewood from his shoulders and deposited it on the ground not far from Fenwick's feet' (WHWA, 180).

creeping out / is ash: Ash is important in both Christian and Hindu religions. God in Genesis 3. 19 tells Adam and Eve: 'for dust thou art, and unto dust shalt thou return'. This in turn has influenced the death rites from *The Book of Common Prayer*: 'we commit his body to the ground; earth to earth, ashes to ashes, dust to dust'. On Ash Wednesday, Christians wear a mark of ash on their foreheads in mourning for Christ's death. In Hinduism holy ash is used to mark the forehead, as a sign of Shiva burning away human ignorance and material concerns.

'Ground doves' *(153)*

Three draft manuscripts, one undated and titled 'Ground Doves', one dated 1 July 1979, and titled '~~Doves~~ Ground-doves', and one untitled and undated. First published in *Poems of Affinity*, pp.42-43 (p.43), with an illustration by Stanley Greaves.

ground / doves: A type of pigeon, also known as 'duppy-birds' in Jamaica, where they are regarded with suspicion (OS, 165).

They / fall: in the dated draft Carter writes after these words: 'Aghast / ~~Time will~~ pick them up, / we shall / and burn our hands'.

'Our voice betrays' *(153)*

Undated and untitled fair copy manuscript. The text of this poem is published as the first half of 'Show Me a Little Freedom', *Kaie*, 16 (July 1979), p.86 (for the second half, see 'Some kind of fury'). First published as 'Our voice betrays' in *Poems of Affinity*, pp.44-45 (p.45). Retitled 'Show Me A Little Freedom' in the two editions of *Selected Poems* (p.148; p.190).

Orion: There are many Greek stories about how Orion, the Titan hunter, died. Some suggest that he pursued the goddess, Artemis, and she punished him, sending a scorpion to kill him. Others suggest that he was killed by the scorpion on the order of Gaia, the earth goddess, because he boasted that he could kill all or any wild beasts. A further story has him fleeing from the scorpion into the sea, only to be shot and killed accidentally by his lover, Artemis.

to surrender: (1) to hand over; (2) to abandon.

COLLATION

7. devoured] devour [*Kaie* 1979]

'Being always' *(154)*

Draft manuscript dated 13 January 1979 and titled 'Replaceable', with a former title, 'Time Itself Arranges', having been crossed out. First published in *Poems of Affinity*, pp.46-47 (p.47).

Being: DCEU states that in Guyana this word is used as a conjunction equivalent to 'since' or 'seeing that'.

'Too much waiting' *(154)*

Undated, untitled draft manuscript. Titled 'Too Much Waiting' on the draft contents page. First published in *Poems of Affinity*, pp.48-49 (p.49), with an illustration by Stanley Greaves.

jumbie umbrella: An inedible mushroom that grows in damp, shaded places. DCEU states that it is also known as 'duppy-parasol' and 'jumbie-parasol' in other parts of the Caribbean. A 'jumbie' is a ghost or evil spirit.

cones: A rare verb meaning 'to shape like a cone' (OED).

last of a lost world: Arthur Conan Doyle's *The Lost World* (1912) is set in the South American interior, taking the plateau of Roraima as its inspiration. In Guyanese Creole *last* and *lost* are pronounced with the same vowel.

an owl hoots: Compare 'In a certain time'. Owls are also known as 'jumbie-birds' in Guyana.

gone sun's: This draws on Creole phrasing; compare the 'the went jaguar's roar' ('What For Now?').

COLLATION

12-13. wild memory of a parasol / sky] wild memory of a parasol sky [SP1989, SP1997]

'As well is' *(155)*

Undated, untitled draft manuscript. Titled 'A Dead Land' on the draft contents page. First published in *Poems of Affinity*, pp.50-51 (p.51), with an illustration by Stanley Greaves.

black outs: Electricity shortages are common occurrences in Guyana, and are known as 'blackout'.

candle flies: See note to *candle fly* in 'No Consolation'.

cutexed: 'Cutex' is the generic name in Guyana for nail polish.

error...cause: The manuscript begins 'If seeing you I make a bold an old / mistake, it is because seeing / you, I confuse cause / with an ancient and mutual / fault, reasoning how a bold / eye, one which sees that making / old error may see as well'.

'Some kind of fury' *(155)*

Two draft manuscripts. The first draft is titled 'Calendar' with the parenthetical note: '(Written in Rayman [Mandal]'s house where the spirit came. For Agnes and the children from Martin, Phyllis and my own children with love. I have learnt how to refuse to be afraid.) Martin 25/10/78'. The second draft is undated and untitled, but on the draft contents page it is named as 'Some Kind of Fury'. The text of this poem was first published as the second half of 'Show Me a Little Freedom', *Kaie*, 16 (July 1979), p.86 (for the first half, see 'Our voice betrays'). First published as 'Some kind of fury' in *Poems of Affinity*, pp.52-53 (p.53).

On the lintel: In the draft titled 'Calendar' the poem opens: 'A lifetime it took to learn / to write a line. On the lintel / of my mind's wrist, and sky's / opaque and apparent window, my / ungrace is the world's same open / book; the not green enough Bible / of the insufficient pasture of / of failed human love.'

I / keep working for a storm: Compare 'so river flood, drown not my pillar feet' ('The Knife of Dawn') and 'I wish this world would sink and drown again' in the final poem of *Conversations*.

vile calendar and book: Compare 'our vileness' ('Bastille Day – Georgetown').

'Inventor' *(156)*

Two draft manuscripts. The first draft is undated and untitled. The second draft is dated 9 January 1979 and titled 'Dining Table'. On the draft contents page 'Dining Table' and 'I Evacuate' are crossed out and replaced with 'Inventor'. First published in *Poems of Affinity*, pp.54-55 (p.55), with an illustration by Stanley Greaves.

I, inventor of the law / I break, am more criminal: possible reference to (1) Carter's role as law-maker while a minister of government; (2) Carter's role as poet, and therefore as a linguistic rule-maker; (3) Kant's belief in *Groundwork of the Metaphysics of Morals* that 'the will of a rational being must always be regarded as at the same time *lawgiving*, since otherwise it could not be thought as an *end in itself*' (IK, 42). In the untitled manuscript Carter writes: 'I am ~~More~~ criminal than them, I, inventor / of lov [sic], am a poet.'

COLLATION

12. in people's] in a people's [SP1989, SP1997]

'Rag of wonder' *(156)*

Draft manuscript dated 12 October 1978. First published in *Poems of Affinity*, pp.56-57 (p.57).

'Anywhere' *(157)*

Undated draft manuscript. First published in *Poems of Affinity*, pp.58-59 (p.59), with an illustration by Stanley Greaves.

air starer: Carter's neologism.

I am so severely one: Compare 'all-o(f)-we-is-one!', which the DCEU describes as a catchphrase of the Caribbean region meaning: 'All of us are the same (class of people)!; There is no real social difference between us!; We are all black people together'.

'The Sun's accordion' *(157)*

Two undated draft manuscripts. One is titled 'The sun's accordian' and one is titled 'The Sun's Work'. It is the final poem named on the draft contents page. First published in *Poems of Affinity*, pp.60-61 (p.61).

comparisoned: Obsolete in SE, meaning 'to compare' or 'to contend'.

'For César Vallejo I' *(158)*

Two draft manuscripts (one a fair copy), both dated 10 July 1979 and titled 'For Cesar Vallejo'. It is not named on the draft contents page. First published in *Poems of Affinity*, pp.62-63 (p.63). Carter was introduced to the work of Vallejo in the 1970s by Rayman Mandal.

César Vallejo: Peruvian poet (1892-1938), grandchild of two Chimu Indian women and two Spanish Catholic priests. He worked on a sugar estate in Peru in his early adulthood, publishing *Los heraldos negros* in 1918 and *Trilce* in 1922. He moved to Paris and became a founder member of the Peruvian Socialist Party, visiting Russia several times. He joined the Spanish Communist Party in support of the new republic. Absorbed by the anti-Fascist movement, he wrote collections, *España, aparta de mí este cáliz* (1939) and *Poemas humanos* (1939).

and to have a name: in both drafts of the poem this is not the final line. The drafts end: 'I, who wanted to be / a poet, and to have a name / like yours.'

COLLATION

4. world a small] world is a small [SP1997].

'For César Vallejo II' *(158)*
Draft manuscript, dated 6 September 1978 and titled 'For Cesar Vallejo'. It
is not named on the draft contents page. First published in *Poems of Affinity*,
pp.64-65 (p.65), with an illustration by Stanley Greaves.

'Bastille Day – Georgetown' *(159)*
Three draft manuscripts, two dated 14 July 1979. It is not named on the draft
contents page. First published in *Poems of Affinity*, pp.66-67 (p.67). 'Bastille
Day – Georgetown (on the murder of Father Darke)' is the full title used on
the contents page of *Poems of Affinity*, but the parenthetical statement does
not appear on p.66. Phyllis Carter remembers her husband returning home
the day of Fr Darke's attack, saying that he had to write about the event.

OUR DAY OBSCENE ANTS
I denied it. Not wanting
to believe it. On this
Bastille day, this day
of the fourteenth of July
I woke up wanting to deny
it. But I saw; with my own
eyes, the faces of the fierce
killers. Men, if I may call them
so, with long sticks, sharp
knives, and impulses worse
than the greed of hungry
infants, which I have seen.
Not human infants I mean.
I mean the progeny rather
of ants who steal the eggs
in the obscenity of theft, of
other obscene ants
    Martin Carter
    July 14, 1979

OUR BASTILLE DAY
(For Walter, Rupert,
Not wanting to deny, I
Believed it. Not wanting
To believe it. I denied. on
On Bastille day, this day
Of July, I saw with my own
Eyes, the fierce barbarians killers, those:
Of criminal want. I saw
a creature, something, once,
I saw, the man a man of death,
The sticks of a hungry lepers
who wants to make hunger
the leprosy of their his own want.
On Bastille today day is today.
We do not want your gates.
You will perish. I say so

    Martin Carter 14/7/79

Fr Darke: In the late 1970s the PNC's plans for constitutional change were
contested within Guyana, particularly by the political party, the Working
Peoples Alliance. There were mass anti-referendum demonstrations in 1978,
but 'the PNC slave constitution' (to use the words of the WPA's *Dayclean*)
was voted through by a referendum on 10 July 1978. Physical attacks on critics
of the government were common and Martin Carter was among those beaten
during the anti-referendum demonstrations. However, in 1979 support for
the opposition, and particularly Walter Rodney (a founder member of the
WPA), was growing. When the offices of the General Secretary of the PNC
and the Ministry of National Development were burnt down during that year,
Walter Rodney and Rupert Roopnaraine (another WPA founder member) were
arrested and charged with arson. As the trial was in progress, large crowds,
including Carter, gathered in Georgetown to protest against the arrests. Members
of the House of Israel – a cult led by the self-named Rabbi Washington and
alleged to be working for the PNC – also came to the demonstrations to split
up the protesters. 'As the cult grew in numbers, they were used [...] to form

289

crowds for PNC meetings [...]. More seriously, they were assigned to break up Opposition political meetings, often using violence and smashing up or making away with public address systems while police stood by passively' (AM, 169).

On 14 July 1979, during one of the demonstrations, a photographer for *The Catholic Standard*, Father Darke, was beaten and stabbed to death by members of the cult. The image of Fr Darke being killed became an enduring emblem of the criminality permitted in Guyana. 'They beat him with staves and, as he fell on the grass verge, continued to beat him. One of them then pulled out an old bayonet and stabbed him in the back' (AM, 141).

nothing to storm: A reference to the storming of the Bastille prison, Paris, on 14 July 1789.

criminal passing for citizen: Compare 'claw a triumph like a citizen' ('Black Friday 1962') and 'Rude citizen' ('After One Year').

weapon, a piece of wood: Fr Darke was attacked with wooden staves.

we shall fight: (1) united, we shall fight against our vileness; (2) we shall fight against each other.

'Let every child run wild' *(160)*

Two untitled draft manuscripts, one dated 29 July 1979. It is not named on the draft contents page. First published in *Poems of Affinity*, pp.68-69 (p.69), with an illustration by Stanley Greaves

throw a flower: Flowers are thrown over the bride and groom in Hindu wedding ceremonies.

of a such instrument: Possible Creole inversion.

a child's wild guitar...silence / of parents: The dated manuscript reads: 'one of our / children's wild guitar, shuddering / with melody in the silence, ~~the~~ harmony / of ~~his parents~~ a house, of time's / love and kitchen.'

'I tremble' *(160)*

Untitled and undated draft manuscript. It is not named on the draft contents page. First published in *Poems of Affinity*, pp.70-71 (p.71).

curse: See note to curse in 'I Clench My Fist'.

a green lip: DCEU states that in Guyana 'green verbs' refer to 'incorrect English, especially as spoken by somebody who is trying or expected to speak correct English...Green in the jocular sense of "unripe, immature".'

dreadful: Draws on Rastafarian meanings of 'dread' that can be positive or negative.

COLLATION

16-17. when I see a green tree, I / tremble] when I see a green tree, I tremble [SP1989, SP1997]

'Faces' *(161)*

Undated draft manuscript. It is not named on the draft contents page. First published in *Poems of Affinity*, pp.72-73 (p.73), with an illustration by Stanley Greaves.

my mother and wife: Carter and Phyllis lived with Violet Carter when they were first married. Phyllis and Violet were good friends and Violet – a midwife – delivered Phyllis's first two children.

'Watch my language' *(161)*

Draft manuscript, dated 31 January 1980. It is not named on the draft contents page. First published in *Poems of Affinity*, pp.74-75 (p.75), with an illustration by Stanley Greaves.

decidingly: decisively.

I walk decidingly about / disappear: Compare 'The man of time whose look can stain a sky / who walks a pavement, walks and disappears' ('Who Walks a Pavement').

Watch my language: Compare 'Watch me good!', a phrase DCEU states is used in Guyana to check someone's seriousness or truthfulness, or to insist on one's own seriousness or truthfulness.

'For Michael Aarons' *(162)*

Draft manuscript, titled 'For Michael', dated 5 October 1978. It is not named on the draft contents page. First published in *Poems of Affinity*, pp.76-77 (p.77), with an illustration by Stanley Greaves.

Michael Aarons: Guyanese poet from Soesdyke, East Bank Demerara. He worked in the library of the University of Guyana. Carter wrote the introduction to the selection of poems by Aarons that appeared in *Release* in 1978.

'He (for Farro)' *(162)*

Undated draft manuscript, titled 'He', held in Poems of Affinity Manuscript Book. A partial draft is contained in Carter's Brown Notebook, titled 'The Poet' and dated 10 October 1979. The poem is not named on the draft contents page. First published in *Poems of Affinity*, pp.78-79 (p.79), with an illustration by Stanley Greaves.

Farro: Ivan Forrester, friend of Carter, poet, painter and fisherman. A painting by Farro of the two of them fishing hangs in the Carters' living-room.

they be: subjunctive in formal English grammar.

'Census' *(163)*

Undated, untitled draft manuscript. It is not named on the draft contents page. First published in *Poems of Affinity*, pp.80-81 (p.81), with an illustration by Stanley Greaves.

'Is why' *(163)*

Draft manuscript, titled 'Is Why' and dated 7 March 1980. It is not named on the draft contents page. First published in *Poems of Affinity*, pp.82-83 (p.83), with an illustration by Stanley Greaves.

incomparable city: Georgetown.

Was real: Creole phrasing (SE: 'It was real').

Was true: Creole phrasing (SE: 'It was true').

walk about: DCEU defines as 'A woman who is a busy-body and gossip; a restless news-carrier', often followed by a name.

FOUR POEMS AND DEMERARA NIGGER (1984) *(164-66)*

Carter continued to write poetry after the publication of *Poems of Affinity*, stopping only when he suffered a stroke in 1993 (after which he was unable to write with ease). 'Four Poems and Demerara Nigger' was published in *Kyk-Over-Al* in 1984. Carter wrote to Seymour on 12 November 1984:

'My dear Arthur,

Sorry to be so tardy and you will have to be careful with the accuracy as indicated in handwriting on the typescript.

As a group I would be grateful if [sic] will publish them under the title: '~~THREE~~ FOUR POEMS AND DEMERARA NIGGER'.

Martin'

These poems comprise some of Carter's most syntactically and semantically opaque work. In *Poems of Affinity* Carter had declared that he was starting new work to be collected as *Poems of Mortality*. In *Four Poems and Demerara Nigger* we find the first expressions of this (never-to-be-published) collection. The manuscripts referred to below are held by Ian McDonald in his *Kyk-Over-Al* Files.

'One' *(164)*

Fair copy handwritten manuscript. First published in *Kyk-Over-Al*, 30 (December 1984), 7-9 (p.7). This poem was most likely a late insertion into the collection of poems, given that Carter corrected his title from 'Three' to 'Four Poems and Demerara Nigger' and the other poems all show Carter's attempts to number the poems and his rejections of these prospective orders.

'Two' *(164)*

Typed manuscript with handwritten revisions. Initially titled, 'On Reading a Young Poet'. First published in *Kyk-Over-Al*, 30 (December 1984), 7-9 (p.7). When Carter was still imagining this as a four-poem sequence, this poem was originally ordered third, then changed to first.

so: An implied reference to the poem that Carter is reading.

yester just so: This might draw on Creole phrasing but it is not a Creole phrase.

a poet cannot truly speak / to himself save in his / own country: Note that Carter, unlike many of his peers, did not emigrate from Guyana. Compare first poem in *Conversations*: 'They say I am a poet write for them'.

standard-bearers: changed from Carter's 'standard bearers' in Bloodaxe edition.

Just so: Creole phrase (SE: 'without warning').

'Three' *(165)*

Typed manuscript with handwritten revisions. First published in *Kyk-Over-Al*, 30 (December 1984), 7-9 (p.8). When Carter was still imagining this as a four-poem sequence, this poem was originally ordered second.

flute: Wilson Harris writes in his 'Note on the Genesis of *The Guyana Quartet*': 'The Carib flute was hollowed from the bone of enemy in time of war. Flesh was plucked and consumed and in the process secrets were digested. Spectres arose from, or reposed in, the flute' (WHGQ, 9).

delta: Guyana's coastline is dominated by dramatic estuaries, from its own Essequibo to Venezuela's Orinoco and Brazil's Amazon.

'Four' *(165)*

Typed manuscript with handwritten revisons. The manuscript shows that the poem was originally titled, 'Renewal'. First published in *Kyk-Over-Al*, 30 (December 1984), 7-9 (p.8). When Carter was still imagining this as a four-poem sequence, this poem was originally ordered first, then changed to third.

The spared are not the saved: Compare Primo Levi, *The Drowned and the Saved*, trans. by R. Rosenthal (London: Abacus, 1989).

wood ants: Caribbean English term for woodworm.

'**Demerara Nigger**' *(166)*
Fair copy manuscript. First published in *Caribbean Contact* (May 1983). Re-published in *Kyk-Over-Al*, 30 (December 1984), 7-9 (p.9).
Farinata: A 13th-century Italian leader of the Ghibellines. In Dante's *Inferno* he lives in the circle of heretics, having been posthumously charged with heresy and excommunicated.
Ghibelline: Political faction in 13th-century Italy that supported the Hohenstaufen dynasty of the Holy Roman Empire and opposed the pro-papal Guelphs, to which Dante belonged. Both factions sought to unite the divided Italian states.
'entertained great scorn of hell / and asked about ancestors': Dante writes of Farinata in *Inferno*, Canto X (40-42): 'As soon as I was at the foot of his tomb / Somewhat he eyed me, and, as if disdainful, / Then asked of me, "Who were thine ancestors?".'
Demerara nigger: Thomas Carlyle, 'Occasional Discourse on the Nigger Question' (1853): 'If precisely the wisest man were at the top of society, and the next wisest next, and so on till we reached the Demerara nigger (from whom down-wards, through the horse, &c., there is no question hitherto,) then were this a perfect world, the extreme *maximum* of wisdom produced in it. That is how you might produce your maximum, would some god assist. And I can tell you also how the *minimum* were producible. Let no man in particular be put at the top; let all men he accounted equally wise and worthy, and the notion get abroad that anybody or nobody will do well enough at the top; that money (to which may be added success in stump oratory) is the real symbol of wisdom, and supply and demand the all-sufficient substitute for command and obedience among two-legged animals of the unfeathered class: accomplish all those remarkable convictions in your thinking department; and then in your practical, as is fit, decide by count of heads, the vote of a Demerara nigger equal, and no more, to that of a Chancellor Bacon: this, I perceive, will (so soon as it is fairly under way, and *all* obstructions left behind) give the *minimum* of wisdom in your proceedings.' (TC, 310).
if no messenger rode: (1) Jesus entering Jerusalem on a donkey; (2) the horses of the Apocalypse.
a horse of hell: Horse of the Apocalypse.

BITTER WOOD AND FOUR POEMS FROM *KYK-OVER-AL* (1993) *(167-69)*
These poems were collected together in the second edition of *Selected Poems*. Vanda Radzik, co-editor of *Kyk-Over-Al*, remembers writing down 'Horses', 'No Easy Thing' and 'The Poems Man' for Carter, as he spoke them to her.

'**Bitter Wood**' *(167)*
Fair copy manuscript dated 1988 held by Ian McDonald in *Kyk-Over-Al* File. First published in *Selected Poems* as a proem, p.v.
Here be dragons: the 16th-century Lenox Globe bears the phrase 'hic sunt dracones' (here are dragons) to mark the edge of the known world.
bitter / cups: DCEU defines the phrase: 'a cup carved out of the wood of the lignum vitae tree...in which water, placed overnight, draws the bitterness of the wood, to be drunk as a medicine against fevers or loss of appetite'. See note to *I taste the bitter world* ('I Walk and Walk).
spoil / of splendid maps: The map that accompanied Walter Ralegh's *Discoverie*

of the Rich and Bewtiful Empire of Guiana is dominated by the guessed site of El Dorado.

green sight: (1) indigenous Guyanese wood, greenheart; (2) unripe.

'The Conjunction' *(168)*
No manuscript exists. First published in *Martin Carter Prose Sampler*, *Kyk-Over-Al*, 44 (1993), 1-4 (p.1).

the sought conjunction: In an interview Carter said: 'Everything borders with something else. When you speak to me about something, I usually see it one way, then in another in one flat second. And that is what I'm trying to do – to deal with two things simultaneously, not separately' (FB, 228).

'Horses' *(168)*
Draft manuscript held by Phyllis Carter in her private collection of Carter's papers. First published in *Martin Carter Prose Sampler*, *Kyk-Over-Al*, 44 (1993), 1-4 (p.2).

horses: Moses Nagamootoo tells an apocryphal story about the editor of the *Chronicle* finding Carter drunk, talking to a horse. Carter was heard to say that nobody understood him, only the horse.

they climb the sky: Pegasus, the winged horse, was tamed by Bellerophon, who used Pegasus in defeating the monster, Chimaera. Bellerophon died when he was thrown from the horse while trying to reach Mount Olympus. Pegasus in turn was transformed into a constellation.

'No Easy Thing' *(169)*
No manuscript exists. First published in *Martin Carter Prose Sampler*, *Kyk-Over-Al*, 44 (1993), 1-4 (p.3).

'The Poems Man' *(169)*
No manuscript exists. First published in *Martin Carter Prose Sampler*, *Kyk-Over-Al*, 44 (1993), 1-4 (p.4).

the poems man: Carter confirmed that this encounter did take place.

SUITE OF FIVE POEMS (2000) *(170-72)*
These poems were first published posthumously in *Kyk-Over-Al*, 49/50 (June 2000), pp.45-49, with the following editorial note: 'A handful of poems written by Martin Carter in 1961, have recently come across the Editor's Desk and a selection of these are here published for the first time in this special edition of *Kyk-Over-Al* which is dedicated to his memory and his life's work.' The manuscripts are held by Ian McDonald in his *Kyk-Over-Al* files.

Rainer Maria Rilke: This prefatory quotation is from Rainer Maria Rilke, '[Ich finde dich in allen diesen Dingen]', *The Book of Hours* (1905) (RR, 4-5).

'1' *(170)*
Fair copy manuscript. First published in *Kyk-Over-Al: Martin Carter Tribute*, 49/50 (2000), 44-49 (p.45).
COLLATION
grows] grown [*Kyk-Over-Al* 2000]

'2' *(170)*

Fair copy manuscript. First published in *Kyk-Over-Al: Martin Carter Tribute*, 49/50 (2000), 44-49 (p.46).

sky bends: Compare 'University Of Hunger' and 'Bent'.

love's magnetic north pole of desire: Compare John Donne's 'A Valediction: forbidding Mourning': 'And though it in the centre sit, / Yet when the other far doth roam, / It leans, and hearkens after it, / And grows erect, as that comes home' (JDP, 84-85).

'3' *(171)*

Fair copy manuscript. First published in *Kyk-Over-Al: Martin Carter Tribute*, 49/50 (2000), 44-49 (p.47).

I'll hang like a bat: Compare 'turn bat and confuse clocks' ('Demerara Nigger').

'4' *(171)*

Fair copy manuscript. First published in *Kyk-Over-Al: Martin Carter Tribute*, 49/50 (2000), 44-49 (p.48).

I will always be speaking with you: Compare 'Death of a Comrade'.

'5' *(172)*

Manuscript. First published in *Kyk-Over-Al: Martin Carter Tribute*, 49/50 (2000), 44-49 (p.49).

seeds that war with God and die: See note to *born again* in '[They say I am a poet write for them]'.

UNCOLLECTED POEMS *(173-90)*

This section includes miscellaneous unpublished and uncollected individual poems that Carter withheld from re-release or that cannot be placed in the previous sequences in this edition. Some we can speculate would have formed the projected *Poems of Mortality*. Some have been recovered from private collections. The incomplete information that is available about the poems or the manuscripts means that it is impossible to reproduce completely these poems in the order of their composition. The poems are ordered by composition date where possible or else publication date. The publication dates range from 1948 to 1993. The composition dates range from 1948 to the 1970s.

'From "An Ode to Midnight"' *(175)*

No manuscript exists. First published in *Kyk-Over-Al*, 6 (June 1948), pp.5-6. The full text of this poem is no longer extant. This is the only Carter poem published during the 1940s, and the only extant from this period, even though Roy Heath remembers the period between 1947 and 1948 as one of great poetic activity for Carter (RH, 326). The fire at Carter's family home in Anira Street presumably destroyed this juvenilia.

Ode to Midnight: Carter read Keats closely as a teenager and as a young man, and the ode form, if not the style, is indebted to that reading.

O: Archaism that Carter uses repeatedly until 1977.

why must thy time be sad: Compare John Keats's pairing of sadness and midnight in 'To Hope': 'O let me think it is not quite in vain / To sigh out sonnets to the midnight air!' (JK, 41-42 [*ll.* 26-27]).

Art thou: Poetic archaism was still current in contemporary Caribbean poetry in the 1940s. See A.J. Seymour's poem VI in *Six Songs*: 'So huge, so incomplete, so passionate / my love for thee' (AJS, 113).

E'en: Line scans as iambic pentameter – a metre that Carter uses throughout his work.

'The Indian Woman' *(176)*

No manuscript exists. First published in *Thunder*, 1.9 (September 1950), 9, under the name, M. Black. Roy Heath remembers 'The Indian Woman' as a poem composed between 1947 and 1948 – a 'period of fermentation, of search for form and subject' (RH, 326).

green lettuce: illegal farming of salad crops, mainly by Indian-Guyanese women, took place along the railway line between Georgetown and East Coast Demerara. I would like to thank Dudley Kissoore for this information.

the rusted railway line: this detail places the Indian woman as living and working along the coastal belt of British Guiana, where from the 1840s to the 1970s there was a railway line.

rice field: In the 20th century rice was becoming as prominent as sugar in Guyana's agricultural economy.

No ! No! The: The spacing here follows the *Thunder* text.

And they whose eyes are dim with this: the final 12 lines are printed as a long stanza. This could have been a decision about layout made by Carter, as the subject of the lines work as a unit. More likely the final three stanzas were compacted to enable the editor, Janet Jagan, to fit in two adverts and a PPP announcement.

dark face: Carter encourages us to read 'dark face' against the syntax of the sentence, as adjective and noun.

'Poem of Prison' *(178)*

A fair copy manuscript was sent to A.J. Seymour on 19 May 1952, with the accompanying note: 'Dear Mr Seymour, If you have any space left in *Kyk*, will you be so good as to consider the above for publication? Martin Carter.' Not published in *The Kind Eagle (Poems of Prison)* or in *Kyk-Over-Al*, 15 (1952), with the rest of 'Poems of Prison'. It is not clear if it was refused, overlooked or withdrawn. It was not published subsequently in *Poems of Resistance from British Guiana*, *Poems of Succession* or *Selected Poems*. A facsimile was published posthumously in *Kyk-Over-Al*, 49/50 (June 2000), p.52. The manuscript is held in the A.J. Seymour Collection, University of Guyana.

dark slab of iron: Compare 'O wall of prison, iron, stone and sorrow / where are those human hands that built you up?' ('Where Are Those Human Hands?').

I go back, I return, I sink into the floor: Compare 'A prison is go back, go back, go back' ('Who Walks a Pavement').

'If Today' *(178)*

No manuscript exists. First published in *Thunder*, 2.7 (31 July 1954), p.3. At Carter's request this poem was not published in *Selected Poems*.

our city: Georgetown.

death rides: Revelations 6.8: 'And behold, a pale horse, and he who sat on it, his name was Death.'

heart into stone: See Yeats's 'Easter, 1916': 'Hearts with one purpose alone / Through summer and winter seem / Enchanted to a stone' (WBY, 181).

'Where Are Those Human Hands' *(179)*

No manuscript exists. First published in *Thunder*, 2.11 (20 November 1954), p.3. At Carter's request this poem was not republished in *Selected Poems*.

prison: Camp Street Prison, Georgetown. Carter was imprisoned in his former workplace in 1954, arrested for taking part in an illegal procession during the Emergency. Phyllis Carter remembers being allowed to visit her husband. Visits were restricted to 15 minutes, and inmates and visitors would stand and speak to each other across a counter. Wearing a khaki and grey prison uniform, Carter would remove his cap and place it on the counter. Hidden underneath the cap would be a letter for a comrade or a poem. Mrs Carter believes that this poem could have been smuggled out in this way.

the bird of hope: Compare the symbolism of *The Kind Eagle (Poems of Prison)*.

'Immortal Like the Earth' *(179)*

No manuscript exists. First published in *Thunder*, 2.12 (18 December 1954), p.7. At Carter's request this poem was not published in *Selected Poems*. Phyllis Carter believes that she could have smuggled this poem out of Camp Street Prison. See note to 'Where Are Those Human Hands'.

fire furious fire: Compare 'It Is for This That I Am Furious', 'I Am No Soldier', and 'Our time'.

They cannot make a poet turn a beast...They cannot kill a poet: Carter draws on the Christian notion of a chain of being, ordering mankind above beasts. Carter's interest in Yeats's Ireland would have taught him that the Irish poet and teacher, Padraig Pearse, was shot for treason after the 1916 Uprising.

immortal like a kiss: Compare Marlowe's *Doctor Faustus*: 'Sweet Helen, make me immortal with a kiss' (12.83).

'For My Son' *(180)*

Fair copy manuscript of this poem is held in Box File 'Non-AJS Poems – submitted for "Kyk"', A.J. Seymour Room, University of Guyana. First published in *Kyk-Over-Al*, 19 (year end 1954), p.125. The poem was not published in 'The When Time' in *Poems of Succession*, but in *Selected Poems* it is added to 'The When Time' as the first poem in the sequence.

For My Son: Keith Carter, born on 13 May 1953.

Flowers will bloom: In the manuscript, Carter ends this line with an exclamation mark.

'For Morton Sobell in Alcatraz' *(181)*

No manuscript exists. First published in *Thunder*, 6.52 (26 March 1955), p.3. The title incorrectly names Sobell as 'Milton Sobell', but names him correctly in the body of the poem.

Morton Sobell: Co-defendant with Julius and Ethel Rosenberg in the famous US atomic spy trial, in which they were charged with conspiring to commit espionage. All were found guilty in 1951, a verdict whose legality has since been questioned. The Rosenbergs were sentenced to death and executed in 1953. Sobell was sentenced to 30 years' imprisonment, the first five years of which were served in Alcatraz. He was released in 1969.

by blows of courage on a brittle sky: compare the prosecutor's claim that as Ethel Rosenberg was typing out secret documents, she 'struck the keys, blow by blow, against her own country and in the interests of the Soviets' (MM, n.p.).

you will not soil those hands of yours: Sobell refused to testify during the trial or subsequently, and still maintains his innocence. It is these acts that may have occasioned the final two lines of the poem.

'Cane Cutter' *(181)*
No manuscript exists. First published in *Thunder*, 3.5, 14 May 1955, p.3.
cutlass: Harvesting by hand was still the norm in Guyana in 1955.
ocean: Many Guyanese sugar estates are located along the coast in Berbice and on East and West Coast Demerara.
blackened fragments of green cane: The sugar canes are set alight before harvesting.
I long to see you flash it at the sun: During the Emergency between 1953 and 1957, the PPP promoted non-cooperation as the best response to the authorities. According to Phyllis Carter, Carter approved of the protest burning of canefields.

'In the Shadow of a Soldier' *(182)*
First published in *Thunder*, 3.7, 9 July 1955, p.2. No manuscript exists. At Carter's request this poem was not published in *Selected Poems*.
Two long years: Troops landed in Guyana on 8 October 1953.
in ships and fields where time was like a shroud: A possible reference to the middle passage, plantation life, and the repressive colonial history of the Caribbean.
cleaned sometimes with fire: Reference to burning of canefields during plantation slavery. During the Emergency there were several incidents in which bombs were planted in Georgetown and cane fields were set alight.
the roots we cannot grow without: Compare 'Baffled and like a root / stopped by a stone you turn back questioning / the tree you feed' ('Proem').

'Wind of Life' *(182)*
No manuscript exists. Previously unpublished. First broadcast on *Caribbean Voices*, 1 July 1956. Transcript housed in *Caribbean Voices*, BBC Radio Archives, Reading. V.S. Naipaul edited the programme at the time. Phyllis Carter does not remember Carter submitting this poem to *Caribbean Voices*. Other poems broadcast on the series were 'I Walk Slowly in the Wind' ('Number One' in *Three Poems of Shape and Motion*) and 'University of Hunger' on 27 July 1958.

'Ancestor Accabreh' *(183)*
First published in a sequence of two poems titled 'Yesterday and Tomorrow' [with 'I Come from the Nigger Yard'], *Masses & Mainstream*, 10.2 (February 1957), 1-6 (pp.3-6). Carter and his PPP comrades had been researching slave rebellions in the Guianas. He discussed the example of the Berbice Slave Rebellion of 1763 and the Demerara Slave Rebellion of 1823 in *Thunder* (see 'The Lesson of August'). Here Carter narrates the final days of the revolutionary Accabreh during the 1763 rebellion.
1. *Was:* Creole phrasing with a specific introductory function. DCEU compares this sense of 'was' to ''Twas' in dialect Standard English.
1. *Accabreh:* See note to Accabreh in 'I Am No Soldier'.
32. *like the sea for Moses:* Moses parted the Red Sea in order for the Israelites to escape from Egypt.
44. *Wikki:* A river in the upper Berbice region and site of a significant victory

for the rebels under the military leadership of Accabreh.

51. *The great rough cayman with red eyes:* crocodile indigenous to Guyana.

52. *the shy agouti:* small rodent indigenous to the interior of Guyana.

52. *the wild tapir:* mammal related to horses and rhinos, indigenous to the interior of Guyana.

83. *the far white god of grief:* Christian God, brought to enslaved peoples in the Americas through European (i.e. white) colonialism.

85. *a laugh of scorn deep in his mouth:* Aphra Behn's *Oroonoko* (1688) depicts another slave rebellion leader scorning the pain of a torturous death: 'Then they hacked off one of his arms, and still he bore up' (AB, 140).

100. *broke him on a wheel:* Accabreh was killed on the wheel (CG, 491).

[Let my greatnesses transcend my indecencies] *(186)*

Unpublished fair copy manuscript is held in the New Beacon papers on Martin Carter, George Padmore Institute, London. The manuscript is dated 2 August 1971. As it is held among correspondence concerning *Poems of Succession*, it is possible that the poem was considered for this collection.

[Having, as I do, a profound hatred for humans and alcohol] *(187)*

Unpublished fair copy manuscript is held in the New Beacon papers on Martin Carter, George Padmore Institute, London. The manuscript is undated, but as it is held with '[Let my greatnesses transcend my indecencies]', it could be dated *circa* 1971.

benab: See note to *l*. 180 in *To a Dead Slave*.

poison arrow: common hunting method for Amerindians.

[Star code and tree fruit. Shout] *(187)*

Fair copy typescript, dated 28 June 1976, held in Box File 'Non-AJS Poems', A.J. Seymour Room, University of Guyana. First published in *Kaie: Carifesta '76*, 14 July 1976, p.83. The poem was published as the close of a discussion by Carter titled, 'About Poetry':

> From a particular position it seems more than ordinarily useful to think of poems as codes. Also since poets are conventionally lumped with artists it is also to suggest that while the poet makes use of art in the organisation of his code or codes, he is not an artist in the same way, for instance, as is a musician or a painter or a sculptor. Whitman in his preface to his *Leaves of Grass* said: 'The poetic quality is not marshalled in rhyme or uniformity or abstract addresses to things nor in melancholy complaints or good precepts, but is the life of these and much else...'.
>
> Every time someone construes a true poem he makes one. He completes, as it were, the poet's "breaking into the chain"'. Every proper reading is also another kind of completion. But every proper reading is only as significant as the original code is significant; which is as much to say that the code itself is a true poem.
>
> So what elevates a given code to the status of a true poem? To attempt an answer one must attempt an interpretation of a true code. If as is advanced here, a code is something based on mutuality; something itself which provides the ground or the possibility of expression, then herein the code becomes a knack.
>
> A knack is the mutuality of simulability. Hence follows what follows.

Note that in the typescript, the final published line is replaced with: 'while my feet scuffle dust, and the code of leaves remember / What stars talk, as do the leaves of trees / a rattle of eternity, or a cat in a kitchen / only waiting for a real kiss, a real kiss, / for which I would give up my mind'.

[As the eyes move and her hands] *(188)*
Unpublished fair copy typescript held in 'Non-AJS Poems' File in the A.J. Seymour Room, University of Guyana, dated in Seymour's hand: 'Jca [Jamaica]. July 1976'.
flambouyant: variant spelling of flamboyant: a Caribbean tree with flaming red, yellow or orange flowers.

'Talking Names' *(188)*
No manuscript exists. First published in 'New Poems', *The Georgetown Review*, 1.1 (August 1978), 127-34 (p.131). This poem has not been republished. It is possible that Carter felt he had expressed sufficiently the themes of silence and dancing present here (in *Conversations* and 'Shines the Beauty of my Darling') to warrant discarding this poem.
dance / on the coals: In Trinidad and Tobago, worship of the Hindu Goddess, Kali, involves 'Fire-pass', the walking over a pit of glowing coals.

'For Walter Rodney' *(188)*
No manuscript exists. First published in *Caribbean Contact*, September 1980. Reprinted in *Walter Rodney: Poetic Tributes* (London: Bogle L'Ouverture, 1985), p.51.
Assassins of conversation: Walter Rodney was killed in June 1980, by a bomb concealed in a walkie-talkie given to him by an agent of the Guyana Defence Force. The government reported that an unidentified body had been found, but only admitted that Rodney had been killed when photographs of his body were leaked to the press. The inquest, finally held in 1988, issued a verdict of 'death by accident or misadventure'. Critics of the PNC government maintain that Rodney's death was a political assassination.
Risker, risk: See 'Free Community of Valid Persons'. In the 'Foreword' to *Walter Rodney: Poetic Tributes*, David Dabydeen quoted from one of Rodney's 1976 speeches: 'Some of our finest comrades will fall, have fallen, in struggle, and we don't set about to get the best of our workers and revolutionaries killed just so that we can write poetry to celebrate them subsequently. When they are lost, they are lost, it's an irreparable loss and may in fact qualitatively affect the development of struggle in another phase. And even for those whom we might not remember in poetry and song, what about their lives, their decision to risk all?' (p. i).
I intend to turn a sky / of tears: Compare 'lift your face / to the gift of the roof of / clouds we owe you' ('For Angela Davis').

'For the Students of St Rose's' *(189)*
First published in *Kyk-Over-Al*, 49/50 (2000), p.19.
St Rose's: St Rose's High School was founded in the 19th century as a girl's school. Boys were admitted in 1975.

[My hand shadows my page] *(189)*
Undated and unfinished manuscript from Martin Carter Private Papers. Ian

McDonald edited the draft after Carter's death, and read this version at the first Martin Carter Memorial Dinner, 20 December 2003. McDonald's version is published here.

[The sweet memory of] *(190)*
Undated and unfinished manuscript in Martin Carter Private Papers, file 'Milton's & Others'.

SELECTED PROSE

'The Lesson of August' *(193)*
First published in *Thunder*, 5.8 (31 July 1954), p.1. Reprinted in *Kyk-Over-Al*, 29/50 (June 2000), pp.64-66.
1833: The Act of Emancipation (1833) became law in 1834, but a period of apprenticeship, that tied emancipated people to the plantations on which they worked, followed for a four-year period until 1838.
the head of the statue of Queen Victoria: In May 1954 the statue of Queen Victoria outside the Law Courts building in Georgetown was blown up. Nobody was charged for the crime, although Carter and Rory Westmaas were implicated.
Capitalism and Slavery: Eric Williams's book was published in Chapel Hill by the University of North Carolina Press in 1944.
insurrection of 1823: Better known as the Demerara Slave Rebellion. See EdC.
John Smith: Also known as 'the Demerara Martyr'. He was a missionary priest at the time of the Demerara Slave Rebellion of 1823, who was arrested, charged and sentenced to death for his alleged role in the plot. He died in prison from pulmonary consumption, waiting for his sentence to be commuted. In his researches on Smith, Carter read Edwin A. Wallbridge, *The Demerara Martyr, Memoirs of the Rev John Smith, Missionary to Demerara* (London: London Missionary Society, 1848). Also see note to *Quamina, l.* 59 in *To a Dead Slave*.
West Indian Freedom and West Indian Literature: P.H. Daly's book was self-published in Georgetown, 1951.
the indenture system: A system by which workers from Portugal, China and India were contracted to work in British Guiana for a fixed period of time, after which they could then return to their country of origin or receive a plot of land in the colony. Compare Carter's essay a year later: 'Because August is the month in which both Emancipation and Swaraj (Indian National Independence) are celebrated, there can be few occasions better suited for discussion of some of the points relating to the unity of the people of African and Indian descent who live, work, and struggle in the country. Furthermore, within the period between 1st August and this one, a split occurred in the popular movement, raising a host of new problems and complicating the already complicated relationship between person and person, social group and racial group and consequently colonial Guianese as a whole people and metropolitan Britain as overlord', 'The Lesson of August – Revisited', *Thunder*, 6.70, 30 July 1955, p.1.
the people of India: Cheddi Jagan and Linden Forbes Burnham visited India in November 1953.
local editors of newspapers: The *Argosy, Sunday Argosy*, the *Daily Chronicle, Sunday Chronicle* and the *Guiana Graphic* were the major newspapers; all were seen to defend the interests of big business.

'Time of Crisis' *(195)*
No manuscripts exists. First published in *Thunder*, 5.42 (15 January 1955), p.4.
Reprinted in *Kyk-Over-Al*, 49/50 (June 2000), pp.67-70.
S.P.C.C. (Society for the Prevention of Cruelty to Colonials): the NSPCC (National
Society for the Prevention of Cruelty to Children) was founded in 1884.
conditions of emergency such as we now live under: These included restrictions on
the movement of members of the PPP, a ban on public meetings and public
demonstrations.
Polyphemus: one-eyed giant in Greek mythology, also known as the Cyclops.

'A Dark Foundation' *(198)*
No manuscript exists. First published in *Thunder*, 6.55 (April 16 1955), p.5.
Reprinted in *Kyk-Over-Al*, 44 (May 1993), 57-59.
the black race is a master race: Carter is likely to be thinking of the beliefs of
Marcus Garvey.
John Smith: See note to John Smith, 'The Lesson of August'. The quotation is
from Smith's 'private letter to a friend in England', signed 'Demerara 1822'
(EW, 39-42).
1763 when the slaves in Berbice rose up: See note to Accabreh, 1. 49, 'I Am No
Soldier'.
Hoogenheim: Wolfert Simon van Hoogenheim, Governor of Berbice from
1760 to 1764.
Accabreh, Atta, Coffy and Accara: See note to *Accabreh*, *l.* 49, 'I Am No Soldier'.

'This Race Business' *(200)*
No manuscript exists. First published in *Thunder*, 6.9 (10 September 1955), p.4.
Reprinted in *Kyk-Over-Al*, 44 (May 1993), 68-70.
bad-mindedness: spite, malevolence, malignant attitude (DCEU).

'Wanted – A Great Obeah Man' *(202)*
No manuscript exists. First published in *Thunder*, 6.10 (22 October 1955), p.5.
Reprinted in *Kyk-Over-Al*, 44 (May 1993), pp.72-73.
'Wanted Now: Leaders': Daily Argosy, Sunday 16 October 1955, p.7.
Giordano Bruno: Italian philosopher-scientist-poet (1548-1600), who believed
in the Copernican doctrine and was charged before the Inquisition and sen-
tenced to death.
John Brown: 19th-century abolitionist who believed in armed rebellion to end
slavery in the United States. After stealing Federal weapons and fighting local
militia, Brown was captured and convicted of treason. He was sentenced to
death and hanged in 1859.
John Smith: See note to *John Smith*, 'The Lesson of August'.
Accabreh, Accra: See note to *Accabreh*, *l.* 49, 'I Am No Soldier'.
great obeahman: healer or practitioner of benign or malignant medicine. Compare:
'He alone appeared to possess powers which were beyond the reach of the
slave owner or the planter. He alone appeared to be able to alleviate distress.
In a world in which the only choice available was a choice of the manner of
dying, the obeahman was not the charlatan he would become when the struc-
ture of life relationships provided a range of choices in addition to and dif-
ferent from the one limited to a manner of dying. Instead, the obeahman was
the living repository of the beliefs, the hopes and the fears of his community,

be it the nigger-yard or the plantation as a whole. But even in his role as obeahman, as living repository, and without being a charlatan, he was already capable of being a victimiser. For he could refuse to use, on behalf of others, the power he was believed to possess and so put himself in a position to reduce a client to the status of victim. Thus even before the transformation of obeahman as obeahman into obeahman as charlatan, the capacity for him to be maker of victims was already established. And one reason which his contemporary performance has more in common with the latter position than with the former position is related to the social and political and therefore psychological changes which have occurred since the abolition of slavery. What during slavery was on his part a positive contribution to sheer survival has in our time been taken over by the political leader. And hand in hand with this has been too the taking over by the political leader of certain negative aspects of the obeahman's performance as charlatan', Martin Carter, *The Edgar Mittelhozer Memorial Lectures: Man and Making – Victim and Vehicle* (Georgetown: Guyana Lithographic, 1974), pp.20-21.

'Sensibility and the Search' *(204)*
No manuscript exists. First published in *Argosy*, 26 January 1958, p.7. Reprinted in *Kyk-Over-Al*, 44 (May 1993), pp.77-81.
Professor J.H. Parry: See J.H. Parry, 'The Teaching of History in the Americas: A Study of the place of National and Continental History in the curriculum of School and University', *Caribbean Quarterly*, 4.2 (1955), 87-98 (p.97).
Dom Basil Matthews: Dom Basil Matthews, *Crisis of the West Indian family* (Mona: Extra Mural Dept., University College of the West Indies, 1953), p.66.
published in the 1955 Mid-year issue of Kyk-Over-Al: *Kyk-Over-Al*, 20 (mid-year 1955), pp.188-203. Other contributors were A.J. Seymour, Frank Williams, H.M.E. Cholmondeley, Ruby Samlallsingh, P.H. Daly, Edgar Mittelholzer, E.S.M. Pilgrim. Carter's words are direct quotation (p.193).
Dr Raymond Smith: author of *The Negro Family in British Guiana* (London: Routledge & Kegan Paul, 1956). The quotation is from Chapter 8, 'The Family System in the Context of Guianese Society', pp.195-201.
the 'Big House': Gilberto Freyre, *The Masters and the Slaves: A Study in the Development of Brazilian Civilisation [Casa-grande & senzala]*, trans. by Samuel Putnam (New York: Mark Knopf, 1944).
porknockers: Independent prospectors for gold or diamonds in the rivers of the interior of Guyana. The name is thought to come from their diet of pickled wild pig.
the emigration of West Indians to Britain: From 1945 there was mass emigration from the West Indies to Britain.
even this rhythm is not our own, in the sense of having been created by us: the examples of Calypso, Ska, and steel pan music would contradict Carter's claim.
Dylan Thomas...Edgar Allan Poe: Compare Carter's own poem, 'From "An Ode to Midnight"'.
Salzberger...Hölderlin: L.S. Salzberger, *Hölderlin* (Cambridge: Bowes & Bowes, 1952), p.37.

'A Letter' *(208)*
No manuscript exists. First published in *New World Fortnightly*, 1 (30 October 1964), pp.2-3. Carter was approached by David deCaires and Miles Fitzpatrick

to write a piece for the first issue of their cultural and political journal, *New World Fortnightly*.

B.G.: common abbreviation of British Guiana, also sometimes sardonically translated as 'Booker's Guiana' (CJ, 73).

'A Question of Self-Contempt' *(209)*

No manuscript exists. First published in *New World Quarterly: Guyana Independence Issue*, 3.2 (1966), pp.10-12. The issue, edited by Carter and the Barbadian novelist George Lamming, included work by leading Caribbean writers and theorists: Frantz Fanon, Aimé Césaire, Wilson Harris, C.L.R. James, Walter Rodney, Nicolas Guillén. Reprinted in *Kyk-Over-Al*, 49/50 (June 2000), pp.103-09.

member of an organisation: In 1946 Cheddi Jagan, Janet Jagan, Jocelyn Hubbard and Ashton Chase formed the Political Affairs Committee (PAC). The People's Progressive Party was formed in 1950.

desperate obeahman: See note to *great obeahman*, 'Wanted – A Great Obeahman'.

A black man in South Africa: Apartheid in South Africa was reported in *Thunder*.

cane-pieces: Plots of land owned by small landowners where sugar cane is grown and sold to local refineries.

Jenny von Westphalen: Karl Marx's wife

you think if was like you so: Creole phrasing, possibly contemptuous (SE: 'You think it was because of you (lot)').

'A Free Community of Valid Persons' *(213)*

No manuscript exists. Delivered as an address to the the University of Guyana's Eighth Convocation Ceremony, October 19, 1974. Published in *Kyk-Over-Al*, 44 (May 1993), pp.30-32.

In the year 1865: Carter's description of the axolotl, and the metamorphosis of some specimens in Paris in 1865, is accurate.

'All gone': See note to *all is gone*, ([Now there was one whom I knew long ago]).

respect of the riskers: See note to *risker, risk*, 'For Walter Rodney'.

'Open Letter to the People of Guyana' *(216)*

No manuscript exists. First published in *Dayclean* (1979). Also published in *Caribbean Contact* (September 1979), p.9. Reprinted in *Kyk-Over-Al*, 44 (May 1993), pp.88-89.

Hamilton Green: prominent member of the PNC.

Father Darke: See 'Bastille Day – Georgetown', and notes.

régime's rigidly controlled mass media: In 1968 the PNC government took over the radio station, Guyana Broadcasting Service (GBS). Radio Demerara was bought by the government in 1979. In the 1970s the PNC government bought the *Daily Chronicle*, *Evening Post* (closed down), *Argosy* (closed down), *Sunday Chronicle*, *Guyana Graphic* (merged with *Chronicle*). As Minister of Information Carter was the governmental head of the Guyana Information Services.

threats against individuals and groups openly advertised: Eusi Kwayana remembers hearing Burnham say to his political opponents in May 1978: 'May I wish happy requiem to those who are dying.'

playing militia: Compare Carter's 1979 poem, 'Playing Militia'.

'Out, Out the Fire' *(219)*

Incomplete 9-page manuscript of 'Out, Out the Fire', held by Nigel Westmaas [numbered, pp.8-16]. Carter submitted a 20,000 word manuscript (now thought to be lost) in 1956 to C. Day Lewis at Chatto & Windus, who liked the story and suggested that Carter submit more work. Carter submitted two more pieces (*Dead, like Eugene* and *A new life*) in 1957, but they were rejected. Carter does not appear to have tried to publish his prose fiction until this extract was first published in *Kyk-Over-Al*, 23 (May 1958), pp.37-42. Reprinted in *Kyk-Over-Al*, 44 (May 1993), pp.36-42.

wallaba: Arawak name for Caesalpiniaceaeae, a flowering tree whose wood is used for building.

white dust: Many Guyanese roads were surfaced with white lime.

Crapauds: toads.

pickney: young child.

marabuntas: wasps.

'A Note on Vic Reid's *New Day*' (225)

No manuscript exists. First published in *Kyk-Over-Al*, 24 (December 1958), pp.81-82. Reprinted in *Kyk-Over-Al*, 44 (May 1993), pp.93-94.

Vic Reid: Author of *New Day* (New York: Knopf, 1949).

Arthur Seymour: For Seymour's article, 'The Novel in the West Indies', see *Kyk-Over-Al* (year-end 1953), pp.221-27. The quotation that Seymour uses is from VR, 32-33.

'Sambo at Large' (227)

Manuscript held by Nigel Westmaas, written *circa* 1965. First published in *Kyk-Over-Al: Martin Carter Prose Sampler*, 44 (May 1993), pp.100-01. Subtitled 'Unpublished Essay on Experiences of Cardiff Conference, 1965'.

perai: piranha.

Poetry Conference at Cardiff: Carter was invited to the Commonwealth Writers Conference in 1965.

sambo: An 18th-century term to describe a person of mixed descent, especially having one Black and one mulatto parent. In American-Spanish *zambo* is a kind of yellow monkey, therefore the term became a derogatory and racially offensive nickname referring to a subservient manner or attitude supposed to be typical of slaves (OED).

Jean-Paul Sartre: Jean-Paul Sartre, 'Orphée Noir' (Black Orpheus), introduction to *Anthologie de la nouvelle poésie nègre et malgache de langue française*, ed. by Léopold Sédar Senghor (1948) (Paris: Presses universitaires de France, 1969). Sartre writes 'le mépris intéressé' (p.xlv).

'Apart from Both' (229)

No manuscript exists. First published in *GISRA* [The Guyana Institute for Social Research and Action], 5.4 (December 1974), pp.45-46. The editors noted: 'We asked him [Carter] to write an article for *GISRA* on the general subject of "Culture and the Artist in Guyana".' Reprinted in *Kyk-Over-Al*, 44 (May 1993), pp.102-04.

It is decidedly not to reduce the human person into an object of use, a convenient thing: Compare Immanuel Kant's Categorical Imperative (Formula of the End in Itself): 'So act that you use humanity, whether in your own person or in the person of any other, always at the same time as an end, never merely as a means' (IK, 38).

Ernst Cassirer: Ernst Cassirer, *Language and Myth*, trans. by Susanne K. Langer (New York: Dover, 1946). The quotations are from p.81 and p.99.

Frederick Hölderlin: Friedrich Hölderlin, *Poems and Fragments*, trans. by Michael Hamburger (London: Routledge and Kegan Paul, 1966), pp.173-77. The quotation is from pp.175-77.

'Man is a god...': Friedrich Hölderlin, *Hyperion* (1797), quoted in *Poems and Fragments*, p.5.

'It is the alternation...': Michael Hamburger, Introduction to *Hölderlin, Poems and Fragments*, p.5.

The Book of the Dead: Carter quotes from Chapter 25. See *The Book of the Dead: The Hieroglyphic Transcript and Translation into English of the Ancient Egyptian Papyrus of Ani,* ed. by E.A. Wallis Budge (New York: Gramercy Books, 1999), pp.436-37.

'The Location of the Artist' *(232)*

Manuscript held in *Kyk-Over-Al* File. First published in *Release*, 8 & 9 (1979), pp.3-4. Reprinted in *Kyk-Over-Al*, 44 (May 1993), pp.111-12.

Winwood Reade: Winwood Reade, *The Martyrdom of Man* (London: Trübner & Co., 1982), p.273.

the prohibition of excellence: Hannah Arendt, *The Human Condition* (Chicago: University of Chicago Press, 1958), p.54.

if one monk becomes proud: See Arendt, p.54 n. 48. Arendt quotes E. Levasseur, *Histoire des classes ouvrières et le de l'industrie en France avant 1789* (1900), p.187 on Article 57 of the Benedictine rule.

LIST OF ABBREVIATIONS

Works by Martin Carter

C. *Conversations* (first published in *Kyk-Over-Al*, 28 [1961], pp.154-55).

HF. *The Hill of Fire Glows Red* (Georgetown: author, 1951).

HM. *The Hidden Man (Other Poems of Prison)* (Georgetown: author, 1952).

JQ1964. *Jail Me Quickly*, first sequence (first published in *New World Fortnightly*, 2, 3 & 4 [1964], pp.5-6, 7 & 34-5).

JQ1966. *Jail Me Quickly*, second sequence (first published in *New World Fortnightly*, 34 [1966], pp.19-25).

KE. *The Kind Eagle (Poems of Prison)* (Georgetown: author, 1952).

KMCT. *Kyk-Over-Al: Martin Carter Tribute*, 49/50 (June 2000).

PA. *Poems of Affinity* (Georgetown: Release, 1980).

PR. *Poems of Resistance* (Georgetown: n.p., n.d. [*c*. 1953]).

PRMagnet. Six anonymous poems seized by colonial authorities from the Magnet Printery, Georgetown, 29 October 1953.

PRMasses. 'Six Poems of Resistance', *Masses & Mainstream*, 6.12 (December 1953), 20-23.

PRWIIP. *I Sing My Song of Freedom: Poems of Resistance* (Port of Spain: Education Department of the West Indian Independence Party, n.d. [*c*. 1953]).

PR1954. *Poems of Resistance from British Guiana* (London: Lawrence & Wishart, 1954).

PR1964. *Poems of Resistance* (Georgetown: University of Guyana, 1964).

PR1979. *Poems of Resistance from Guyana* (Georgetown: Release, 1979).

PS. *Poems of Succession* (London and Port of Spain: New Beacon, 1977).

SP1989. *Selected Poems* (Georgetown: Demerara Publishers, 1989).

SP1997. *Selected Poems* (Georgetown: Red Thread Women's Press, 1997).

AB. Aphra Behn, *Oroonoko, The Rover and Other Works*, ed. by Janet Todd (London: Penguin, 1992).

AC. *Aimé Césaire, Notebook of a Return to My Native Land / Cahier d'un retour au pays natal* (1956), trans. by Mireille Rosello with Annie Pritchard (Newcastle: Bloodaxe Books, 1995).

ACMS. Albert Camus, *The Myth of Sisyphus*, trans. by Justin O'Brien (Harmondsworth: Penguin, 1975).

ACR. al creighton, '"The poet is speaking": Martin Carter's politics of communication', in SB, pp.225-36.

AJS. A.J. Seymour, *Collected Poems, 1937-1989*, ed. by Ian McDonald and J. de Weever (New York: Blue Parrot Press, 2000).

AJSP. A.J. Seymour, 'Publishing in the Caribbean', *Caricom Perspective* (January-March 1987), p.33.

AM. Fr Andrew Morrison, SJ, *Justice: The Struggle for Democracy in Guyana, 1952-1992* (Georgetown: author, 1998).

BB. Bertolt Brecht, *Poems 1913-1956*, ed. by John Willett and Ralph Manheim (New York and London: Methuen, 1976).

BP. Blaise Pascal, *Pascal's Pensées*, trans. by Martin Turnell (London: Harvill Press, 1962).

CG. Cornelis Ch. Goslinga, *The Dutch in the Caribbean and in the Guianas 1680-1791* (Assen and Dover: Van Goraim, 1985).

CJ. Cheddi Jagan, *The West on Trial: My Fight for Guyana's Freedom* (London: Michael Joseph, 1966; St John's, Antigua: Hansib Caribbean, 1997).

CO. Colonial Office official documents, held at National Archives, UK.

DCEU. *Dictionary of Caribbean English Usage*, ed. by Richard Allsopp (Oxford: Oxford University Press, 1996).

DD. David Dabydeen, *Turner* (London: Jonathan Cape, 1994).

DHL. D. H. Lawrence, *Sons and Lovers* (1913) (Cambridge: Cambridge University Press, 1992).

DWCP. Derek Walcott, *Collected Poems, 1948-1984* (London: Faber, 1992).

DWHC. Derek Walcott, *Henri Christophe: A Chronicle in Seven Scenes* (Bridgetown: Barbados Advocate, 1950).

EB. Edward [Kamau] Brathwaite, *The Arrivants, A New World Trilogy: Rights of Passage, Islands, Masks* (Oxford: Oxford University Press, 1973). *Rights of Passage* was first published separately in 1967.

EdC. Emilia Viotti da Costa, *Crowns of Glory, Tears of Blood: The Demerara Slave Rebellion of 1823* (Oxford: Oxford University Press, 1994).

ED. Emily Dickinson, *Complete Poems*, ed. by Thomas H. Johnson (London: Faber, 1976).

EH. Errol Hill, *The Trinidad Carnival: Mandate for a National Theatre* (London and Port of Spain: New Beacon, 1992).

EK. Eusi Kwayana, 'The Politics of the Heart', in SB, pp.159-82.

EKI. Eusi Kwayana, Interview with Gemma Robinson, 20 October 1998.

EW. Edwin A. Wallbridge, *The Demerara Martyr: Memoirs of the Rev John Smith, Missionary to Demerara* (London: London Missionary Society, 1848).

FB. Frank Birbalsingh, 'Interview with Martin Carter' in *Kyk-Over-Al*, 46/47 (1995), pp.218-34.

FY. Frances Yates, *Giordano Bruno and the Hermetic Tradition* (London: Routledge & Kegan Paul, 1964).

HMP. Herman Melville, *Pierre; Or the Ambiguities* (1852) (New York: Russell & Russell, 1963).

IK. Immanuel Kant, *Groundwork of the Metaphysics of Morals* (1785), trans. by Mary Gregor (Cambridge: Cambridge University Press, 1998).

IM. Ian McDonald, 'Note to *Jail Me Quickly*', *New World Fortnightly*, 34 (18 February 1966), pp.19-25.

JD. Joan Dayan, *Haiti, History, and the Gods* (Berkeley: California University Press, 1995).

JDP. John Donne, *The Complete English Poems*, ed. by A.J. Smith (Harmondsworth: Penguin, 1971).

JK. John Keats, *The Complete Poems*, ed. by John Barnard (Harmondsworth: Penguin, 1973).

JR. Jacques Roumain, *Masters of the Dew [Gouverneurs de la rosée* (1944)], trans. by Mercer Cook and Langston Hughes (1947; London: Heinemann, 1978).

JWF. J. Walter Fewkes, 'Relations of Aboriginal Culture and Environment in the Lesser Antilles', *The Bulletin of the American Geographical Society*, 46.9 (1914).

KMFE. Karl Marx and Friedrich Engels, *The German Ideology*, ed. by C.J. Arthur (London: Lawrence & Wishart, 1970).

LT. Leon Trotsky, Literature and Revolution (1924) trans. by Rose Strunsky (Ann Arbor: The University of Michigan Press, 1960).

L&W. *Lawrence & Wishart 1954 Catalogue* (London: Lawrence & Wishart, 1954).

LW. Ludwig Wittgenstein, *Philosophical Investigations* (Oxford: Blackwell, 1953).

MH. Martin Heidegger, *Elucidations of Hölderlin's Poetry*, trans. by Keith Hoeller (Amherst: Humanity Books, 2000).

MM. Michael Meeropol, 'The Significance of the Rosenberg Case', speech delivered at Vassar College, 21 September 1995 (http://www.rosenbergtrial.org/docmerpol.html [November 2005]).

MRKF. Michael Richardson and Krzysztof Fikalkowski, eds, *Refusal of the Shadow: Surrealism and the Caribbean* (London: Verso, 1996).

MS. Morton Sobell, *On Doing Time* (New York: Bantam, 1974).

MVW. Milton Vishnu Williams, *Years of Fighting Exile* (Leeds: Peepal Tree, 1986).

NF. Northrop Frye, *Anatomy of Criticism: Four Essays* (Princeton: Princeton University Press, 1957).

OED. *Oxford English Dictionary.*

OS. Olive Senior, ed., *Encyclopedia of Jamaican Heritage* (St Andrew, Jamaica: Twin Guinep Publishers, 2003).

PB. Paul Bremen, ed., *You Better Believe It* (Harmondsworth: Penguin, 1974).

RB. Roland Barthes, *Image Music Text* (New York: Hill and Wang, 1977).

RH. Roy Heath, 'A Gimlet Eye…', in SB, pp.326-27.

RR. Rainer Maria Rilke, *The Selected Poetry of Rainer Maria Rilke*, trans. by Stephen Mitchell (New York: Vintage, 1989).

SB. Stewart Brown, ed., *All Are Involved: The Art of Martin Carter* (Leeds: Peepal Tree Press, 2000).

SD. Sonia Dolphin, Interview with Gemma Robinson, 27 November 1999.

SE. Standard English.

TC. Thomas Carlyle, 'Occasional Discourse on the Nigger Question', in 'Fifteen Years of Emancipation in the West Indies', *The Old Guard*, 4.5 (May 1866), 308-11.

TCOCCL. *The Concise Oxford Companion to Classical Literature*, ed. by M.C. Howatson and Ian Chilvers (Oxford: Oxford University Press, 1993).

VR. V.S. Reid, *New Day* (1949) (London: Heinemann, 1973).

WB. William Blake, *Complete Poems*, Second Edition, ed. by W.H. Stevenson (London: Longman, 1989).

WBY. W.B. Yeats, *The Poems, A New Edition*, ed. by Richard Finneran (London: Macmillan, 1983).

WHES. Wilson Harris, *Eternity to Season* (Georgetown: author, 1954).

WHPP. Wilson Harris, *Palace of the Peacock* (London: Faber, 1960).

WHGQ. Wilson Harris, *The Guyana Quartet* (London: Faber, 1985).

WHWA. Wilson Harris, *The Whole Armour and The Secret Ladder* (London: Faber, 1973).

WM. William Morris, *News From Nowhere and Selected Writings and Designs*, ed. by Asa Briggs (Harmondsworth: Penguin, 1962; repr. 1984).

WMMC. Wordsworth McAndrew, '"You do not organise or want to control culture, but let it flower": Interview with Martin Carter', *Caribbean Contact* (February 1979), p.9.

WOM. Wunyabari O. Malaba, *Mau Mau and Kenya* (Oxford: James Currey, 1993).

WR. Walter Roth, *An Inquiry into the Animism and Folk-Lore of the Guiana Indians*, Thirtieth Annual Report of the Bureau of American Ethnology, 1908-09 (Washington DC, 1915).

WRS. Walter Roth, ed., *The Story of the Slave Rebellion in Berbice, 1763*, in *Journal of the British Guiana Museum and Zoo*, 21-27 (December 1958 – September 1960).

WW. Walt Whitman, *Complete Poems*, ed. by Ellman Crasnow (London: Everyman, 1993).

WWP. William Wordsworth, *Poetical Works*, ed. by Thomas Hutchinson, rev. ed. by Ernest de Selincourt (Oxford: Oxford University Press, 1936).

INDEX

INDEX OF TITLES

INDEX OF FIRST LINES

Gemma Robinson is a Lecturer in the Department of English Studies at the University of Stirling. She taught at the University of Newcastle upon Tyne until 2006, and before then at Trinity College Dublin. Her research focuses on Guyanese writing and she has published articles in *Moving Worlds*, *Small Axe* and the *Journal of Caribbean Literatures*. In 2004, she gave the inaugural Martin Carter Memorial Lecture in Georgetown, and she was a judge for the 2005 Guyana Prize for Literature.

Milton Keynes UK
Ingram Content Group UK Ltd.
UKHW021824190124
436347UK00010B/614